POLITICS ON DEMAND

New Directions in Media

POLITICS ON DEMAND

The Effects of 24-Hour News on American Politics

Alison Dagnes

New Directions in Media
Robin Andersen, Series Editor

 PRAEGER

AN IMPRINT OF ABC-CLIO, LLC
Santa Barbara, California • Denver, Colorado • Oxford, England

Library of Congress Cataloging-in-Publication Data

Dagnes, Alison.
    Politics on demand : the effects of 24-hour news on American politics / Alison Dagnes.
        p. cm. — (New directions in media)
    Includes bibliographical references and index.
    ISBN 978–0–313–38278–9 (hard copy : alk. paper) — ISBN 978–0–313–38279–6
(ebook)
1. Press and politics—United States. 2. Journalism—Political aspects—United States.
3. Mass media—Political aspects—United States. 4. Digital media—Political aspects—
United States. 5. United States—Politics and government—2001–2009—Press coverage.
6. Mass media and public opinion—United States. I. Title.
PN4888.P6D34 2010
320.973—dc22   2009053321

ISBN: 978–0–313–38278–9
EISBN: 978–0–313–38279–6

14 13 12 11   2 3 4 5

This book is also available on the World Wide Web as an eBook.
Visit www.abc-clio.com for details.

Praeger
An Imprint of ABC-CLIO, LLC

ABC-CLIO, LLC
130 Cremona Drive, P.O. Box 1911
Santa Barbara, California 93116-1911

This book is printed on acid-free paper ∞

Manufactured in the United States of America

For Pete

CONTENTS

ACKNOWLEDGMENTS

A book project is no small undertaking, and many people have helped me out along the way. I have to thank a number of important people who have selflessly assisted in this endeavor.

First, and perhaps most notably, I would like to thank those who afforded me their time and attention during the numerous interviews I conducted for this project. Special thanks to Alex Baze from *Saturday Night Live*, C-SPAN Chairman Brian Lamb, former Assistant Army Secretary Sara Lister, and James Poniewozik from *Time* magazine.

I thank Michael Millman of Praeger for his editorial wisdom and kindness. Thanks also to Herbert Levine for his assistance, and to the anonymous readers whose comments helped to make this a better book.

Throughout my professional career I have received shrewd and prudent guidance from a number of wise, generous, and considerate advisors, and so my deepest gratitude goes to them: Fred Exoo from St. Lawrence University, Jeff Sedgwick and Jerome Mileur, both formerly of the University of Massachusetts, and Sara Grove from Shippensburg University.

And speaking of Ship, thanks to the wonderful Shippensburg University for giving me a professional home and a career that is magnificent, with deepest gratitude to my friends, colleagues, and students. Special thanks go out to the three fantastic students who assisted in this project: Stephanie Kelly, John Kalathas, and Chris Gray. Their good humor and keen insight made this a truly fun project to work on.

My family Dagneses and Spokanys alike have supplied varying types of support in remarkable abundance, and I owe them more than a thank you. In fact, I think I owe them money.

Monica Gocial's support and love have been life sustaining, and I'm not sure I can ever thank her enough. I'll probably just buy her a lot of stuff instead.

Finally, I want to express gratitude to the three people who make every day a joy, even when the day kind of stinks. Thanks to Maddy and Caroline, who make my heart fill with love and joy, and thanks to Pete, for all that he does and all that he is. To properly express gratitude would take another book in itself, and he'd be forced to read every incarnation of that one too. So, simply, thank you.

Tempting though it is to blame any of these remarkable people for any mistakes in this book—and there are undoubtedly several unintended ones—any error contained within is purely my own.

INTRODUCTION: HOW THE MEDIA ARE FAILING AMERICAN GOVERNMENT

You can fool all of the people all of the time if the advertising is right and the budget is big enough.

—Joseph Levine

Senator George Allen of Virginia should have been an unbeatable candidate for reelection. He was an incumbent Republican from a GOP-leaning state, he had served as governor for a term before running for his Senate seat, his father was a legendary football coach, and his hair was perfect. But campaigning in the summer before election day he blew his whole reelection effort with one annoyed and terse statement to a college student who was volunteering for his opponent's campaign. Spotting 20-year-old S. R. Sidarth, who was conducting opposition research by videotaping an Allen event in southwestern Virginia for Democratic candidate Jim Webb, the senator pointed at the young volunteer and said:

> This fellow here, over here with the yellow shirt, Macaca, or whatever his name is. He's with my opponent. He's following us around everywhere. And it's just great. . . . Let's give a welcome to Macaca, here. Welcome to America and the real world of Virginia.[1]

With that, George Allen's reelection bid came to a screeching halt. His "Macaca" remark was viewed as offensive given Sidarth's Indian heritage and the widespread interpretation that "Macaca" was a racial slur. Allen spent the rest of his campaign trying to explain and defend himself while Webb came from behind to become a formidable challenger. Allen lost the election by a little more than 7,000 votes, just .3 percent of the ballots cast.

Allen lost not because what he said was particularly stupid, since politicians have been saying stupid things for generations. The crowd to which Allen was speaking even laughed at the "Macaca" comment at the time, and the senator probably never gave the statement another thought—until the video of his "Macaca moment" hit the Internet and the airwaves and spread like wildfire well beyond Virginia's borders. It all happened because of YouTube, which was just about a year old at the time.

We all know about YouTube now, but in 2006 it was an emerging technological tool and was untested in political media. S. R. Sidarth brought the "Macaca" video he shot back to a computer, uploaded it, and then sent it to Virginia voters, news outlets, and the rest of the world. George Allen never saw it coming. The spread of the "Macaca moment" changed American politics not just because it happened so quickly, effectively, and inexpensively, but because it marked a sea change in the way Americans got their news and in the way the media reported it.

The American news media have developed and grown throughout time, but they have always been a bit unruly. Journalists—especially political journalists— have traditionally been seen as instigators and rebel antagonists, not only reporting on the news but also uncovering the nastiness of American politics, business, and society. At one time journalism was the work of amateurs, who were viewed as dirt-diggers. Even when it became formalized and professionalized, however, journalists were seen as antiestablishmentarians. Today, journalists are something else entirely: a colossal tangle of professional newspersons, political insiders, pundits, academics, and "citizen journalists." With an American electorate that sifts through a tidal wave of information and opinion that changes its format so regularly, it takes real effort to keep up with these changes, and an even greater effort to find real news within them.

This fundamental shift in American political media would not have happened were it not for four crucial developments. First, technological changes led to a wider variety of mechanisms to deliver news media content very quickly and in many different forms. Second, the abundance of media options, evidenced by so many cable channels, radio stations, and endless Internet Web sites, led to fierce competition among media outlets that include news content. This competition has forced an emphasis on entertaining news (to attract viewers) and fast and constant information delivery (so as not to lose them). Third, the immense amount of programming time that needs to be filled and the proliferation of Web sites have led to an emphasis on opinion over actual journalism. These developments occurred concomitantly with a sharp partisan polarization in American politics, these divisions accentuated by a 24-hour news cycle that now contains very little actual "news." Finally, politicians and journalists have had to mold themselves and their messages into these new media format confines and work within the demands for rapidity and diversion. This means that the old ways of making the news and delivering it have all but been forgotten, and new mechanisms have led the way to new political media norms. These norms include sound-bite politics, ideological shout-fests, and the near constant public awareness of every action and statement made by a politician. The effects of these new norms on the audience consist of cynicism about our political leaders and the journalists who cover them as well as the search for authenticity amidst an overall skepticism of the truth. The news today is not so much a dissemination of facts as much as it is an interpretation of events, personalities, and debates that comprise the political landscape. The effects of this shift in American political media are striking. Journalism has been permanently altered as the lines between average citizens, pundits, and reporters have blurred to accommodate entertainment. Politicians rely on dramatics and loud language within this entertainment-driven format, and the extremity of political rhetoric in the name of entertainment has all but killed substantive debate.

With so many media choices available, we have lost that communal feeling engendered by reading a hometown newspaper, listening to a national radio broadcast, or watching one of the three nightly network news programs on television. I do not suggest we return to the age of horses and buggies, but instead I argue that all of our media options have caused us to become more insular and misanthropic. So many selections have led the media to become fragmented, polarized, and angry. Each individual station, channel, Web site, magazine, or newspaper must fight on a crowded field for attention, which only encourages the highly specified niche programming that is turning the news into a particularized endeavor as well. Ironically, as the media have evolved with amazing technological advancement, somehow we have returned to the kind of partisan media last seen in the Jacksonian era, when certain newspapers acted as house organs of the political parties. Today, Fox News is widely viewed as an outlet that advocates exclusively for the Republican Party, and Internet bloggers are generally seen as soldiers of the left. As a result, the American public no longer trusts the media, once considered the fourth branch of government, and this cynicism breeds a general feeling of distrust for all things political.

This book examines how the news media have changed across the varying mediums because of extensive technological expansion and financial demands, how politicians maneuver within these new and constantly evolving journalistic environments, and how in the course of this maneuvering political discourse has become extreme, oversimplified, and harmful for democracy. The American media system as it exists today is no longer suitable for our political system, and Americans are suffering because of it.

TECHNOLOGICAL AND FINANCIAL DEVELOPMENTS OF THE MEDIA

In the past 30 years, the American media have changed so dramatically that today's versions are virtually unrecognizable from the time of Jimmy Carter's presidency, when the media system included only three television channels and an antenna pinned to the roof of the viewer's house. The media's growth and development have necessitated evolution and metamorphosis into astonishing new communication territories. It is a behemoth of a system that includes print, radio, television, and the Internet, and each technological development has helped to set in motion the enormous media revolution that has ensued.

Technology has historically forced changes to the American media. Steam engine technology gave rise to what Alexis de Tocqueville referred to as our "nation of newspapers." Telegraph and radio technology sped up news delivery even more with their instantaneous information transmission, and then television brought images right into our living rooms. However, since the 1980s it feels like the development is on warp speed. The advancement of cable satellite technology increased the number of television stations from 3 to more than 300. Now, satellite radio has increased listening options for subscribers who have the capability to listen to not one all-news channel, but 13 different ones with varying—and constant—points of view. When the Internet emerged in the mid-1990s, it blew radio and television away with the enormity of its content and the speed of its message delivery. It changed the form and content of the print media because of its own configuration, and it profoundly influenced broadcast media because of its ability to stream video and audio. As a nation, we went from TV stations that played the national anthem before the station went to bed for the evening to a never-sleeping media system where everything is on demand all the time, at all times demanding our attention.

Simultaneously, the financial imperatives of the media grew as more corporate players saw the huge money at stake and began demanding a piece of the pie. Conglomerates that focus on media and entertainment concerns became so lucrative that large corporations began to buy up smaller media outlets as part of their moneymaking efforts. For example, National Amusement Inc. is a privately held media company owned by Sumner Redstone. The company holds controlling voting interests in both CBS Corporation and Viacom, and between these two corporations run cable television channels, publishing houses, and movie studios, plus local TV and radio stations. National Amusement's 2007 revenue earned the company more than $2 billion, and the company employs more than 133,000 people. National Amusement is up against the Walt Disney Company (the number-two media conglomerate behind Time Warner), which also owns cable channels, TV and radio stations, publishing houses and movie studios, plus theme parks, magazines, and recording studios. Disney employs 137,000 people and has an estimated worth of over $4.5 billion. Time Warner and Disney are two of the biggest transnational media corporations that exist in the world today, and they help to illustrate how large the companies can be and how much money is at stake in the current incarnation of the information age. Even nonmedia companies such as General Electric (GE) have found the media to be a rewarding investment. GE owns NBC and MSNBC, but those two media giants comprise only a small part of GE's corporate holdings.

Media diversification within one corporate entity offers a layered approach to product promotion and opens doors for select media offerings, known as vertical integration. An article in the *Journal of Media Business Studies* by Richard Gershon and Ratnadeep Suri about Viacom nicely details the benefits of vertical integration for transnational media corporations:

1. Cross-licensing and marketing opportunities between company-owned media properties.
2. Sharing of newsgathering, printing, and distribution facilities between company-owned media properties.
3. Negotiating licensing, rental, and sales agreements across different media platforms.
4. Offering clients package discounts in advertising that cut across different platforms. Transnational media corporations like Time Warner, Viacom, and News Corp. routinely offer clients package discounts.[2]

In short, vertical integration gives large media corporations more opportunities to make money from a single product. For example, when a political book is published by Simon & Schuster (within the Viacom family), it has a natural discussion place on CBS news media outlets and Comedy Central political shows and integrated advertising on local news outlets. Thus, the book is sold more effectively and makes more money for all of Sumner Redstone's enterprises. This symbiosis means that while paper-print publications may not be as socially valued in today's electronic media environment, they still hold an important place in the political media world, if only because they remain profitable for their corporate ownership. The downside of vertical integration within the media is that if very few large corporations control the means of media production, then it is less likely that alternative or independent work will be produced. What's more, since the multilayered approach to marketing is a significant benefit in vertical integration, then it is unlikely that a media product that lacks the ability to gain interest or marketing potential in other media areas will be produced. Regardless of the weaknesses of vertical integration, it is an accepted fact in today's media world, and cross promotion is an accepted fact among media leaders.[3]

The immensity and constancy of the media—and the corporate competition for ratings that accompany this—lead to a demand for content that is alluring to the largest number of people. The competition for viewers, readers, and Internet surfers necessitates media content that can attract large audiences. Additionally, with so many more media outlets being created, the amount of airtime to fill has increased exponentially. Because radio and television are now 24-hour-a-day enterprises and because the Internet demands instantaneous updates, the constant need to produce and distribute something new is imperative in order to stay competitive among the transnational media corporations fighting for business. Whatever is broadcast must be interesting, entertaining, and new enough to grab the attention of the listeners, viewers, and surfers, who it is hoped will then pass the information along to their friends.

Thus, the sheer immensity of these corporations is beneficial for Americans who want greater choice in their media options. At the same time, however, the size of the media system has made it more difficult to keep the attention of these consumers. As a result, the demand for speedy information delivery and amusing or attention-grabbing content has led to changes in media formats to accommodate such demands. For example, the nightly news used to consist of an anchorman sitting behind a desk, reporting on public affairs and events with 30-second sound bites from policymakers that were contained within four-minute pieces. Today, as the anchormen and anchorwomen move frenetically around a studio filled with countless images from computer and TV monitors, nightly news segments are significantly shorter and are more likely to contain seven-second sound bites and 140 character "Tweets" from "average Americans" as they are from experts or political figures.

Another example concerns the cable news channels or talk radio programs that now include less real news and more opinions from pundits who raise the volume on their "analysis" and often speak extemporaneously and without filter. Since 24 hours of news would be repetitive and uninteresting to most viewers, the rise of the pundit class has emerged on cable. Punditry in America, which is supposed to involve a critical examination of important matters, is today more likely to involve personal invectives amidst observation. This form of journalistic entertainment is popular with viewers and listeners who either adore the pundits with whom they agree, or engage in their own personal battles against those they do not. Pundits are lauded for their efforts not only because they speak on behalf of ideological sides but also because their form of entertainment helps to sell a media organization and its product. The Project for Excellence in Journalism (PEJ) chronicles this phenomenon by dubbing it the "Answer Culture," where punditry supplies both the questions and answers for the viewers:

> In a sense, the debate in many venues is settled—at least for the host. This is something that was once more confined to talk radio, but it is spreading as it draws an audience elsewhere and in more nuanced ways. . . . The Answer Culture in journalism, which is a part of the new branding, represents an appeal more idiosyncratic and less ideological than pure partisan journalism.[4]

While the pundit shows do help news organizations brand themselves, political philosophy still plays an important role in talk radio, television punditry, and Internet blogging, as outlets across the different mediums cater to specific ideologies, using pejorative language to cast aspersions on the opponent. This aspect destroys the ideals of unbiased reporting but supports the goals of entertainment, which make the "Answer Culture" more competitive and profitable for the corporations that own the media businesses.

These angry debates, ferocious monologues, and high-speed information releases are now part of the new media culture and are vested in the changing format of the news media. This format change—from staid and static programs to frenzied and intense spurts of information—occurred not only to keep a competitive edge between mega- transnational media corporations, but to also suit the potential of the new and emerging technological hardware. Improvements in the area of media reception have made it possible to constantly broadcast information to tiny and portable devices that allow access all the time. Bite-sized news works well when a kiwi-sized screen delivers information to an audience with short attention spans, but it results in a media on hyper-drive, able to inform and entertain constantly and instantaneously, yet without much substance or meaning. The "Macaca moment" is an excellent example of this. The video said virtually nothing about George Allen's political beliefs or proposed policies, but it was instead a short and entertaining blip of real life caught on tape, easy to comprehend and delivered quickly.

Another effect of the enormity of the media has been what political scientist Markus Prior refers to as the "real media divide" between those interested in politics and those who turn away from it:

> Now that Americans can choose among countless channels and websites, the role of motivation is key. Many people's reasons for watching television or surfing the Web do not include learning about politics. Today's media users seek out the content they really like. Unfortunately for a political system that benefits from an informed citizenry, few people really like the news.[5]

Prior, like legal scholar Cass Sunstein and media scholar Neil Postman (both of whom made similar arguments), alleges that as a result of so much media choice, citizens learn less about politics and are thus less likely to become politically active. And since politicians pay attention to those who pay attention to them, the cycle of disregard and voter apathy is perpetuated. The abundance of media choice allows many Americans to avoid the news entirely and redefine in their own mind what news is and what it means to them.[6]

EFFECTS OF THESE CHANGES: NEW MEDIA AND THE DEVOLUTION OF POLITICAL EXPRESSION

The technological development of the media has led to greater profit motives, content and format changes, and information hardware advancement. All of these developments, in turn, have led to an emphasis on entertainment over substance. There are those who will argue that these developments in themselves are not negative things. It can be argued that even if the news is more entertaining, there is simply more news available, which is beneficial for society. Further, if more people stumble upon the news in shorter spurts, they are well served by the little information they receive. If this, in turn, sparks debate and deliberation, then the body politic is better off for it.

Additionally, proponents of the abundance of new media choice argue that the technological developments of the Internet have encouraged citizen participation in American politics and political journalism like never before. C-SPAN started this trend with call-in access to newsmakers. During the last two decades, this idea has ballooned into an all-access pass for the general public, where citizens text questions for presidential debates, blog their opinions about politics and society, and drop e-mails to their elected officials with ease. Where once there were three anchormen disseminating the news daily from on high, today five cable news networks staff their channels with 24 hours of news, opinion, and information, and the Internet updates itself to break news instantly and constantly. This development has allowed many more people to act as journalists even if they are not professional journalists. Take Mayhill Fowler, for instance, a volunteer for the *Huffington Post* Weblog. A Weblog (or "blog") is a forum that anyone with a computer can set up, posting his or her own opinion and linking to the opinions of others. The *Huffington Post* is operated by Arianna Huffington, a syndicated columnist and self-described "former right-winger who has evolved into a compassionate and progressive populist." The blog leans to the left of the ideological spectrum and was highly critical of the George W. Bush Administration, but it does not reserve its criticism only for the right. Its unofficial reporters, like Mayhill Fowler, who call themselves "citizen journalists," have broken some big news.

Fowler broke two major stories in the 2008 presidential campaign without a journalistic credential to her name. The first concerned Democratic presidential candidate Barack Obama's comments concerning middle-class voters in times of economic hardship. At a fundraiser in California, Obama stated, "It's not surprising, then, they get bitter, they cling to guns or religion or antipathy to people who aren't like them or anti-immigrant sentiment or anti-trade sentiment as a way to explain their frustrations."[7] Fowler broke this story on the *Huffington Post* Web site, and the mainstream media picked up on it, causing great damage to the Obama campaign just prior to the Pennsylvania primary. Fowler also broke the story about Bill Clinton calling *Vanity Fair* writer Todd Purdham "sleazy" and a "scumbag," which greatly damaged the Hillary Clinton for President campaign prior to the North Carolina primary.

Both were legitimate campaign stories that gained traction in the mainstream press. In both cases, Fowler was present because she was lucky, not because she was accredited. She nailed Bill Clinton on a rope line shaking hands with Hillary Clinton supporters, and she got Obama at a private fundraiser where no press was allowed. Both of these stories had profound effects on the campaign, and both came from a woman who has said, "I have no journalistic training. I just discovered that I'm impelled to get out there and get the truth of the matter."[8] By her own biographical admission, Fowler's previous job experience is characterized as such: "Worked a bit as a teacher, editor, and writer, but mostly raised my two daughters."[9] Her stories were sensational (thus entertaining) and came from someone who was not entrenched in Beltway politics, which lent them an air of Average Joe authenticity.

Blogging has the effect of forcing the mainstream media to catch up with instantaneous news, which by this virtue alone puts the mainstream press on the defensive and at a great disadvantage. The upshot of this switch to a newer, faster, entertaining, and perhaps more authentic form of news can be quite positive, providing more information to more people and challenging the mainstream media to work more rapidly, more vigorously, and more effectively at their jobs. However, there are several important downsides of this new media domination as well. First, since these newer forms of journalism are not governed by traditional journalistic standards—indeed, the Internet is barely regulated at all—they can fall far short of what is necessary to actually inform the public. Traditional journalism conforms to a uniform pattern that mandates information be delivered scrupulously and consistently, with the lead explaining a story and the supporting paragraphs providing substantial explanation. The new media tend to emphasize humor and brevity without adhering to formulaic norms and without being edited for accuracy. The result can be entertaining, but also sloppy and erroneous.[10]

A specific problem with online information dissemination occurs when false stories online are given credence by the mainstream media that are trying to catch up with their new media counterparts. The alacrity of the medium can spread falsities so quickly that rumors become almost impossible to refute. For instance, the *National Review Online*, the Internet arm of one of the most credible and intelligent conservative magazines in the country, posted a report that Barack Obama was born in Kenya (and thus ineligible to run for president), that his middle name was Muhammad (and not Hussein), and that his mother named him Barry (as in White, the walrus of love). Cable television programs picked up these stories and ran with them, giving legs to gossip that was wholly unsubstantiated and entirely untrue.[11] Because the Internet is far too big to be monitored for content accuracy by either a private entity or the government, it is then up to the media and the citizens who use the Internet to monitor themselves. This self-governance is unlikely to occur when the incredible or surprising sells: Who wants to check facts when the alleged is far more entertaining and profitable?

Another downside to this new media upsurge is that it can inspire what scholar Judith Rodin calls the "shallowness, thoughtlessness, oversimplification" of public discourse. Jon Stewart, the host of Comedy Central's *The Daily Show*, has railed against the cable pundit shows and their emphasis on unsophisticated wrestling matches and simplicity over significance, calling it "the theater of it all." Stewart is a curious spokesperson for intellectual sobriety, since so many Americans claim to get their news from *The Daily Show*, the snarky satire program that pretends to examine the news of the day; but he brings up a good point. Television has become a medium where everyone seems to be screaming at one another. Stewart made this point on the CNN show *Crossfire*, which pitted ideological opposites against one another in a shout-fest environment, calling the program (and shows like it) bad for democracy. The hosts were taken aback by

Stewart's attack and didn't defend themselves well. Shortly thereafter, the program was cancelled.

Despite *Crossfire*'s cancellation, the pundit shows that remain on the air continue to feature angry partisanship and lots of shouting. Ratings are high for programs that are incendiary in their nature and provide conflict for viewers to engage in and enjoy, and so they remain successfully on the air. TV shows like *The O'Reilly Factor* and *Countdown with Keith Olbermann* have led to the design of other shows just like them. Both hosts and guests of radio and television chat shows ping-pong between the media, garnering more attention for themselves as they rail against their opponents. As a result, talk radio is—if possible—even more vitriolic than a decade ago at the height of its popularity. Since the crossover between talk radio and cable news is profitable for the media companies that produce the shows and affords the media figures greater public exposure, there is greater incentive than ever to state the shocking and compelling. The incivility occurs online as well. Web sites include invectives so personal and cruel as to be libelous because the anonymity of the Internet allows anyone to say anything and get away with it; and the other media outlets report on such content. If you succeed in inciting an audience, you succeed in general and are rewarded with greater attention.

We are losing a battle for civility in this country because incivility is more fun to watch, and since the media play such an important role in American politics, the consequences of this incivility are grave. The "Macaca moment" marked the start of YouTube in politics, just as Lyndon Johnson's "Daisy" ad marked the start of negative television advertising. More political media developments will arise to further change the electoral landscape, but they will emerge in an environment that is already hostile, personal, and almost entirely devoid of substance.

GENERATIONAL DIVIDE OF THE AUDIENCE

There is a generational divide in the news audience. Audience demographics show that older Americans tend to watch the evening broadcast news or gravitate towards their favorite ideological flavor of cable news, eschewing the newer modes of information dissemination. Younger Americans, on the other hand, who came of age during this considerable media expansion, have been drenched in electronic media from the time they first began processing information. As a result, they are accustomed to the careful construction of a politician's public image and are thus highly skeptical of the media that transmits these depictions. As James Poniewozik of *Time* magazine notes, this younger age bracket more markedly tells the difference between "the way things are, and the way things are on TV."[12] This awareness makes them more cynical of the media in general and of what the media are revealing in particular, and it leads younger Americans to search for authenticity in their news: moments where politicians are caught off guard, hypocrisies that are exposed, flashes where their cynicism is validated.

There are some very good reasons for their cynicism. First, many Americans feel that journalists are no longer interested in exposing the truth but are instead interested in their own personal benefit. The Project for Excellence in Journalism notes that the American public thinks the media are motivated by money, and journalists are motivated by their own ambitions. Second, the journalistic profession has garnered a bad reputation amidst several well-publicized ethical violations. The plagiarism scandals at the *New York Times* and the *USA Today* (to name two) have lent an air of distaste to the profession, as has the shoddy journalism practiced by broadcast news outlets that has been exposed by Internet bloggers. Third, those critical of the media point to the general lack of journalistic aggression (or even mere inquisitiveness) during the Bush Administration's justification for (and conduct during) the war in Iraq. Fourth and finally, the increasing fragmentation of media audiences divides the nation between those who seek out news and those who seek out entertainment, and those who seek out both concomitantly.

All of these reasons, either individually or in combination with one another, create the sense that perhaps the mainstream news media are not to be trusted. This cynicism manifests itself in different ways, such as when Americans simply ignore the news being broadcast around them or are drawn towards a specific (and oftentimes isolated) news organization they deem as trustworthy. For younger Americans, the specific news outlets they prefer are oftentimes not news outlets at all. Younger audiences turn to skeptical sources for their information, which include *The Daily Show* and the inexpert opinions of bloggers on the Internet, all of whom claim proudly "We're not real journalists!" while they disseminate news. These skeptical sources reject the construction of the mainstream news media and provide what the younger, more cynical audiences are craving: authenticity. This authenticity presents itself as more genuine and legitimate than the construction of the mainstream press. It presents itself as exposing the flaws, blunders, and inaccuracies of the American political system because, as mentioned, "real" journalism cannot be trusted.

Today, the authenticity younger Americans crave can go hand-in-hand with entertainment. According to a Pew Research Center study, 39 percent of television viewers aged 18 to 29 stated that they learned about the 2008 presidential election from comedy shows and late-night television programs.[13] One reason for this is, of course, that these shows are funny and enjoyable, but another reason is the very nature of political satire. According to Aaron McGruder, the artist who draws the comic strip "Boondocks," political comedy's greatest strength is when it encourages skepticism: "Good satire goes beyond the specific point it's trying to make and teaches you how to think critically."[14] When the message is to disbelieve the politicians that comedians focus on, it's really quite easy to do so. And comedians have a way of formulating their own truths through humor. According to comedian Bill Maher, politicians are most vulnerable when lots of comedians make the same joke: "If someone does something twice, it becomes a reputation. Hillary becomes a congenital liar [after] all the comedians jump. If they're all making the same joke, that's the danger. Then there's a solidifying effect and it becomes the truth."[15]

And truth—within this entertainment—is exactly what the cynical younger generation is in search of. While older Americans might find comfort in tradition, structure, and authority, younger Americans concern themselves with what they perceive to be insincere or deceitful. In their search for authenticity, this new generation of media users looks to one another and to those perceived as outsiders for the "real story," which helps to explain the attraction of user-generated content on the Internet and the blogging from amateur "citizen journalists."

In a study on the Internet's role in Campaign 2008, the Pew Research Center found that an age gap developed as more young Americans, those aged 18 to 29, went online for their news. While 42 percent of those aged 18 to 29 reported using the Internet as a campaign news source, only 15 percent of those over 50 reported the same. Conversely, only 24 percent of the younger age bracket watched the nightly news, versus 40 percent of the older group. The Internet provides a wide array of options when looking for news, from official Web sites of existing news organizations to homegrown blogs, to sanctioned politician Web pages, to social networking sites such as Facebook. Within this vast range of alternatives, most young Americans opt for such sites as Google, Yahoo!, and MySpace, where they stumble upon the news while amusing themselves. The official news Web sites hold less attraction for the 18- to 29-year-old age group.

In order to reach this younger group, politicians have had to contort themselves into these new realities, which has had mixed results. Certain politicians, such as GOP presidential candidate John McCain, have an easy time working within the confines of political humor, appearing frequently on *The Daily Show* and on *Saturday Night Live*. Democratic presidential candidate Barack Obama worked magic on the Internet with his enormously successful fundraising efforts and his ability to reach the younger audience quickly and effectively. At other times, as in the George Allen "Macaca" moment, politicians are caught in a medium they do not fully understand and cannot operate well within. Thus, politicians have had to work hard to comprehend the new media environment in which they operate and figure out ways to utilize the media to their best advantage.

POLITICIANS WORKING WITHIN NEW CONFINES

The first new development that is catching up with politicians is the absolute lack of privacy available to them now. The good news about the new media is that one can be in constant touch and send out clips of exciting speeches and media events with complete ease. The bad news is that the ability to do anything anonymously is now completely destroyed. Every poorly timed joke, every heartbreaking slip of the tongue, every miserable misstep is now chronicled immediately and spread faster than a case of pink eye at a daycare center.

Pollster John Zogby refers to the "politics at the speed of light" when discussing the new atmosphere for politicians. Because cell phones now almost always include cameras, there are no more moments of privacy for politicians, which makes every single word spoken a public message:

> Of course, the George Allen "Macaca" fiasco was the turning point. It was the end of the private or semi-public political speech as we used to know it. . . . Even politicians used to have private thoughts they could share among friends. That's no longer the case.[16]

One case in point: During the 2008 campaign season clips of inflammatory statements made by then-presidential candidate Obama's Pastor Jeremiah Wright made their way around the Internet and straight to the mainstream news media outlets. Spread just as quickly was Obama's famous "race speech" in which Obama spoke out about the question of race in American history and in current American politics. Delivered at the Constitution Center in Philadelphia, the speech acted as a salve for the campaign to combat the damage done by the pastor's remarks. It also afforded news organizations the opportunity to run a positive story about the electrifying rhetorical powers of the candidate. Obama supporters linked the speech to their own blogs and sent it virally by e-mail to everyone they knew, which helped the campaign just as quickly as the damage it received from Pastor Wright. In Obama's case, the instantaneous gratification of Internet news transmission worked as an instigator and as a pacifier. In all cases, politicians have to be extremely—and constantly—careful about what they say, no matter to who they are speaking.

Politicians also have to work within the confines of the media's need for rapidity, which produces a whole other set of concerns. A policymaker or candidate for office has to compose "sound bites," those short clips from a politician or policymaker that we see on the news. These brief snippets are attractive to the media's need for fast entertainment. Unfortunately, very short sound bites are no way to convey an actual opinion or nuanced series of facts, which then deprives the American public of some much needed detail in forming an opinion. In a study on sound bites, University of Indiana researchers Erik Bucy and Maria Grabe (2008) found that the length of a sound bite has shrunk exponentially since 1968. Their research showed that in 1968, the average sound bite length was one minute, while 40 years later in 2008 they were only eight seconds long.[17]

Thus, when a politician speaks about something as complicated as immigration or health care or Social Security, the sound bite must be compressed, articulate, interesting, and pithy—or else it won't get played in the media at all. This brevity may be easier to accomplish for some politicians than for others, but it has generated a new breed of political consultant: the sloganeer, someone who is able to squeeze a philosophy into sound bite while creating a brand for a candidate or a policy working its way through the political system. These handlers often advise politicians not to speak extemporaneously to the media because they know that bad things happen when politicians go off-message. The messages have been painstakingly crafted and tested on focus groups, and political consultants are sure of their efficacy. But political journalists and the American public do not trust the politicians who are so well handled and over-messaged, and so the call for authenticity emerges once again. It is an endless cycle.

Authenticity sometimes emerges in the form of nontraditional media coverage, such as candidate appearances on ESPN, House & Garden Television, and the *Oprah Winfrey Show*. Candidates appear on niche programming shows to prove that they are "just like us" in their interest in sports, home decor, and personal introspection. It helps to humanize a political candidate and make them more relatable to the average American. During the 2008 campaign, Hillary Clinton, Barack Obama, and John McCain actually appeared on the World Wrestling Enterprise *Smackdown* program. During his tenure in office, President Bush called in to *American Idol* to speak to the contestants and to the 40 million people who watched the show. President Obama appeared on *The Late Show with David Letterman* and was the first sitting president to do so. While he spoke for most of the time about his health care reform plan, he also discussed his children's adjustment to the White House. This served to connect him with viewers who had school-age children, and he appeared genuine in his parental role. These appearances help bolster a politician's perception of authenticity, and at the same time they increase his or her visibility, which is also important to politicians. In these efforts, the abundance of media outlets serves cross-purposes. They entertain Americans and offer politicians visibility and the opportunity to appear authentic in the construction of their public persona. The availability of so much media has served to blur the lines between news and entertainment.[18]

Politicians can avoid news media programs altogether, if they so choose, due to the multitude of media venues that are accessible to them. The process of leaving the journalists behind, which began 80 years ago with Franklin Roosevelt's "Fireside Chats," is an important development for politicians who want to control their message. In the new world of politics and media, journalists are almost becoming unnecessary because politicians can go straight to the public with their information, either through their Web site or through the staged events they host for their supporters. In the 2008 campaign, Hillary Clinton announced her presidential candidacy on her Web site, and Barack Obama texted his vice presidential nominee announcement to his supporters several hours before the formal press announcement. However, even in these cases the mainstream news organizations were vital to the political needs of the candidates, and they picked up the stories after the fact. Politicians can only avoid the modern news environment for so long before the citizen journalists are on to them, which then triggers the mainstream press to catch up with the story. Politicians must now work within these new structures—working inside and outside the mainstream news media—in order to be successful.

Today, a politician must be brief *and* appear to be genuine in his or her message, as someone just telling the truth but telling it quickly and without error, a dependable and flawless bona fide person who is realistic in the unrealistic demands we place upon him or her. When they fail in this futile endeavor, the shouting begins within an immense media system that operates constantly and without nuance or distinction. The news media are no longer the watchdog of American democracy as they contort themselves to appeal to an uninterested public by reporting only the most attention-grabbing and compelling stories. The lethal combination of financial imperatives for an entertainment-driven media and the harsh polarization of the current American political system have led to a weakened news media more interested in the fight than the resolution of conflict and an entertainment media saddled with the duty to inform that they are ill-equipped to handle. The fact that the American public looks to *Saturday Night Live* and the *Daily Show* for its news is hardly the fault of these entertainment shows. It is, instead, the fault of the news media that have abdicated their responsibility to inform. It is also the fault of the public, who has relinquished its duty to inform itself. To borrow from the sentiment of a country/western song: we are looking for news in all the wrong places. Our ignorance is beginning to overwhelm us as a result.

OUTLINE OF THE BOOK

This book argues that technological progress across the media has led to dramatic changes in the way politicians use the media and in the way the voting public receives their messages. As a result, American politics cannot work well within the modern media boundaries. To that end, much of the book focuses specifically on the different media: their structures, financial imperatives, and political uses. By examining the way each individual medium has evolved, it is far easier to see how they work together. But first there needs to be an exploration of the partisanship that has a stranglehold on American politics as well as an examination of the importance of the media in American culture.

The first chapter delves into partisanship, theories about media reception, audience response, media content theory, and issue framing. All of these concepts are important because they offer an understanding of how the polarization in Washington has evolved, how the media are used as weapons in these partisan battles, and how these media affect the way the American public understands the political system. Politicians of all stripes use the American media system to their advantage, yet within the current ideological media politicians use different media for similar purposes. For example, it is currently the fashion for politicians to write autobiographies in order to advertise themselves, but there are certain book publishers that cater to conservatives. Likewise, all politicians want to appear on television, but liberals tend to eschew Fox News while conservatives flock to it, and CBS has been categorically denounced as biased by conservatives while liberals find it perfectly acceptable. Those on the right use talk radio and those on the left utilize the Internet. These media outlets are becoming increasingly insular, catering to specific audiences and ramping up the rhetoric to pull in the readers, viewers, and listeners necessary to turn a profit. In advertising themselves as disseminators of "the truth," these media outlets demonize their competition, forcing the public to pick sides and defend their choices.

Scholars are divided in their assessment of the media's significance in American politics. Some think there is a strong media influence that colors the way Americans view candidates and issues, while others disagree, arguing that the media can be used simply for entertainment and without grave consequences. Other scholars examine the "gatekeeping" function of the press and look at how the media helps to shape the debate in American life, while others study the way the media frame the issues they report on and also the way that politicians try to frame their stands and those of their opponents. Framing, which is how a topic is approached in a news story, plays a crucial role in political media today. Since brevity is essential for the modern media environment, the way a message is framed is central to political communication. All of these influences and aspects of media theory are examined in Chapter 1. Also discussed are governmental oversight of the modern American media and laws regulating media content.

The next chapters of the book focus specifically on the different forms of the media, exploring their own technical evolutions and the results that have ensued. Chapter 2 looks at print journalism and book publishing. Since the founding of the Republic, when the imposition of the Stamp Act by the British authorities helped lead to the Revolutionary War, Americans have demanded printed materials, and politicians have used such publications to deliver their messages. Despite the popularity of broadcast media, print media remains important. Within the media consolidation of the last decades, both newspapers and publishing houses have been bought by larger media conglomerates and continue to be profitable components of transnational media corporations. As mentioned earlier, the position these publishing houses hold within the larger media conglomerates provides them with ample opportunities to be part of larger, coordinated media efforts aimed at both corporate self-promotion and political message dissemination or candidate marketing. If a candidate writes a book—something now deemed necessary in order to run for high office—he or she is afforded the opportunity to build upon this exposure by hawking the book on a cable or broadcast news program owned by the same transnational media corporation. This gives the politician extra exposure from one publication. Concomitantly, the media entity that owns the publishing house that produced the book also owns other media outlets that can advertise its publication. This strategy is called "vertical integration," where one corporation owns the means of production and distribution, and it results in a win-win for both the corporation in control of all the media outlets and the author of the published book.

Even if the book promotion extends beyond the transnational media corporation that published it, a political candidate is more likely to gain cable and broadcast airtime when speaking not just about his or her candidacy, but also about that individual's story. It is no coincidence that prior to his election as president, Barack Obama published three books and that his rival for the Oval Office, John McCain, authored or coauthored almost two dozen books. Chapter 2 explores the print publication industry and its relationship to politicians, its financial imperatives, and the role it plays in American politics.

Chapter 3 examines radio, a technology that is more than a century old but one that is still evolving and emergent in its political significance. Calvin Coolidge was the first president to use radio expansively, and since then the intimacy of the medium has lured politicians to the microphone. To this day, even with the dominance of visual media, the president delivers a weekly radio address to the nation and speaks for 10 minutes on a topic of his choice. The popularity of talk radio, which reached its zenith in the 1990s but remains significant today, is another important way that politicians reach out to the American public. Often, radio talk show hosts advocate for issues or candidates, and often they argue fiercely against them; but all the time radio is entertaining, and most of the time it is profitable. The more recent rise of satellite radio has added more news and opinion programming options to the airwaves, and added to that is the Internet's ability to stream audio. All of these developments present new ways for citizens to hear radio stations from around the world through their computer, and it helps maintain radio as an important player in American politics.

In technological development, radio led the way to the true heavyweight of modern media: television. Television was born in the 1950s and went through a painful adolescence until its tremendous growth spurt with cable satellite technology in the 1980s. The explosion of airtime has led to an increasingly politicized pundit class, which in turn has helped to shape the political debate in America as well as the way the debate is constructed. The abundance of choice afforded by so many cable channels has forced immense competition between the companies that own them, which in turn has helped usher in a new emphasis on entertaining content. These financial requirements that changed the format and style of television in order to attract new audiences have also helped alter the way politicians appear on TV. Chapter 4 studies the impact and development of television in American politics.

All of these components together—newspaper and book publication, radio programming, cable satellite technology—make for an extensive media network. As important as all of these components are for political discourse, however, none has had greater impact on the way Americans get news as the Internet. The sheer immediacy of message dissemination and the impact of instantaneous image transmission have served to permanently alter the meaning of the term *journalist*. Chapter 5 looks in greater detail at the Internet to show how the Wild West of American media is forcing immense changes in journalism today. There exists now a divide between "old" and "new" media, where tensions between the journalists of older media and the new "citizen journalists" from the Internet force battles for attention and validity.

Certainly, the new media have compelled dramatic alterations in the way news is recognized. As a result, politicians have had to reconfigure themselves as well. For not only has journalism changed, but the politicians who the journalists cover have had to change, too. As the "Macaca moment" clearly exemplified, the old ways of campaigning for office or for policy no longer work. Chapter 5 analyzes the information uncovered and addresses the two major questions that arise from all of this media development: How is political discourse influenced when politicians maneuver themselves within these new media confines? What are the consequences of this new political rhetoric for the American public? Answering both of these key questions will help illustrate the effects of a 24-hour news media on American politicians, citizens, and civility.

We live in a two-party system, and entertaining and angry partisanship is a staple of American political media today. From the moment that Patrick Buchanan coined the term *culture war* at the 1992 Republican National Convention, the divide in America has been quantified, labeled, and used as fodder for political media across the board. Partisanship isn't new to American politics, but giving it a catchy name allows it to be used as an entertainment vehicle, and the modern American media act as a conduit of this partisan-entertainment. Politicians use the media as a weapon in their ideological battles. For example, conservatives have successfully used what media scholar Kathleen Hall Jamieson terms the "Echo Chamber" of several specific conservative news outlets that broadcast the political right's viewpoint almost exclusively. The left has tried to emulate this formula with its own news outlets, and there has emerged a brand of partisan press not seen since the Jacksonian era.

And so the three rings of the media circus are established. The modern media broadcast the bitter and spiteful environs in which politicians and political groups operate today because such hostility is good theater and attracts good ratings. Politicians use the media as weapons to fight one another in their campaign and policy battles. At the same time, the viewing, listening, reading, and surfing public are able to tune into only what reinforces their political beliefs and to ignore those who oppose them. As an electorate, we can have our current events spun the way we like them without challenging our own conceptions of a situation. We have insulated ourselves against debate at the same time we reward heated arguments as theater. On both sides of the political spectrum, liberals and conservatives—and even moderates in the middle—ramp up their language and volume to gain attention in an entertainment-driven media world. With politicians using all the new technology available to best gain traction for their agenda, politics has become an "on demand" entity, devoid of substance and antithetical to democracy.

NOTES

1. Tim Craig and Michael D. Shear, "Allen Quip Provokes Outrage, Apology: Name Insults Webb Volunteer," *Washington Post*, Washington, D.C., August 15, 2006, A01.

2. Richard A. Gershon and Ratnadeep Suri, "Viacom Inc: A Case Study in Transitional Media Management," *Journal of Media and Business Studies* 1, no. 1 (2004): 60.

3. Several scholars examine the economic market forces of the media in great depth, including Robert Entman (*Democracy without Citizens*, 1989) and Robert McChesney (*The Global Media*, 1997). Both of these authors detail the effect of commercialism in the news, among other relevant matters.

4. State of the News Media 2007, The Project for Excellence in Journalism, http://www.journalism.org/.

5. Markus Prior, "Liberated Viewers, Polarized Voters—the Implication of Increased Media Choice for Democratic Politics," *The Good Society* 11 (2002): A15.

6. Please see work by Marcus Prior (2002, 2005) and Cass Sunstein (2002) for much more on this topic.

7. Jim Kuhnhenn and Charles Babington, "Obama Says Remarks on 'Bitter' Working-Class Voters Ill Chosen," *Boston Globe*, April 13, 2008.

8. Howard Kurtz, "Blogging without Warning," *Washington Post*, June 19, 2008, http://www.washingtonpost.com/wp-dyn/context/article/2008.

9. Ibid.

10. Much has been written recently on the impact of the Internet on the American political system, including work by Richard Davis (*The Web of Politics: The Internet's Impact on the American Political System*), Doris Graber (*Processing Politics*, 2001) and Andrew Chadwick (*Internet Politics: States, Citizens, and New Communications Technologies*, 2006).

11. Karen Tumulty, "Can Obama Shred the Rumors?" *Time*, June 23, 2008, 40.

12. James Poniewozik, Personal interview with author, June 9, 2008.

13. Michael Cavna, "Comedians of Clout," *Washington Post*, June 12, 2008, C01.

14. Ibid.

15. Ibid.

16. John Zogby, "Politics at the Speed of Light," *Politics*, June 2008, 54.

17. Michael Schudson and Danielle Haas, "Getting Bit: When Sound Bites Get Snacksized," *Columbia Journalism Review* (May/June 2008).

18. This is an especially rich area of inquiry for both political scientists and media theorists and includes work from Douglas Kellner (*Media Culture: Cultural Studies, Identity, and Politics between the Modern and Postmodern*, 1995), John Thompson (*Ideology and Modern Culture*, 1991, and *Media and Modernity*, 1996), Bonnie Anderson (*News Flash*, 2004), and Daya Thussu (*News as Entertainment*, 2008).

Chapter 1

The Media: Partisanship, Media Regulation, and Audience Reception

> In Washington, the FCC voted to allow big media companies to own more television stations and newspapers. They believe that this improves the American peoples' ability to get a single viewpoint rather than be confused by a bunch of different ones.
>
> —Jay Leno

The American news media hold a longstanding and important place in American politics, and from the very start of our nation we have taken seriously the role and responsibility of the press. In fact, the American people would not recognize the practice of politics without the accompanying media presence. The link between politics and the media is so close that the two create an illusion that they are one entity, or at least that the press serves as the "fourth branch" of government. The perception that the media are so closely tied to the institutions of government is reinforced by several modern phenomena. First is the revolving door that politicians use to move between elected political positions and media analyst positions. Often those who have held office move seamlessly to the media after their tenure in office has ended, being offered a lucrative spot in the news in which they provide expert opinion and analysis. One case in point: Joe Scarborough was once a Republican member of the U.S. House and now hosts his own show (*Morning Joe*) on the MSNBC cable network. This common practice not only provides a politician with job security after losing an election, but it also provides broadcast media outlets with an authority to provide commentary and fill the many hours of programming time available. Another reason the American public sees such close ties between elected officials and the press is because they tend to socialize in the same circles, frequently at high-profile Washington events that gain media attention themselves, such as the Gridiron Dinner, the various Correspondents Dinners, and White House affairs. These occasions present the public with the perception of a friendly bond between those elected to office and those covering such offices. This connection is not problematic in itself, but if the press is supposed to be a watchdog of democracy it is difficult for the press to act in that capacity at social gatherings. Finally, the desire of most politicians to appear in the media, no matter how hot and danger-ous the spotlight, also lends an air of connectivity between those elected officials and the press.

No matter how closely associated these two entities are, the fact remains that the press in America is at times an antagonistic one. Even as the public views their elected officials and press comingling, they also see the press aggressively pursuing a story, attacking said officials and often taking sides, and fragmented between ideological camps. This partisan press mirrors the polarization of the voting public, which is sharply divided in their politics. While the nation has always adhered to a two-party system, of late it feels like the rhetoric has become angrier and divisions have become more severe. Additionally, the media system of today is far more complex than it has been in the past, and the consequences of such an enormous construction include the resurgence of a partisan press not seen in the past century. This results in a media system seen as too cozy with the politicians they cover and at the same time too adherent to their own political beliefs to fairly cover their subject matter. This chapter examines the importance and place of the media in a highly partisan and polarized American political system.

MEDIA DEVELOPMENT

The First Amendment of the Constitution guarantees press freedom and pre-serves the right of journalists to cover politicians and institutions. Throughout our history American journalism has often acted as a mirror of the political mood of American society, and because of this reflection our news media have often served the political system well. From the time of the founding of the American Republic until the present day, the technological developments of the media have evolved to create new means of information dissemination, which have sped up the development of the media and made them more sophisticated and better able to inform the public quickly and effectively. In the earliest days of the nation, the press consisted of newspapers and pamphlets, many of which were printed to convey the political messages of the time. The newspapers carried the news of the day, but the pamphlets were specific, one sided, and exuberant polemics on the most important issues, including the question of whether or not to go to war with Great Britain. This emerging press reflected the American government in its infancy, learning how to become independent from England and excited about the potential for democracy. Technology pushed journalism forward in the years that followed, creating a news media that grew increasingly quick in their reporting abilities. The steam engine printing press, telegraph, radio, televi-sion, computer, and Internet technologies are just a few of the major changes that altered news journalism. All along the way, technological advances were increas-ing the speed of information delivery and circulation, enlarging the number of journalists in the ranks, and professionalizing the industry.

Throughout this evolution, politicians have had to adjust their own relationships with journalists in order to operate most effectively. The norms and standards of what could and should be covered have changed dramatically as the media have evolved. It is now common knowledge that Franklin Delano Roosevelt was wheelchair bound, something the contemporary press never reported, and stories of John F. Kennedy's infidelities were similarly ignored by the news media. As the media changed, however, so too did the boundaries of good taste, and stories once deemed too unseemly for family newspapers or beneath the high standards of news anchors became commonplace and perfectly acceptable to report upon. Such stories include the 1974 incident where the very married Congressman Wilber Mills was pulled over for a traffic violation in the company of stripper Fanne Foxe, which then led to press coverage of the 1987 incident where Democratic presidential candidate Gary Hart was caught cheating on his wife on a yacht called "Monkey Business." This led to the announcement of Bill Clinton's sexual relationship with a 22-year-old intern in the White House during the mid-1990s, and now the limits of press coverage have extended well beyond simple adultery to fellatio. As these norms changed and the press began to cover more about a politician than he or she wanted, the relationship between elected officials and the press became more strained. When politicians' personal lives are equal fodder to their policy stands, suddenly the press is viewed less as a critic and more as a voyeur. When the technology of the media allows constant observation this voyeuristic impulse grows even greater.

The perception of ideological bias in the mainstream media has also added tension to the relationship between politicians and the press. William Safire, a *New York Times* columnist and former speechwriter for President Nixon, coined the term "nattering nabobs of negativism" to describe the press. This conception of the news media continued after Nixon left office and has evolved into an even more disapproving characterization. After two *Washington Post* reporters brought down the Nixon administration after breaking the Watergate story, many Republicans alleged that the press was out to get them, and this idea took hold throughout much of American society. While many conservatives were denouncing the mainstream media, some affluent and powerful conservatives were establishing their own media counterpart, and thus an intentionally conservative-dominated press has emerged in the past decade that is committed to providing a foil to the perceived liberalism in other media outlets.[1] This has opened the door to politicians selectively choosing their media, using varying outlets for specific purposes. In recent years, political partisans have used the media as weapons against their political opponents. Because the tension in partisanship is entertaining, the media encourages such discord. The partisan divide in America makes for good radio, television, and Internet broadcasting, and it sells books, newspapers, and magazines as well.

In the world of political media, nothing entertains as much as a heated debate between two opposing sides. The good news for political journalists and media outlets coveting entertainment is that the sharp partisan divide in America today is chock-full of conflict. Even after the election of Barack Obama in 2008 amidst the promises of a "post partisan" America, the polarization continues, indicated by aggressive attacks against the new government by many conservative media players. Additionally, since most positions on the hot-button issues of the day are (to say the least) bifurcated, the fights regarding abortion rights, the war in Iraq, oil production, and environmental concerns can easily be turned into political theater. As an additional bonus, the opposing sides truly seem to despise one another, and thus partisanship in America is not only compelling entertainment but has also had a tremendous impact on the audience watching the fight. The media may generate good ratings when they underscore the tension between warring political factions, but the effect on the citizenry can be pernicious.

Some argue that partisanship is good for America: that it encourages debate, that it helps represent differing priorities in a highly diverse nation, and that it allows greater connection among citizens. This may be true, but partisanship today is not so much adherence to one party as much as a wholesale rejection of another, and with this shift come personal invectives and characterizations that border on the defamatory. Today's political polarization is vicious but not unprecedented, and U.S. history is filled with times of great partisan divide and political acrimony between citizens. What is unique to this new period of partisanship, however, is the powerful media system that has developed, which projects the strong views of political actors more broadly and with greater speed than in the past. If one assumes that the media are a strong influence in America today, then the media's propagation of the partisan divide has more serious consequences than if one thinks the media are harmless.

PARTISANSHIP IN AMERICA AND PARTISANSHIP IN THE PRESS

When discussing the partisanship, of course, we are talking about the divide between Democrats and Republicans, which manifests itself in the very structure of American government, in electoral politics at all levels, and within our electorate itself. This divide is one that helps to organize the political system and provides citizens with a side to choose. A 2008 study conducted by the *Washington Post*, the Henry J. Kaiser Family Foundation, and Harvard University found that 3 in 10 Americans self-identified as Independent.[2] These Americans may be moving away from party identification either because of a dislike of the two parties—feeling that they are too moderate, too extreme, or generally out of touch with voter concerns—or because of a general apathy about politics altogether. In an age when a growing number of Americans call themselves Independent, the question arises: Does party identification even matter? The answer is yes. The United States is driven by the two-party system, and as long as that remains true, then all the real money, power, and trappings are controlled by those two entities. Since political parties oppose each other so dramatically on major issues affecting American life, the drive to woo these Independent voters is strong. The fight for the Independent voters who could swing an election in either direction is an important one at a time when elections are won by the narrowest of majorities and at a time when the majorities in Congress are terribly slim. As a result, the parties have tried their level best to attract these Independent voters and bring them into their respective tents, at least for the purposes of winning elections. Thus, party identification matters greatly on a practical level for candidates and for party leaders engaged in electioneering.

Additionally, scholarship on party identification and core political values shows that the way voters view the political parties themselves is more enduring than their beliefs about specific issues or events.[3] The issues of the day fluctuate from election to election, and what might be crucial in one election cycle may not have the same impact in the next. The parties, however, remain enduring symbols of American politics and the vehicles by which politicians are elected. Thus, political parties do matter, even in an age when people are moving away from party identification individually, and thus it makes sense that the effects of partisanship influence American politics. As noted by more than one political scientist, the battles in Washington now wage well beyond the election stage and head right into battles for policy adoption and implementation. These policy campaigns are often waged to combat partisan opposition and sell an ideological policy stand. The use of media outlets in these efforts is commonplace now and reaffirms the connection between politicians and specific news media outlets. Certain partisan news organizations trumpet policy programs while others demonize them, amplifying the battles being fought in Washington outside the Beltway. The American public watches, reads, and listens to these arguments and picks sides.

The bottom line is that the nation is sharply divided. Although political scientists argue that this division is neither new nor especially debilitating, the current environment in Washington is, as one Capitol Hill staffer calls it, "fairly toxic."[4] Since the American political system is divided into three branches, it can be assumed that the levels of polarization differ among these political institutions. For example, the legislative partisanship on Capitol Hill remains consistently sharp despite leadership changes, while executive partisanship is directly tied to the primary occupant of 1600 Pennsylvania Avenue and his leadership style.

The reasons for the rancor in the legislative branch, according to noted political scientist James Q. Wilson, are threefold. First, party realignments in the South and in New England have strengthened partisan adherence and party-line voting. Because these regions have become more unified in their ideology, their representatives hold on more closely to their party lines concerning policy and politics. Second, the philosophical disparity between parties is growing. The Republican Party has become more conservative in the past 25 years, broadening the difference between it and the Democratic counterparts. Third, redistricting shenanigans where state legislatures have redrawn congressional districts to favor one political party over another have lessened the competitiveness of House elections, which has served to make seats safer and their occupants more ideologically radical.[5] Add the slim majorities in Congress in the past two decades that demand allegiance to ensure policymaking success, and you have a legislative body unwilling to compromise, and policymaking that is mediocre at best.

In their book on lawmaking, *The Broken Branch*, scholars Norm Ornstein and Thomas Mann argue that the partisanship on Capitol Hill has led Congressional leaders from both parties to play fast and loose with the rules in order to win, which comes at a cost to the legislation passed: "The eschewal of the regular order, the abandonment of deliberation, the core value that political ends justify the legislative means, the lack of concern about legislative craftsmanship . . . result in the production of poor laws and flawed legislation."[6] Capitol Hill journalist Juliet Eilperin affirms this argument in her book, *Fight Club Politics*, when she maintains that the polarization on Capitol Hill has resulted in such aggressive tactics that the American body politic is left behind amidst all of the wrangling. As others have noted, the fighting is exacerbated in election years, but the growing length of campaigns extends electoral fighting to a near-constant level. Amplifying it all is the media, from the staid C-SPAN, which simply records every floor fight and angry debate, to the rest of the more than 7,000-strong Capitol Hill press corps that aim to report, analyze, and portray the workings of our legislative branch in such a way as to attract attention to the beat. These reporters, producers, camera technicians, and staffers come from every media mode—print, broadcast, and cyberspace—and their goal is to report the happenings on the Hill in a manner that is both informative and interesting. Partisanship is definitely interesting.

Partisanship can play a major role in the executive branch as well, confirmed most clearly in the executive style of President George W. Bush. The politicization of both foreign and domestic policymaking made his White House one that valued party loyalty over all else. In order to put his policy program into effect, Bush relied on a "take no prisoners" style, perhaps best exemplified in his statement to the international community in our war on terror: You're either with us or against us. Examples of this abounded, from the 2001 punishment of Vermont Senator Jim Jeffords that led to his defection from the GOP, to the outing of undercover CIA agent Valerie Plame as retribution against her husband, to the executive decision to fire U.S. Attorneys not seen as "loyal Bushies."[7] The upshot of such a divisive and loyalty-bound administrative style is the rejection of oppositional thought and strict adherence to a sole ideological philosophy, which served President Bush and the GOP well in the first years of the Bush administration.

The Bush administration used partisan media outlets to its advantage, employing what political media scholar Kathleen Hall Jamieson calls the "conservative echo chamber" of television, radio, and newspaper to stay on point and reify the message of the day. The Bush White House understood that there were two types of journalists in Washington at the time: those friendly to the administration and everyone else. In the course of the Bush presidency, consequently, the White House communications office was accused several times of rewarding supportive journalists. In the first case, White House briefing room seats were given on a temporary basis to unaccredited "journalists" who would throw soft-ball and supportive questions to the president or his spokesperson.[8] The process of allotting daily passes for various journalists was neither new nor newsworthy, but what was out of the ordinary was that these daily passes were given to someone so egregiously friendly to administration. The Bush administration also punished journalists it deemed to be hostile by stripping them of their briefing room credentials. In the case of White House press queen Helen Thomas, it was declared that she was not to be called upon again.

The Obama White House strived for a less-partisan approach to executive policymaking in the earliest days of the presidency, but eventually it lost its bipartisan fervor amidst attacks from the right, and thus the entrenched partisan environment of Washington did not change with the new administration. However, the White House press office has yet to use briefing room seats as leverage, opting instead to reward new media outlets such as the *Huffington Post* blog and underutilized ones such as Black Entertainment Television (BET) with first-time access.

Studies have shown that while members of the media are personally more liberal on social issues, they trend conservative on economic ones, and most deny any ideological influence in their journalism. However, in the modern American news media there are cable channels, newspapers, and radio talk show hosts who obviously, if not openly, favor one political side over the other. This makes for a highly politicized media environment in which politicians operate. Conservatives have developed an intricate and sophisticated media network that has become immensely popular, featuring Fox News Channel on cable television, talk radio hosts such as Rush Limbaugh, Glenn Beck, and Sean Hannity, and newspaper editorial pages such as *The Wall Street Journal*. The potent combination of newspapers, talk radio, cable news, and book publishing has assisted conservative politicians in their efforts to spread their ideological messages. All of this together has made conservatism in America an incredibly potent force to be reckoned with, while putting liberalism on the defense. The right uses these media organizations to communicate its messages for a very specific reason: their base is uniformly adherent to these formats. For example, media mogul Rupert Murdoch specifically established Fox News to counter the so-called liberal media; and despite its slogan "fair and balanced," in reality Fox News is anything but. By acknowledging its conservative philosophy—employing well-known conservative anchors, pundits, and analysts, countered by far fewer leftist voices employed specifically as opposition—Fox News seeks out conservative viewers and rewards them with an antagonistic view of the left. Fox adheres to conservative religious values (Bill O'Reilly's constant drumbeat against "secular progressives") and to conservative economic philosophies (Neil Cavuto's

Common Sense financial programming) as well as to conservative philosophies that rail against big government, both Bill and Hillary Clinton, and Michael Moore. All of this combined made Fox the chosen media outlet of the Bush White House and the conservative GOP leaders on the Hill. After Vice President Dick Cheney accidentally shot a lawyer in the face during a hunting party, Cheney granted only one interview: to Fox News correspondent Brit Hume. Hume is an outstanding journalist, but he was chosen by Cheney for his ideological predilection and his Fox News Channel affiliation.

The fact that these news outlets lean conservative might support Hillary Clinton's contention that there exists a "vast right wing conspiracy." In fact, the right wing media is less about conspiracy and more about a well-oiled public relations machine. During the 12 years Republicans were in charge of a united government, lawmakers worked in conjunction with lobbyists and conservative media organizations to advance their political agenda.[9] This was not about secretly amassing power, but instead about not-so-secretly advancing the right's policy programs while assisting big business, both of which fit in very well with conservative ideological philosophy. Through painstaking organization and strict adherence to GOP leadership, those on the right were rewarded with programmatic success and further governmental dismantling. The right-wing news organizations were present to aid in this success and advertise the victories when they happened.

In recent years, political operatives on the left have looked to their counterparts on the right with envy at the tremendous infrastructure that the right has established. The left is currently trying to emulate this infrastructure by organizing its own networks, channeling money into developing connections between lobbying, business, and media interests with their own political goals. National Public Radio (NPR) reported in 2004 that then-Senator Hillary Clinton spoke to a meeting of liberal activists and addressed this disparity:

> It didn't happen by accident. It happened because people with a very particular point of view—they didn't like labor unions, they didn't like civil rights, they didn't like women's rights—they came together, literally, starting 50 years ago. They created think tanks. They invested in endowed professorships. They set up other media outlets. And so, they very slowly, but surely, tried to change American politics. And you've got to give them credit. They've done a good job.[10]

To try and remedy the situation, according to NPR, the left has taken to the Internet to coordinate efforts, spread their messages, and raise money. And the left is not exactly impotent—it just amasses its power differently. Liberals and Democrats are fully capable of making piles of money (see Clinton and Obama's 2008 election fundraising), but they are less wont to coordinate together to enact one strict ideology. This is most likely because the left values diversity more than uniformity and independence more than adherence. Look at any Democratic effort on Capitol Hill to see how Speaker Nancy Pelosi tries to coordinate efforts among her partisan peers. Getting the Blue Dogs (i.e., conservative Southern congresspersons), the Congressional Black Caucus, and the New England liberals to agree on policymaking is astonishingly difficult. The Democratic Party may have shifted right since the 1960s, but its members became even more diverse during this time. The multiplicity of voices within the left has caused a fragmentation with which the right has never had to contend. Add to that the bottom-line philosophy on the left that eschews big business (see Franklin D. Roosevelt), assists demographic groups in need (see Lyndon B. Johnson), and helps low-yield causes such as the environment (see Al Gore), and you have a recipe for a cacophony of speakers without one common audience.

The differing means of communication used in partisan messaging today are remarkably consistent with the ethos of the two ends of the ideological range. Even though the two major political parties use different media modes in their attempts to advertise and antagonize, the end result is the increasing insularity of the messaging. Conservative voices are heard in one place, liberal voices in others, and when the two are paired it is not for actual deliberation but instead for the gladiator-style clash that serves as entertainment.

THEORIES OF MEDIA INFLUENCE AND CONSTRUCTION

None of this would matter if the American press was unimportant, but the press has played a crucial role in American politics throughout history. The question arises as to its precise importance, and here scholarly opinions vary. The late media scholar Neil Postman, author of *Amusing Ourselves to Death*, best illustrated the "Strong Media Theory" when he argued that the media would turn the viewing/listening/reading public into practical zombies. Postman argued that television in particular has conditioned the American public to covet dumbed-down, simplistic programming at the cost of deliberation and sophisticated debate. Postman's argument falls into the theory known as the "hypodermic theory" of media, which sees the audience as victim to a powerful media that possesses seemingly unlimited control. Those who prescribe to the hypodermic theory are wary of the shift in information dissemination to "soft news," which emphasizes entertainment over intelligence and style over substance. If the hypodermic theory of a strong media is true, then the shift towards more pundit-driven opinion shows on cable TV and the impact of talk radio shock-jocks are immensely troubling.[11]

The opposing theory, exemplified by media scholar Joseph Klapper in the 1960s, posits the idea that the American public is stronger than the hypodermic theory gives it credit for, and as a result the media are far weaker than one might think. The "minimal effects approach" consists of several elements that help to explain why the media are harmless. The first concerns a viewer's own filter system, which seeks out information that is comfortable to him or her already and absorbs this information in a way that suits that individual's existing views. The other limits to the media's power include the political socialization process that influences the reception of information, where friends, family, and group membership help shape how the message is received.[12] Additionally, political and social leaders help shape the media through their own actions, and economic and social conditions play roles as well. According to the minimal effects approach, these factors help an audience shape its impressions of a media message. As a result, the audience is not viewed as individual and weak actors, but as group members more powerfully affected by their environments.[13]

While scholars may argue about the consequences of the media's impact on the public, what is not in dispute is the sheer ubiquity of media in American society today. As technology developments allow both affordability and portability, it seems practically impossible to escape the media that bombard us from all corners. Much of this media are entertainment-driven, but a significant portion is news related. And so with all the available means of information transmission, there is a super-abundance of news for the American public to accept or disregard.

"Gatekeeping" and "framing" are two central theories concerning message dissemination and construction. Gatekeeping, according to media scholar Doris Graber, is the process by which news stories are selected by news organizations for print or broadcast.[14] The myriad newsworthy events that occur in a given day are far too many to broadcast on an evening news program or even during a one-hour pundit opinion show. Even on the seemingly endless open space of the Internet, there is only so much room on Web pages for a finite number of story links. Thus, the decision must be made regarding what to discuss, report on, or stress. There are two branches of gatekeeping as defined by Gary Woodward: "ideological gatekeeping," in which stories are selected by virtue of their political slant, and "structural gatekeeping," in which stories are chosen based on how well they fit into the type of media involved and that media's particular emphasis, organizational structure, or financial imperative.[15] Both ideological and structural gatekeeping afford a great deal of power to those in charge of editorial decision making, for it is the gatekeepers who help to set the agenda. In cases of partisan slants in the media, this gatekeeping function determines which messages are carried, reinforced, and absorbed by the public. Many in the media today argue that there are fewer instances of ideological gatekeeping than structural gatekeeping, since the financial imperatives of the mainstream media mandate a certain kind of story to attract the most readers, listeners, and viewers. However, since ideology is so important in American politics, it is important in the media as well, and therefore perhaps both types are used more often in conjunction with one another than individually.

Another factor concerns framing. "Issue framing" is a process by which someone constructs and defines a story or an issue, placing emphasis on certain events or issues over others. Political scientist William Jacoby argues that framing is an "explicitly *political* phenomenon," where issue frames are created by political leaders and the media "serves as the conduits through which their messages flow."[16] Political scientist J. N. Druckman wrote that a framing effect occurs when "in the course of describing an issue or event a speaker's emphasis on a subset of potentially relevant considerations causes individuals to focus on these considerations when constructing their opinions."[17] Framing is used effectively during political campaigns. For example, during the 2008 presidential campaign the issue of Republican John McCain's selection of Alaska governor Sarah Palin as his vice presidential running mate was covered extensively in the media, which generally framed the story not in terms of her political strengths but rather in terms of her personal characteristics, such as her young special-needs child, her son going to war in Iraq, and her pregnant daughter. In this framing, a substantive discussion of Palin's qualifications for the office was generally ignored in favor of debate about her children, her hair, and her glasses.

Framing remains important well after election day. In today's media heavy world the campaigning never ends for a politician, as he is either running for election or he is campaigning for public policy. Today, many political scientists address the question of whether one can govern in this country without having to campaign for policy.[18] Scholars Norm Ornstein and Thomas Mann write: "The line between campaigning and governing has all but disappeared, with campaigning increasingly dominant."[19] When those campaigning for policy craft message frames in order to sell the policy to the American public, they emphasize certain elements over others in order to appeal to the greatest number of Americans. Framing stresses specific elements of a topic, boiling down a multifaceted issue and placing it within a central context. The result is that whoever most effectively frames the argument is afforded a tremendous amount of power and is able to set agendas or shape issues for the body politic.

Both gatekeeping and framing provide essential theories concerning how the media impact what Americans listen to, watch, or read. With the power to choose what stories are important, and the power to define the way these stories are constructed, the media are able to steer the American public agenda in one direction or another. For example, in the 2008 presidential campaign Democratic candidate Barack Obama was questioned by Joe Wurzelbacher, a man who came to be known as "Joe the Plumber." Wurzelbacher was a plumber from Ohio who aggressively questioned Obama's economic policy, stating that Obama's tax policy was at odds with the American dream. This questioning was caught on camera by ABC News, and "Joe the Plumber" was then used by Republican candidate John McCain in a presidential debate in two important ways. First, he was designated as a sort of American "Everyman," someone who was emblematic of American values and standards. Second, McCain used "Joe the Plumber" to illustrate middle-class opposition to then-candidate Obama and his policies. Immediately after the debate, the media seized this "Joe the Plumber" construction as a way to frame their own stories about economic matters. Media organizations camped out on "Joe the Plumber's" front lawn, he was interviewed incessantly, and he even gained representation by an agent once the media made *him* the story. In doing so, the media made "Joe the Plumber" the tool to explain the economic debate in the election. McCain supporters all over the country carried signs stating, "I am Joe the Plumber!" regardless of their own vocation or—more awkwardly—their gender.

The use of "Joe the Plumber" as the metaphor and frame of economic matters in the 2008 presidential election is also a good example of "soft news." As explained by political communications scholar Matthew Baum, soft news includes the following characteristics: "The absence of a public policy component, a sensationalized presentation, human-interest themes and an emphasis on dramatic subject matter, like crime and disaster."[20] Soft news is emphasized because it is viewer/reader friendly, which is beneficial for the financial imperatives of a ratings-obsessed news media. The soft-news emphasis on entertainment and human interest stories is appealing to Americans who have little interest in actual policymaking or political debates. Even though sometimes political scientists do not want to believe this is true, there are those who are not really interested in politics. In fact, not only do these citizens exist, but they also far outnumber the political junkies in America today. Despite their general disinterest in American politics and government, these citizens still want to be informed, and so many news programs intersperse gossip, entertainment, weather, and other human interest stories with so-called hard news in order to woo those Americans to their network, station, or site.

According to media scholar Lance Bennett, the emphasis on soft news has inspired four information biases with which the news is now riddled: personalization, which focuses on the people engaged in political combat instead of on process or policymaking and which also demands stories that connect to an audience personally; dramatization, which emphasizes news items that are easily simplified into dramatic terms, "emphasizing civic crisis over continuity, the present over the past or future, and the personalities at their center"; fragmentation, which occurs when news stories become isolated chunks of information without being part of a broader context; and authority-disorder, where authority figures are either overemphasized to add legitimacy or demonized in order to make the story more dramatic.[21] All of these biases result from an emphasis on soft news and help to neuter the strength of the news and its impact on the American body politic. Soft news, combined with the effects of framing, help to create an environment that is not particularly informative.

Scholars have examined the role of the news and entertainment media on electoral politics and nonelected political activity, and several scholars have looked specifically at the effects of the sheer size of the media on American politics. In one study, University of Chicago law professor Cass Sunstein determined that the abundance of choices available to Americans has had a polarizing effect on the electorate. Sunstein argues that with a multitude of choices available on television and on the Internet, media consumers will select only the outlets that they find the most comfortable or familiar. Because of the vastness of the new media technology, many news outlets today are highly partisan in nature, and thus citizens looking for a Web site or channel that reinforces their existing opinions can do so without any challenge to their position. Sunstein warns that this serves to end debate and discourse, encouraging the kind of one-sided thinking that leads to deep political division. When the media become obviously ideologically partisan, the self-selection of viewers can lead to the polarization of which Sunstein writes.[22] When liberals watch Keith Olbermann or Rachel Maddow and conservatives stick to Bill O'Reilly and Sean Hannity, two important things happen. First, these viewers are deprived an opposing view. Second, when these outlets disparage their opponents, the viewers are directed towards greater division.

Another recent study examined the effect of media choice on political attitudes. Political scientist Markus Prior proposes that a system with so many media options has important consequences. First, and as touched upon in the Introduction, the vast number of media outlets makes it easier for people interested in current events to find out more about the news and are thus more likely to participate in politics.[23] So-called news junkies now have 24-hour-a-day access to cable networks catering to niche news areas (such as C-SPAN for congressional and public affairs coverage and CNBC for economic news) and also to the Internet, which provides highly specified information for the most addicted news fan. Because of the immediacy of these media, those individuals with an interest in news can look for constant developments and updates in emergent news stories. All of the information available educates citizens to partake in the process, from voting to political activism, but the recent consequence of this media saturation, according to Prior, is that so much media also afford those who are uninterested in the news with even more options for entertainment. As a result, it is far easier for these people to abandon the news and seek out different media alternatives. Additionally, this very abundance of news may only serve to irritate those with a minimal interest in the topic, since those people are more subject to information overload. This kind of "news fatigue" is more likely for people who are suspicious of politicians to begin with, and thus more news information can paradoxically lead to even less interest and less participation in the system.

So it is within a polarized, partisan environment that the American news media operate, gaining an audience and ratings for the big fights and giving undue attention to those who speak out most aggressively, angrily, and entertainingly. None of this matters if one adheres to the minimal effects school of thought that the media do not play important roles in American politics. However, if one subscribes to the theory that the way the messages are formed contributes to the way the electorate understands American politics, then the media are essential. Not only do they inform the public, but they also help shape political debates and, in certain circumstances, advocate for one political position or another. The media become even more important if one believes in the theory that the American public is a receptive audience, susceptible to the information delivered by a powerful media force. Partisanship is not new to American politics, and neither is ideological polarization. What is new is the constancy of the modern news media that broadcast information and opinion all the time. If the media are vital to democracy, the impact of their message is not just noteworthy, it is critical.

MEDIA REGULATION

American media are controlled by laws, regulations, and judicial decisions that rein them in, monitor their ownership and content, and aim to prevent abuse. The media are concomitantly protected from government pressure by these same edicts. In the past 20 years as the media have exploded in growth and technology has developed with alarming speed, often the government has had to react retrospectively to fix the problems of the media rather than act prospectively to address problems that may arise in the future. Since our governmental system is one of checks and balances, oftentimes the legislature passes laws that are then examined by the judiciary, which then leads to a reexamination of the rules and the handing down of edicts. Thus, the laws, regulations, and judicial decisions concerning the media are almost constantly in flux.

The Telecommunications Act of 1934 that regulated the American media system during much of the twentieth century was amended when Congress passed the Telecommunications Act of 1996. The 1996 legislation, which came about when the Internet became more readily available and digital broadcasting was on the horizon, is immense in size and scope and divided into four general areas.[24] The first area concerns television and radio broadcasting; the second addresses issues relating to cable broadcasting and phone transmission; the third focuses on the Internet and online technology; and the last area concentrates on telecommunications equipment manufacturing.[25] Once the 1996 legislation was signed into law by President Clinton, it was almost immediately challenged in the courts, and various portions of the legislation have been addressed and examined and overturned or upheld in the past decade.

One important upshot of all this legal maneuvering over the Telecommunications Act is that the Supreme Court has given the Federal Communications Commission (FCC) very broad latitude in regulating the broadcast industry. The government oversees the airwaves because they are viewed as a public trust, and the FCC is the agency that regulates radio, television, satellite, cable, and wire communications technology. The bureaucratic agency has two primary purposes: to control media ownership and to monitor content to protect citizens from obscene or inciting content. Comprising five political appointees, the FCC must always have at least two members of each party on the commission. The president has the opportunity to fill open seats with his choice of appointee, however, and thus the balance normally swings to the party in office.

Recent FCC actions have focused on ownership rules, allowing one company to own multiple media outlets in the same city. Another issue the FCC has dealt with of late is station licensing. Since it is in charge of authorizing television and radio stations to broadcast, the issue of licensing has been an important one in the agency's history. It used to be that stations were required to renew their license every three years and were held to standards of about 14 different guidelines concerning coverage of communities and public services. Recently the FCC changed its licensing rules so that stations need only fill out a marginal license renewal application every eight years, which takes the regulatory responsibility out of the hands of the FCC and allows stations to self-regulate their content. As the media continue to expand their reach and capabilities and as technology advances, the government will be forced to increase its oversight.

The courts have long ruled that not all speech is protected, and the Supreme Court has taken a medium-by-medium approach to the First Amendment, where radio and television broadcasts are not necessarily entitled to the same protections as newspapers. In general terms, however, the First Amendment covers both print and broadcast similarly in order to preserve a free press. While these standards have changed through the twentieth and twenty-first centuries, there remain very few legal precedents that allow the government to infringe on a citizen's or news organization's First Amendment rights. As journalists try to do their jobs, they are often faced with dilemmas that interfere with their responsibilities to report the news and that threaten the First Amendment free-expression protections that all Americans are afforded.

FIRST AMENDMENT PROTECTIONS AND POLITICS

The First Amendment, which affords us a free press, is sacrosanct but not absolute. Journalists are afforded great protections, but they cannot use the First Amendment as a shield against absolutely everything. These protections are in place to safeguard the press—and also those investigated by the press.

When journalists investigate a story, they are usually relying on information they received from a source. These sources can be named (meaning they are "on the record,") or unnamed (meaning the source is anonymous). The use of anonymous sources is considered fairly standard practice as long as the news organization verifies the facts of the case with supporting evidence, and ever since Mark Felt went undercover as "Deep Throat" during the Watergate investigation news organizations have used anonymous sources to help break major stories.

Journalists do not want to rely on anonymous sources entirely because they tend to carry less weight than their named counterparts. According to Jill Abramson of the *New York Times*, "Reporters really recognize, as do editors, that when you can name sources, you have a much more authoritative first draft of history than you do with one larded with anonymous sources."[26] Furthermore, there have been cases where journalists have fabricated anonymous source material in order to break a story. In the past decade, scandals have occurred at major newspapers when reporters fabricated stories in order to advance at their papers, including the *USA Today* and the *New York Times*. Another difficulty with using anonymous sources is that journalists promise anonymity but cannot be bound legally to their promise. Put another way, there are no legal protections for a journalist who refuses to reveal the name of his or her source, a situation that has landed more than a few journalists in jail for contempt of court citations.

Most famously, in July 2003 the name of a CIA analyst, Valerie Plame, was leaked by White House officials to members of the press in an effort to damage the reputation of Plame's husband, Joe Wilson. Wilson had been sent to Niger in 2002 by the CIA to look into the matter raised in President Bush's State of the Union address that the British government had learned that Saddam Hussein had recently sought significant quantities of uranium from Africa.[27] This claim, which originated with Italian reports of uranium acquisition but was never authenticated, was made by the president in order to bolster public support for the invasion of Iraq. However, after Wilson returned from Niger and reported to the CIA his doubts that the president's accusations were true, Wilson wrote a piece in the *Washington Post* that succeeded in undermining the administration's claim. In response, several high-ranking Bush officials contacted other members of the Washington press establishment to counter Wilson's assertions, and in doing so revealed Plame's name and occupation. In a story titled "Mission to Niger," *Washington Post* writer Robert Novak wrote the following: "Wilson never worked for the CIA, but his wife, Valerie Plame, is an agency operative on weapons of mass destruction. Two senior administration officials told me that Wilson's wife suggested sending him to Niger to investigate the Italian report."[28] The disclosure of Plame's name was a violation of a federal law barring the disclosure of a covert operative, and thus began a four-year investigation to try and find the person who revealed Plame's name to the press.

Among the journalists who had been contacted with Plame's information was *New York Times* reporter Judith Miller, who was instructed by a federal court judge to divulge the name of her sources. She refused, and spent almost three months in jail. The entire investigation, which included testimony from some of the biggest names in the Washington media establishment, resulted in the sole conviction of Lewis "Scooter" Libby, who was chief of staff to former vice president Dick Cheney. Libby was convicted of obstruction of justice, perjury, and making false statements. President Bush later commuted his sentence. But Miller, in her refusal to expose her sources, stayed in jail until Libby came forward to release her. This is one example of how the use of anonymous sources can go terribly awry.

Journalistic standards have changed through the twentieth and twenty-first centuries, but there remain very few legal precedents allowing the government to infringe on a citizen's or news organization's First Amendment rights. Essentially, there are two basic areas of restraint on free speech: prior restraint, which applies before speech is expressed; and accountability, which applies after expression through laws addressing libel, slander, obscenity, incitement to commit a crime, contempt of court, or seditious utterance. With respect to prior restraint, there has consistently been a hesitancy to allow the government to prohibit free speech. This principle was established in the Supreme Court decision *Near v. Minnesota* (1931), which established the legal tenet that a "heavy burden of justification" is necessary before the government can suppress media content prior to publication. This means that the government has to show good reason to prevent the publication of written material. This "heavy burden" model was upheld in *New York Times v. United States* (1971), also known as the "Pentagon Papers" case. This was the first case involving an effort by the national government to restrain newspaper publication of material in its possession. Prior restraint holds except in time of war or other national emergency.

Accountability after expression, on the other hand, is provided by laws regulating the risk to public safety, defamation of character, either written (libel) or spoken (slander), and invasion of privacy. When speech can generate harm to others or causes a group to fear danger, the risk to public safety overrides First Amendment speech protections. What first began as the "Clear and Present Danger" test in the early twentieth century modernized into what is today referred to as the incitement standard, which determines if speech is dangerous enough to be restricted. The incitement standard aims to ascertain if harm or malice is intended in the speech, which would therefore constitute a threat to public safety.

Other limits to free speech are found in libel and slander rules that protect the citizenry from rogue journalism that spreads falsities or innuendo. Both libel and slander are used to define statements that expose a person to hatred, contempt, or ridicule, that injure his or her reputation, or that harm the person in his or her trade or profession. These laws act as a protection for citizens against an unchecked press that would print or broadcast material that is patently false or damaging to a private citizen. Such protections are different for public officials, who are held to a higher standard of proof in post-expression cases. In the decision *New York Times v. Sullivan* (1964), the Supreme Court determined that even false statements made against public officials were not libelous unless there was actual malice shown within the statement. This decision was made to further preserve the First Amendment protections for the press, since they need to be able to criticize and report without fear of political retribution.

Finally, rules concerning invasion of privacy places checks upon the First Amendment as well. This issue includes name or likeness use of both celebrities and average Americans, the disclosure of private facts, and disclosure of information illegally obtained. There are remedies for all of these problems, from release form signatures to legal rulings that allow disclosure in the public interest. Illegally obtained information is never supposed to be used in journalism, and rules prohibit its use to protect the public from an unfettered press. With the massive amounts of information available, however, it is sometimes impossible to do anything after the fact. Thus, when illegally obtained material makes its way onto the Internet, there is little one can do to stop the public impact of such information. Those who obtain this material are subject to prosecution under state and federal laws, but sometimes the promise of scooping a story or breaking exciting news trumps deterrence. This exemplifies the difficult line of speech freedom. A press needs to be free to investigate public officials and opine on those elected to office, but at the same time there must be protections to prevent the press from doing harm by spreading rumors or half-truths as fact. All of these legal doctrines serve to protect journalists from undue political and governmental pressure and also protect citizens from excessive press actions.

There are those who argue that there should be accountability guidelines to prohibit anonymous Internet users from abusing their freedom of speech. According to legal scholar Jennifer O'Brien, there are several arguments for these guidelines. The first is that the Internet has significant potential to disseminate information that sticks—it can be downloaded, saved, printed, posted, and sent off to other computer users much more readily and easily than other media. The result is that material disseminated over the Internet has much greater staying power than other published or broadcast material. The damage, therefore, is more significant. O'Brien's second argument is that, while some opponents of regulation frame this debate in terms of a David and Goliath match between one small user and a giant Internet service provider (ISP), the reality is that in some cases David might be a bad guy. Therefore, framing the argument as such does not really show the extent of the damage that can be wreaked by a single person—perhaps an unscrupulous person. O'Brien's last argument is that anonymity shields posters from psychological filters that might control what they say or do. It is harder, for example, to speak one's mind in public than it is in the solitude of one's home, facing not a crowd of people but a computer screen instead. This gives greater license to those who do not feel accountable for their actions. These arguments, according to O'Brien, mean that there should be systems in place to prohibit unidentified Internet users from speaking in an uncontrolled manner.[29]

The other side of the argument reaches to the protections guaranteed by the First Amendment. Opponents point to the power of anonymous writers to speak the unpopular truths and voice the position of the unaccepted minority in the marketplace of ideas. For this reason, the courts have been loath to force anonymous users to reveal their identities unless there is a prima facie case of liability proven. This means that unless the wronged party can prove damage, the accused maintains his or her secrecy online, which gives online media content a very different degree of regulation.

Government regulations exist to keep the American press free and able to do its job as watchdogs while also protecting the public from corrupt media content. The side that argues vehemently for a free press and for fewer media laws and regulations often invokes the First Amendment as its shield against government control, and this argument is not without merit. Certainly, the very basis of our democracy is rooted in freedom of expression, and without these protections the press cannot watch the government for us. However, the side that argues media content has become so unruly as to need greater regulation is correct as well, since the profitability of outrageous media content drives the media organizations to air and print content that is harmful or extreme. A driving force behind the question of regulation is the issue of media significance. If one believes the media to be an important and commanding force in America, then more regulation is necessary.

Regardless of the protections afforded by government regulation, however, the press cannot be sheltered from itself. For while the American news media have always played an integral part in the American political system, today that system is complicated by profit motives, partisanship, and structural norms that have made the system challenging for democracy.

NOTES

1. Analysis of the right-wing media has been written that exhaustively addresses the conservative media system, and I encourage readers interested in a more thorough examination of this topic to see Eric Alterman (2003), Eric Brock (2004), Kathleen Hall Jamieson (2008), and Gerry Spence (2006).

2. Dan Balz and Jon Cohn, "A Political Force with Many Philosophies: Survey of Independents, Who Could Be Key in 2008, Finds Attitudes from Partisan to Apathetic," *Washington Post*, July 1, 2007, http://www.washingtonpost.com/wp-dyn/content/article/2007/06/30/AR2007063000859.html?hpid%3Dtopnews&sub=AR (accessed September 22, 2009).

3. Paul Goren, "Party Identification and Core Political Values," *American Journal of Political Science* 49 (October 2005): 881–896.

4. Thomas Dunn, Personal interview with author, April 2007.

5. James Q. Wilson, "How Divided Are We?" *Commentary Magazine*, February 2006.

6. Thomas Mann and Norman Ornstein, *The Broken Branch* (New York: Oxford University Press, 2006), 146.

7. Dan Eggan and Paul Kane, "Justice Department Would Have Kept 'Loyal' Prosecutors," *Washington Post*, March 16, 2007, A02.

8. This was exposed most embarrassingly when blogger James Dale Guckert, operating under the nom de plume of "Jeff Gannon," was outed as a Bush loyalist (and not a journalist) after asking an especially egregious question during a White House press briefing.

9. For more on this phenomenon, called the "K Street Project," see Nicholas Confessore's article titled "Welcome to the Machine: How the GOP Disciplined K Street and Made Bush Supreme," *Washington Monthly* (July/August 2003).

10. Mara Liasson, "Political Left Launches Its Own Attack," *NPR*, June 19, 2007, http://www.npr.org/template.story.story.php?storyId=11181167 (accessed June 19, 2007).

11. Neil Postman, *Amusing Ourselves to Death* (New York: Penguin Books, 1985).

12. David Paletz, *The Media in American Politics* (New York: Longman Publications, 2002).

13. Ibid.

14. Doris Graber, *Mass Media and American Politics*, 6th edition (Washington, D.C.: CQ Press, 2002), 99.

15. Gary Woodward, *Perspectives on American Political Media* (New York: Allyn and Bacon, 1997), 73–75.

16. William G. Jacoby, "Issue Framing and Public Opinion on Government Spending," *American Journal of Political Science*, Vol. 44, No. 4 (October 2000): 750–767. Emphasis in the original.

17. James Druckman, "On the Limits of Framing Effects: Who Can Frame," *Journal of Politics* (November 2001): 1042.

18. Please see Blumenthal (1982), Ornstein and Mann (2000), Jacobs and Shapiro (2000), and Lathrop (2003), among many others.

19. Thomas Mann and Norman Ornstein, *The Broken Branch* (New York: Oxford University Press, 2006), vii.

20. Matthew Baum, "Talking the Vote: Why Presidential Candidates Hit the Talk Show Circuit," *American Journal of Political Science* 49 (2005): 213–234.

21. Lance W. Bennett, *News: The Politics of Illusion*, 6th edition (New York: Pearson Longman, 2005), 40–42.

22. Cass Sunstein, *Republic.com* (Princeton: Princeton University Press, 2002).

23. Markus Prior, "The Real Media Divide," *Washington Post*, July 16, 2007, A15.

24. Much more has been written about the 1996 Telecommunications Act in great detail, and I urge readers to examine this in books by Dale E. Lehman and Dennis L. Weisman (2000) and Nicholas Economides (1998).

25. "U.S. Policy: Telecommunications Act of 1996," *The Museum of Broadcasting Communications*, http://www.museum.tv/archives/etv/U/htmlU/uspolicyt/uspolicyt.htm (accessed May 11, 2009).

26. Clark Hoyt, "Those Persistent Anonymous Sources," *New York Times*, March 21, 2009, http://www.nytimes.com/2009/03/22/opinion/22pubed.html (accessed May 12, 2009).

27. "Timeline of the Iraq Uranium Imbroglio," ABC News, October 1, 2003, http://abcnews.go.com/International/story?id=79393 (accessed May 12, 2009).

28. Robert Novak, "Mission to Niger," *Washington Post*, July 14, 2003, A21.

29. Jennifer O'Brien, "Putting a Face to a (Screen) Name: The First Amendment Implications of Compelling ISPs to Reveal the Identities of Anonymous Internet Speakers in Online Defamation Cases," *Fordham Law Review* (2001), 2745.

Chapter 2

PRINT MEDIA: NEWSPAPERS, MAGAZINES, AND BOOK PUBLISHING

George W. Bush is seen crossing the Potomac River on foot.
The Washington Post: "President Bush crosses the Potomac River."
The Washington Times: "Bush's conservative approach saves taxpayers a boat."
Mother Jones: "Bush can't swim."

—2008 Internet Joke

On October 28, 2008, the vaunted and well-respected *Christian Science Monitor* became the first national newspaper to announce that it was shutting its print operation and moving its news publication operations entirely online. The *Seattle Post Intelligencer* is now available only online as well, as these two papers made the move in an effort to stay alive as many of their peers folded their pages for good. In Michigan, the *Ann Arbor News* shut down publication, began again as a Web site, and then launched a newspaper version of the Web site called *AnnArbor*.com.[1] Major newspapers, such as the *Rocky Mountain News*, have gone under entirely, and the *Baltimore Sun* and the *Boston Globe* are teetering on the verge of collapse. The print media have a long and storied history in American politics, but in recent years the broadcast industry has become so vast and ubiquitous to the point that many people are writing the obituaries for the newspaper and magazine trades. Consistent with the trend to move online for reading material, book publication has declined in profitability as well.

It is true that more and more people are resorting to electronic devices for their information and entertainment purposes, and it is true that fewer people are reading newspapers than in past years. It is also true that the magazine industry is struggling, and many small publishing houses have been bought by larger media conglomerates and folded into bigger publishing entities. But all of this does not mean the printed word is a thing of the past. American politicians use the print media now, albeit in different ways than before, primarily in conjunction with other media. In fact, today's politicians had best make use of print media or they will miss out on an impressive opportunity to create a multifaceted campaign approach. Since politicians want to control the way the media broadcast the messages about them, the print media offer great opportunity. Print journalism, often hard hitting and investigative, can also be fawning, offering politicians the ability to deliver their version of themselves or their opinions of events. Magazines offer similar abilities to delve deeper into personality than broadcast segments, and book publication gives politicians the chance to define themselves, their actions, and their opinions in their own words.

The public continues to read print media, even if at smaller rates than before. The various print industries are happy to announce that advertising in their publications is a smart thing to do because readership remains high even as the numbers dwindle. One example proves the effectiveness of print media in American politics. In 1994, when then-representative Newt Gingrich (R-GA) was promoting the Republican Party's "Contract with America," a 10-point plan aimed at ushering in a Republican-controlled Congress, he printed the Contract on the back page of *TV Guide*. This was, according to Republican consultant Frank Luntz, "a million-dollar proposition but with equally powerful rewards. It was the only magazine people kept in their houses for an entire week and opened on a daily basis—seven unique opportunities to communicate the Contract and all it represented."[2] The "Contract's" publication in *TV Guide* was a tremendously successful effort and paid off for the Republicans, as they gained control of Congress for the first time in 40 years, in no small part thanks to the "Contract with America." Print media was a dynamic part of this effort.

Perhaps "dynamic part" is the best way to view the political use of print media because most politicians use print in conjunction with other types of media. For example, it is wise to gain newspaper endorsements not only because these show support for a political candidate, but also because these endorsements can be used in broadcast political ads to illustrate support for a candidate. Political memoirs and autobiographies are regularly published by politicians, which are then hawked on cable news and talk radio programs by hosts who interview the authors and are featured in other print and Internet articles about the books and their authors. News magazine pieces that will break news and make headlines outside their own readership are leaked well in advance of publication for greater promotion, and all the while print media outlets are used as a larger effort. Political consultants refer to this as "surround sound," where citizens are reached numerous times a day in numerous ways through varying media.

The print industry remains alive in America today, even if the trend within the print industry is to move more content online. Print media are used by politicians as a selective and strategic component of a full-court media press, which keeps print relevant even as Americans shift their attention elsewhere. This chapter examines the way American politicians draw on the newspaper industry, magazine trade, and book publishing houses for their benefit and how the print industry benefits from this attention as well, even as the American public increasingly turns to electronic media instead.

NEWSPAPER INDUSTRY

The United States used to be a "nation of newspapers," and these newspapers have historically played an important role in American politics. Newspapers began in America as the means by which information was communicated, but they quickly became tools of the political parties. Census data from 1850 found that 95 percent of all U.S. newspapers were politically affiliated.[3] However, newspaper partisanship ended in the early part of the twentieth century as advertising made newspapers more lucrative, allowing them the financial independence to break with the parties. This development helped usher in a new set of journalistic norms that emphasized impartiality and neutral reporting. It also helped usher in a reliance on advertising revenue for newspaper survival. In the early years of the twenty-first century, consequently, newspapers are facing an economic crisis because so many readers are moving online, and ad rates drop as a result. According to the Project for Excellence in Journalism, as of 2006—the last time such data was gathered—there were 1,437 daily newspapers in America, a number that has steadily decreased every year since 1990.[4] Many of these newspapers are owned by large corporate chains such as Gannett, which means the financial imperatives of these newspapers are significant.

The newspaper industry in America is extremely fragile right now, with print newspaper circulation dropping annually and ad revenue falling as well. According to the Project for Excellence in Journalism, "Circulation continues to fall at about 2.5 percent year-to-year for dailies and 3.3 percent for Sunday editions."[5] This means that newspaper editors and reporters are panicking as they face increasingly troubled times. The good news for the newspaper industry is that the online readership of these same newspapers is growing as their print readership drops, yet there are still troubles for the trade because the online growth is not commensurate with print declines. Not only does this shift online portend the possible end of print newspapers, but the advertising revenue online is not increasing as much as it has in years past, and oftentimes the ad revenue drops after a move online. The British newspaper, *The Guardian*, reported on a study from City University of London that suggested that ad revenue drops when print publications become exclusively virtual. The study examined the Finnish newspaper *Taloussano*, and the results showed that going online-only cut costs by 50 percent, but ad revenue dropped by 75 percent.[6]

Optimists involved with the newspaper industry argue that the shift to online content keeps newspapers alive in the hearts and minds of the American public. According to advertising executive Marc Brownstein, "We all know that most newspapers are experiencing monthly declines in advertising and circulation. However, many of the readers are now captured online in the newspapers' websites, where the content is current, often compelling, and the writing and presentation gets better every day."[7] The problem is that the business model of the newspaper industry is changing dramatically, and with these changes comes the downsizing of newspaper staffs and the elimination of some well-regarded papers.

In the past several years, major newspaper companies such as the Tribune Company and Dow Jones have faced corporate sales to other media companies. Layoffs within the industry abound. To decrease costs, many newspapers have cut jobs and have also taken the steps to outsource advertising production (such as the *Sacramento Bee*, which produces its ads in India) and hire subcontractors for printing (such as the *Boston Herald*, which is actually printed by its rival, the *Boston Globe*).[8] The reason for this dramatic drop in circulation numbers can be directly attributed to the Internet revolution, but there are other factors at play as well. In addition to the migration of young readers to their computers for news, the advent and prosperity of free dailies distributed in major cities have helped cause the downturn as well. These free newspapers, far shorter in content than standard newspapers, contain the major stories of the day and include a heavy emphasis on lifestyle and entertainment stories. They are often distributed at spots of mass transit, such as train stations and subway stops, in order to attract commuter readers. The existence of these dailies takes away from the standard newspaper circulation, and the numbers drop as a result.

Circulation numbers are important for two primary reasons. First, circulation helps a newspaper promote itself within a community. While very few cities have competing newspapers today, in the major metropolitan areas with more than one newspaper the competition is intense. In cities like New York and Washington, where two or more newspapers vie for readership, many residents take sides in the newspaper wars and fall into characterizations of the newspapers that include depictions of their readers. For instance, in Washington, D.C., the papers divide by ideology, with the *Washington Times* catering to a more conservative clientele and the *Washington Post* accommodating a more liberal audience. The same thing occurs in New York, where competition exists between the *New York Post* and the *Daily News*. These divisions have never been scientifically proven, but the generalizations do hold. Circulation numbers add fuel to the intra-city debates between social groups.

More important than in-fighting between readership groups, circulation numbers drive advertising rates. When a newspaper can claim a superior readership, it can charge a great deal more for ads placed in its pages. Therefore, there is a financial imperative to show increased circulation that helps determine content, emphasis, and style. As in all media industries, the more popular, the more profitable, and so it should come as no surprise that in an effort to prove profitability, when the emphasis is on newspaper circulation, these numbers are occasionally fudged. In the early 2000s, the Tribune Corporation was caught submitting inflated circulation numbers to the Audit Bureau of Circulation, the independent organization that monitors circulation numbers. Executives from the *Newsday* and *Hoy* newspapers pleaded guilty in a circulation-fraud scheme at the publications and were charged with conspiracy to commit mail fraud.[9]

As circulation numbers continue to fall in the newspaper industry, the temptation will remain for newspapers to inflate their readership information or to find innovative ways to attract readers to their print publications. If this does not occur, then budgets will continue to be cut and resources will become even more limited than they already are.

These resources are already extremely scarce, and the staffs at most newspapers are adjusting to this new environment. This adjustment has had a profound effect on the news that is reported in the print publications. The game plan is to do less with less, but in an artful way that will minimize negative reader reaction. As one executive, ordered by headquarters to plan a fresh round of newsroom cuts for 2008, said, "I'm past bleeding—we're into amputation now."[10] In some smaller newspapers there are not enough journalists to cover the city council. In many larger newspapers there are not enough journalists to cover much else. According to data from the Project for Excellence in Journalism, "Foreign bureaus at all but the biggest papers were decimated in 2006; current targets for deep cuts include satellite bureaus, specialty beats like science and religion, and in-house movie and television critics."[11] These cuts have resulted in a greater reliance on news services to report the hard news and a palpable shift towards reporting soft news. Soft news is easier to report and more cost effective and has the added effect of drawing larger readership numbers, especially from younger readers.

And yet, even with this shift towards entertainment-oriented news, young people continue to avoid reading the newspaper. Data from the Project for Excellence in Journalism shows that currently 33 percent of 18- to 24-year-olds and 34 percent of 25- to 34-year-olds read a newspaper in an average week. That said, it is not only the youngest among us who are turning away from the print news, as the largest drop in readership is seen among those ages 35 to 44.[12] Most of the readership hemorrhaging in this under-45 age bracket is caused by the immense shift to online news consumption.

The movement online was a natural progression accompanying the technological developments that made the Internet the powerhouse it is today. Once content could be downloaded quickly and inexpensively, once people could move easily from Web page to Web page, and once it was possible to access the World Wide Web from anywhere—without even being tied to a desk computer, thanks to hand-held personal digital assistants (PDA) like the Palm Pilot or the iPhone—then mass movement to the online world was inevitable. As a result, the print newspaper industry is facing difficult times and is scrounging for ways to make up the difference in its readership numbers and its associated advertising rates. The most obvious way to do this is to move online, which is precisely what most newspapers did. In the earliest days of the Internet, newspapers worked hard to figure out what worked and, perhaps more importantly, what did not.

Several prominent newspapers, the *New York Times* and the *Wall Street Journal* in particular, began online subscription services that would allow paid subscribers to access content unavailable to those just surfing for fun. These charges annoyed many long-time readers of the newspapers, who were eager to access the publications more easily online, and those with access to Lexus-Nexus could get the "premium" content anyway without paying for it. So even though both papers had paid online subscribers totaling in the hundreds of thousands, the *Times* cancelled their online subscription services in the hopes that "traffic and ad revenues will more than make up for lost subscription revenue."[13] The question, of course, is for how long can newspapers remain viable if they keep giving away their news for free on the Internet. Walter Isaacson, the former managing editor for *Time* magazine wrote a cover article for *Time* called "How to Save Your Newspaper," in which he addressed the future of print news. Isaacson writes, "Even an old print junkie like me has quit subscribing to the *New York Times* because if it doesn't see fit to charge for its content I'd feel like a fool paying for it."[14] As Isaacson notes further, the news industry has traditionally relied on newsstand sales, subscriptions, and advertising for revenue. When a paper moves entirely online, it loses two of those three revenue sources.[15]

The future of newspapers and their online components is up for grabs now, with varying solutions proffered. David Carr of the *New York Times* suggested in early 2009 that an iTunes-style solution—a la carte payments for individual stories—was one option.[16] Another model would be monthly payments to access an entire site, such as the *Wall Street Journal* does now. Other solutions abound, but the one commonality among all of them is that the public will be forced to start paying for something they currently get for free.

The competition between the major newspapers is significant. Two percent of American cities have competing newspapers today, a considerable decline from several decades ago, before the Internet revolution hit.[17] As the newspaper industry tightened its belt, the Internet allowed access to more news from around the world, and so competition among newspapers today occurs not only in metro areas boasting several papers, but also in areas where readers have only one daily paper but a computer with access to news from around the nation. The competition for readers not only continues among newspapers themselves, but also grows significantly with the preponderance of news available online from other sources. Newspapers have Web sites, and so do magazines, broadcast news programs, cable news networks, and political bloggers who link to other content. The sheer amount of news online is staggering. To stand out from the crowd and attract attention, newspapers have turned to an online source to increase their readership and cultivate advertising revenue: Yahoo! In 2006, the Internet search engine Yahoo! launched an effort to bring local newspapers online in order to "increase its local content offerings" and generate more ad revenue and traffic for the company.[18] Today, what is called the "Newspaper Consortium" includes 800 local newspapers that has produced 100 million visits to these sites.[19] This collaborative effort has increased the viability of smaller papers online as it has increased their ad revenue. The ability to link with one of the two largest Internet search engines in the world has improved the outlook for these papers and allowed them to compete with larger ones on a national scale.

Yet while Yahoo! presents somewhat of a solution for struggling newspapers, its main competitor Google presents another challenge. According to Josh Cohen, a content specialist at Google News, the mission of the news division is consistent with that of Google itself: "Organizing the world's information, making it universal, accessible, and useful."[20] However, the way that Google News seems to co-opt the newspapers has competitors concerned. The Google News homepage itemizes news stories by category and then supplies links to the news sources supplying the stories. Because the broadcast news outlets also provide streaming audio and video, Google News is more likely to link to them, and this is why the newspaper folks are apprehensive. If Internet users are more likely to go to a clearinghouse of information than a standard newspaper, this does not bode well for the print outlets trying to gain an online audience or keep their print audience intact.

Even as more people turn to the Internet to access their news, the growing number of online readers is not a panacea that soothes the newspaper industry's concerns. For one thing, advertisers do not view online readers to be as valuable as print readers.[21] This is most likely because online readers often skim content and move from Web site to Web site. Print newspaper readers are believed to pay attention to the material in their hands. Another problem facing the industry concerns the fast-moving technological changes that consistently present new adaptation challenges for newspapers. First, the Internet made immediate news transmission possible, but then the computer and phone technology increased so dramatically that hand-held devices operating wireless and from remote locations forced even more changes within the industry. As cell phones and texting become de rigueur, so too does the ability to spread news instantly, even if the news is in bite-sized snippets. According to an article in the *American Journalism Review (AJR)*, the new Blackberry, iPhone, and text phone technology is "smart" and thus tempting for news consumers. It is "readable, visual, acoustic, and connected, serving readers who access breaking news, sports scores, weather, blogs and stock quotes with mobile Internet."[22]

The *AJR* story argues that this "smart" technology will "complement" traditional news outlets. But at what cost? If the news that people are receiving comes in such small amounts, does it really inform or does it just notify? The distinction between these two ideas is found in the depth of knowledge that is communicated. The newspaper industry is facing hard times because the American public views print media as out of date, lagging in current information, and too cumbersome to read in its entirety. And so many news consumers are moving to faster transmission modes and enjoying the constant updates. But what is missing in these shortcuts is the depth of information and substance present in newspaper stories. The attraction to instant gratification may be too tempting for many to resist, but what they gain in speed, they lose in weight and consequence.

As newspaper circulation numbers take a dive, so too does a certain amount of national comprehension and analysis that is vital for deliberative democracy. It is impossible to return to an age where we were a "nation of newspapers," but it is unwise to become a nation entirely without them.

Another problem with the shift from newspapers to online news concerns journalism itself. While newspapers employ reporters to cover various beats and investigate the government actors and businessmen who run our society, the vast majority of bloggers and online news clearinghouses employ no such journalists. Many online news sites rely on "volunteer citizen journalists" who, by the very nature of their unpaid assistant status, are not held to the same level of journalistic accountability as an established reporter. The number of online news and information sites that investigate rather than opine, report rather than argue, and analyze rather than advocate, are far fewer in number than their print counterparts, and this is true even in the era of declining newspaper numbers. One such Internet-originated news site is the *Chitown Daily News*, which covers the local Chicago news with a staff of four reporters, four freelances, and 100 unpaid contributors.[23] This is a start, but the *Chitown Daily News* faces the same problems as other news organizations. Their main competition, the *Chicago Sun Times* and the *Chicago Tribune*, have both declared bankruptcy. Will the *Chitown Daily News* be able to make enough money to continue? Can it afford to report? And does the reporting meet the journalistic standards we have come to rely upon as a democracy with a free press?

Around the country today there still exists investigative reporting, but it now takes the form of magazine articles or documentaries, and these forms are not as readily available to a voting public. Without newspaper reporting, the depth and breadth of our news would suffer, and so too would our political system. One of the cornerstones of American democracy is a free press, one that can not only speak the unpopular but also investigate those in power. While newspapers still exist and wield power, politicians will continue to pay attention to them.

HOW POLITICIANS USE NEWSPAPERS

Politicians use newspapers for two primary political reasons: to help them get elected and to help them promote their policies. The most widespread use of newspapers for electioneering concerns editorial board endorsements. A study by MIT political scientist Stephen Ansolabehere examined newspaper endorsements and found that while the endorsements were fairly equally divided across party lines, they heavily favored incumbents.[24] This bipartisanship pointed to a general trend towards "valuing individual politicians more and parties less."[25] Ansolabehere's study also found that candidates who received newspaper endorsements did better than those who did not: "Those candidates who received endorsements won approximately 5 percentage points more at the polls than those who were not endorsed."[26] This provides enough evidence to inspire politicians running for office to seek out the endorsement of their local paper if campaigning for local office, or larger papers if campaigning statewide or nationally.

That said, there are those who question the efficacy of newspaper endorsements. In a 2004 article titled "What's the Point?" the *AJR* argued that newspapers carry endorsements in order to assert their own authority and knowledge of a candidate or an election cycle, and it casted doubts upon the influence of the endorsement over the voting public.[27] Gail Collins, the editorial page editor of the *New York Times*, lends credence to this last point: "I don't think anybody who has a job like mine is deluded that many people change their opinion about who they're going to vote for president when they see the *Times* editorial."[28] *Time* magazine's James Poniewozik agreed, stating, "I don't think there's too much to be gained by trying to impress newspaper editorial boards anymore, which I think is a message that at least a lot of candidates have learned at this point."[29]

So why do politicians even bother trying to garner editorial board endorsements at election time? One reason is tradition, because newspaper endorsements have historically played an important role in American politics. Politicians would not be well served to ignore this tradition and raise the ire of those who publish the news. As newspapers lose readers, power, and prestige, however, the need for endorsements feels antiquated and unnecessary. In the end, the simple fact is that any good publicity helps on election day, and the value of a positive endorsement is worth something. Tied into a larger campaign of ads that publicize endorsements, they can be powerful tools. Political candidate endorsements also help advertise the paper, since candidates use the newspaper's name to broadcast their success. Thus, the endorsements serve two purposes: they help validate the usefulness of a newspaper and also provide an easy narrative for other news organizations to report upon.

In addition to affecting politics through political endorsements, newspapers report on campaigns and policy initiatives. Although most news organizations tend to emphasize process over policy, the reporting on policymaking can have profound effects on the success of the policy. Two policy examples that help illustrate this point include President Bill Clinton's 1993 health care reform plan and President George W. Bush's 2005 Social Security reform plan. Although both approaches were dissimilar in terms of ideology, both proposed revolutionary institutional change and both were initiated immediately following elections, at a time when both newly elected presidents believed they had political capital to spend. Both reform plans were bold, proposing serious changes to the status quo of American society, and both presidents who put forward these ideas backed them with well-crafted policy campaigns to sell them to the American public first, in the hope that the public would try to influence their representatives in Congress to agree with the presidents' plans. Both efforts were large, expensive, and well-coordinated public relations campaigns that aimed to rally public support, and both efforts included speeches where the president would travel to cities around the country and sell the policy program. Both efforts also included media appearances from administration officials who were dispatched by the White House to push the presidential initiative.

Interestingly, neither reform proposal proved to be legislatively successful, most likely because the media concentrated on the policy fights taking place on Capitol Hill instead of examining the policy proposals themselves. I researched the *New York Times* and *USA Today* newspapers during these two time periods to understand how they covered the policy debates. More often than not, both newspapers emphasized the process—the fighting, wrangling, and horse trading of the policymaking process—more often than they examined the policy proposals themselves. The reasoning is fairly clear: There were tremendous battles fought over both proposals, and it is infinitely easier to write about the process than it is intricate public policy initiatives. It is also more interesting to read about fights than about numbers. In both cases, when more attention was paid to the battles, the brawling took center stage, and the end result could only be a victory for one side and a loss for another. Within this wrestling frame, the policy focus was lost. One might have expected the *New York Times*, the nation's "newspaper of record" to concern itself with policy more than *USA Today*, a Technicolored light read that was once called the "McPaper." It did not. In the end, both papers paid more attention to the most personality-driven aspects of the stories and included the fighting that occurred within the process of passing policy.

As newspapers face a declining readership, they will continue to emphasize soft news over hard news and process over policy because these are more attractive to reading audiences who wish to be entertained. As stories shrink to headline length to accommodate electronic devices, the easier a story is to convey, the more likely it will be communicated. At risk is the journalism, of course. This is so perilous that President Barack Obama broke from a lighthearted speech at the 2009 White House Correspondent's Dinner to address this very issue:

> This is a season of renewal and reinvention. That is what government must learn to do, that's what businesses must learn to do, and that's what journalism is in the process of doing. And when I look out at this room and think about the dedicated men and women whose questions I've answered over the last few years, I know that for all the challenges this industry faces, it's not short on talent or creativity or passion or commitment. It's not short of young people who are eager to break news or the not-so-young who still manage to ask the tough ones time and time again. These qualities alone will not solve all your problems, but they certainly prove that the problems are worth solving. And that is a good place as any to begin.[30]

MAGAZINE INDUSTRY

The same problems that face the newspaper industry also face magazine publications. Magazines are dealing with hard times in the Internet age and are changing their format and approach as ad revenue drops. Also like their newspaper brothers and sisters, magazines are shifting much of their emphasis online, and in doing so are changing the way their print material looks as well.

News magazines fall roughly into three categories. The first are news weeklies, of which there are a "Big Three"—*Time, Newsweek,* and *U.S. News and World Report.* These magazines take a universal approach to the news, covering hard news items plus lifestyle, sport, arts, culture, and entertainment topics as well. The second category includes the elite magazines, such as *The New Yorker, The Economist,* and *The Week,* which take a more narrow approach to the news and generally eschew the lighter material that might give the news wider appeal. The final category consists of ideologically leaning magazines, such as *The National Review, The Weekly Standard, The New Republic,* and *The Nation.* These magazines cover the news from a consistent ideological viewpoint and include criticism and commentary. Other magazines cater to niche interests. According to *The Christian Science Monitor,* there are 200 magazines that focus on three subjects alone: golf, dogs, and interior design.[31]

The magazine industry is a large one, and one that can, by virtue of its own diversity, attract a wide variety of demographics. Because there are magazines that are targeted to very specific interests, the industry can be viewed as far reaching yet shallow, with many magazines bringing in a small number of subscribers. Each magazine has to ascertain its own level of viability since ad rates are drawn from circulation and readership numbers, and magazines earn their profits from ad revenue and subscriptions. Most magazines are owned by large media organizations, the largest being Time Warner, which owns more than 70 magazine publications worldwide, including such major magazines as *Time, Fortune,* and *People* and such niche publications as *Land Rover World, Sporting Gun,* and *Horse and Hound.*[32] The top five magazine publishers account for about one-third of total magazine revenue generated in the United States.[33]

Independent magazines have much to worry about these days in addition to declining readership numbers. In 2007, the Postal Regulatory Commission increased postage rates for magazines significantly, but did so in a way that clearly favored larger publications. Magazines with circulations over 250,000 saw a postage increase of 10 percent. For magazines with lower circulations, the increase was sometimes twice or three times more. According to an article in *New York Review of Magazines,* "The new suggested rate system changed from a flat rate per pound, like a stamp for a first-class letter that costs the same no matter how far the letter travels within the United States, to a new piece-by-piece rate, like determining how much the stamp should cost based on how difficult it would be to deliver the letter."[34] The larger magazine publishers would clearly benefit from this structure, and so it should come as no surprise that Time Warner helped engineer the specific postal rate increase plan through months of serious lobbying efforts.[35] Smaller magazine publishers were so outraged that even ideologically disparate magazines such as *Nation* and *National Review* came together to beg Congress for assistance. Although the House Subcommittee on Federal Workforce, Postal Service, and the District of Columbia held a hearing to examine the issue, as one committee member, Congressman Elijah Cummings (D-MD), asked rhetorically, "This is a done deal, isn't it?"[36] The result of this "done deal" could very well be the elimination of smaller magazines that are forced out of business by the immense postal rate increases that hit their publications disproportionately harder and with more devastating effect than the larger publications.

Larger magazines are safe from the hazards of postage rate increases (for now) but are still subject to the problems of readership movement online. The circulation of the "Big Three" newsmagazines has remained "flat" in the past several years, and according to Ball State University journalism professor David Sumner, "The extent of their influence has declined. . . . News has become more of a commodity, and it's cheap and easy to find."[37] And so the "Big Three" newsmagazines are adjusting themselves to compete with broadcast news on television and radio and with the immensity of information on the Internet. According to Sumner, "They're trying hard to provide more interpretation, insight, and context, as well as soft entertainment stuff." In addition to emphasizing more soft news and light reading, the news magazines have cut their news bureaus to cut corners as well.[38] Since the new emphasis is on entertainment, it's not like they need news bureaus anyway.

Time magazine changed its publication date in 2007 from Monday to Friday in order to appeal to weekend readers and now augments its print material with an Internet site that contains more original content than simply rehashing what is in the magazine itself. The others in the "Big Three" are taking different tacks, with *Newsweek* publishing on Mondays and emphasizing analysis. According to publisher Gregory Osberg, "In the past you followed the news. Now we're getting out in front of it and providing analysis."[39] *U.S. News and World Report* remains committed to "serious news" and eschews lighter fare in favor of international coverage. It also maintains its third-place ranking in the newsweeklies' "Big Three." According to the Project for Excellence in Journalism, "The topic breakdown shows that the three magazines are distinctly different and that one, *U.S. News*, is hewing to a more traditional news agenda. It is carving out a hard-news niche among the three magazines and avoiding the broadest 'general-interest news magazine' approach taken by its two bigger-circulation siblings. That may be a factor in the smaller size of the audience for the *U.S. News* but perhaps in the long run it's a more devoted one."[40]

Because news magazines are published only weekly, biweekly, or monthly, it is virtually impossible for them to actually break news. Even if there is a breaking story in a magazine, today that story is often leaked ahead of the publication in order to help sell the magazine. For example, in 2005 *Vanity Fair* magazine broke the biggest story in journalism to date, which was the identity of the Watergate informant known as "Deep Throat." In order to promote this "news breaking" issue, *Vanity Fair* leaked its news to other media outlets that broke the story before the magazine hit the newsstands. Thus, in lieu of breaking news, news magazines have to focus their energy on attracting an audience through broad appeal (and more entertaining content) or on analysis and opinion pieces that draw subscribers and raise ad revenue. While the magazine industry is not facing the devastation that newspapers are, they are still facing hard times as the American public increasingly turns to broadcast media or goes online for their news and information. The result is more of an emphasis on entertainment in order to attract enough readers to stay afloat.

Online news magazines that specialize in politics are successful endeavors that use a hybrid approach to publication. Many have regular columns and columnists but then also have breaking news stories on their sites to keep them current. Online magazines such as *Slate*, *Politico*, and *Salon* are able to stay afloat because they work in conjunction with other news organizations. For instance, *Slate* partners with the *Washington Post*, and *Politico* partners with CBS News. This is a win-win situation for both partners because it allows a free-flow of news information from established media organizations to the online magazines and provides access to additional online vehicles for the established media outfit.

HOW POLITICIANS USE MAGAZINES

Like cable news, magazine publication is a niche-driven industry where most magazines focus exclusively on specific topics and rarely delve into outside matters. However, as politicians try to use the "surround sound" approach, those campaigning often appear in non-news-oriented magazines to help attract attention. Obviously, politicians use magazines in comparable ways to other media outlets: to advertise themselves, construct their own image, and draw attention to the things they value most. In such a niche market, magazines can be especially useful.

Examples from the 2008 presidential campaign help to illustrate how political candidates use magazines. In the two-year campaign that led to Barack Obama's presidential election, the Democratic candidate and his wife, Michelle, were featured in numerous general interest magazines that helped them construct their public image. In these articles, the Obama's marriage, their individual and shared histories, and family matters were addressed in exhaustive detail. In magazines that have a specific focus, such as education and health care periodicals, a prospective Obama presidency and its effect on related industries was examined in similar detail. Women's magazines scrutinized Michelle Obama's fashion sense, her education, her parenting skills, and her possible importance as a role model for all women, especially African-American women. Even niche-oriented magazines took a look at the would-be president, with bridal magazines questioning the impact of an Obama presidency on the wedding industry. A trade magazine for the floral industry featured a story celebrating Obama's purchase of a dozen white roses for Michelle on the occasion of their sixteenth anniversary. The florist interviewed by the magazine about Obama's floral purchase said, "He was very engaging and easy to talk with. This is good for the whole flower industry."[41] Even the most non-political magazines can include political content when politicians are viewed not as policymakers but instead as celebrities.

Magazines can be part of a larger effort to define a politician's image or they can be used to frame a policy discussion. Because it is such a specialized industry, magazine publications are used well when they focus on a particular element of a candidate's personality or policy endeavor. Politicians cannot rely on magazines alone in their political efforts, but magazines can help a politician reach a specific segment of American voters. This allows politicians to tailor their messages to particular audiences in the hope of having a greater impact overall.

THE BOOK INDUSTRY

There are more than a million titles in print today,[42] and in 2007 publishers sold 3.13 billion books.[43] While this would appear to indicate robust sales and a healthy publishing industry, the number of books sold in 2007 remained essentially the same as the year before, which was cause for concern amongst publishing houses.[44] According to David Rosenthal, the publisher of Simon & Schuster, "It is a time of uncertainty and overall economic concern."[45] Publication numbers skyrocket in years when mega-hits such as *Harry Potter* are released, but these numbers dwindle in off years as fewer Americans are willing to pay the $35 for a hardcover book. Best-sellers help buoy the industry that, much like the newspaper and magazine industries, is mainly controlled by large media corporations that have immense financial imperatives. For example, the imprints Random House, Doubleday Crown, Alfred A. Knopf, Bantam, Ballantine, Delacorte, and Dell are all owned by the German company Bertelsmann AG, which also owns radio stations, magazines, and music recording companies like Sony. The publishing house Simon & Schuster is owned by CBS, part of Sumner Redstone's National Amusements corporate entity, which also controls numerous radio and television stations. HarperCollins is owned by Rupert Murdoch's News Corp, which also owns *The Wall Street Journal*, the Fox cable television networks, magazines such as *The Weekly Standard*, and a wide variety of international news organizations. The financial pressures to add to these mega-corporate bottom lines are enormous.

Dan Brown's book *The Da Vinci Code* was such a hit that there are now more than 80 million copies that have been printed. According to Brad Martin, president and CEO of Random House of Canada, "What really moves the needle in this business is a hit, a big hit."[46] As a result, the book publishing business is constantly looking for books that will "move the needle" and supply the sensation that will earn the companies the most money. There is a great deal of money at stake: The Book Industry Study Group (BISG) estimated that total publishers' net revenues in 2007 were $37.26 billion, and they estimate growth at such a pace that revenues will reach $43.46 billion by 2012. If Americans are not willing to spend large sums of money on hardcover books, then the book-buying audience will be very particular in their purchasing. Thus, even though political books garner a different audience than, perhaps, *The Da Vinci Code*, there remains competition for profits. Thus, politicians know that their books must attract attention in order to be considered for publication; for if they are not potentially lucrative, then they are not viable publishing options.

Technological advances in book publication have been a boon to authors, who are now more able to self-publish than ever before. In order to actually place a book in a bookstore and afford it real publicity, however, an author needs a major publishing house behind him. Technological advances have also aided book publishing online, and Google has begun an effort to scan millions of books into its databases, giving the reading public access to these books online. A class-action lawsuit against Google tried to stop the Internet giant from advancing its Google Book Search engine, but in May 2009 a deal was reached that allowed the search engine to proceed with its book project. Authors can opt in to the Google Book Search engine, giving the rights to their books to Google and sharing in any profits garnered from a user acquisition, or they can opt out, whereby Google is supposed to remove the title from its list and allow authors to retail all rights for themselves. According to an article in *The Irish Times*:

> The settlement grants Google the ability to scan all the books it wants, and then use that content in various ways. It might sell entire books via instant printing services; it might sell chunks of material to be used in class reading packs for universities and colleges (a common form of assigned reading in U.S. college courses); it might make material available with targeted advertising running alongside it.[47]

The future of book publishing in the Internet era is daunting. Much like the newspaper and magazine industries, publishing houses are struggling to remain solvent. Despite this uncertainty, politicians continue to write books in order to publicize themselves, for book publication is an excellent way to write and promote themselves to the American public.

HOW POLITICIANS USE BOOK PUBLICATION

Politicians write autobiographies to portray themselves to the public; they write policy books as a call to action; and they write memoirs to recall important and defining life and career moments and to solidify their legacies. These books may vary in their focus, but most are written within the manner described by the U.K.'s *Independent* newspaper as "self-serving, self-congratulatory."[48] The authors of these books, in constructing their own narrative or their call to action, are certain to cast themselves as the hero in their own story. These books provide nice launching pads unto other media venues to increase visibility and enhance name-recognition, and this means the author-as-hero narrative is spread more easily.

There are some politicians who author books because they have a vested interest in the subject matter. Take, for example, Republican Senator and former presidential candidate John McCain who has authored or coauthored almost two dozen books, most of which concern military matters. He coauthored a history of the Naval Academy (from which he graduated) and a book on combat trauma as well as several books on heroic battlefield behavior. All of this makes sense because McCain is a Vietnam combat veteran with an abundance of experience in the armed services. These publications allowed McCain to share his own knowledge at the same time he could advertise himself to the general public, but the fact that McCain has a personal and deeply held interest in this subject matter cannot be denied. The point is that McCain was able to use his personal knowledge of military matters in order to present himself as a patriot, as an expert in the military, and as a leader. Through this book publication, McCain established his military bona fides at the same time he kept his name fresh to the general public.

Politicians have also written books in order to explain bad behavior and to construct their own version of history. For example, former New Jersey Governor James McGreevey resigned from his office in 2004 after he was outed as a homosexual by a staffer who was blackmailing him. In 2009, McGreevey wrote a memoir, titled *The Confession*, that explained his version of events that occurred during and after his tenure in office. The fact that McGreevey lied so egregiously to his wife and his constituents in the course of his career cast a shadow on his political legacy. His memoir was one way to justify the events that took place in an effort to restore his political name. Another example of a politician crafting his own take on history was seen in 2009 when the late Senator Edward Kennedy authorized a comprehensive autobiography to be published immediately following his death from cancer. His book, titled *True Compass: A Memoir*, addressed the Senator's proudest and most humble moments, and in doing so cast his own account as the definitive history of his life. Both examples show how politicians can use book publication to further their own political images.

Self-description provides politicians with the ability to entirely control a message, with the added bonus of repeating this construction on television, on the radio, and in interviews that help spread the image. For politicians, this construction often means exposing one's flaws for self-definition before others characterize them in unflattering terms. For example, before he was elected president, Barack Obama wrote several books that specifically described and characterized his unique international upbringing, a topic that could have been purposely misconstrued by his opponents. When Obama was interviewed about his autobiography on shows like *Late Night with David Letterman*, *The Daily Show with Jon Stewart*, and *The View*, he was able to affirm his story and refute the mischaracterizations made by his political opponents. Also in these narratives, Obama revealed certain elements of his past that could also be detrimental to his electoral aspirations, such as his drug use as a young man. By controlling the report himself in his book, Obama was able to get in front of a potentially damaging story, and in doing so declared the matter dead and dealt with. Obama's drug use was never brought up again in the 2008 presidential campaign, making his telling of the story quite effective in its ability to neutralize a potential scandal. While she was First Lady, Hillary Clinton wrote substantive books about education, in addition to her more general interest publications. Once she was out of the White House and eyeing her next big political effort, however, Hillary Clinton wrote her memoirs, which helped her reframe her public persona and craft herself as a heroic figure—someone who might be a worthy candidate for the Oval Office herself. Thus, the primary reason that political figures write books is to sell themselves. Politicians are wise to define themselves through these books since others will eventually use the books as evidence in the candidates' narratives. This makes these books an important element of a continuous public relations loop, where others refer back to the words of the author as evidence and proof of a story's veracity.

Besides the elected officials themselves, ancillary political figures write books to augment the careful construction of a political figure, which is why First Ladies often publish books of their own. Barbara Bush, the wife of our 41st president George H. W. Bush, wrote a book about her dog, Millie, and Hillary Rodham Clinton did the same when she was First Lady, writing about Socks (her cat) and Buddy (her dog). In the past, First Ladies have mostly written books with wide-ranging appeal, including children's books and books about the White House, its decor, and its place in history. These are somewhat standard topics for First Ladies, whose job it is to add a personal face to the most important office and officeholder in the free world. First Lady Laura Bush maintained this tradition by writing several children's books that focused on literacy and American history, plus a book about Internet safety called *Faux Paw's Adventures in the Internet*.

First Ladies are not the only ones writing books to help further the political ambitions of the men with whom they are attached. In today's heavily mediated environment, the children of politicians are getting in on the act too. One of the Bush twins, Jenna, wrote two books while her father was in office, one coauthored with her mother and one she wrote with a different coauthor about a young woman in Latin America. During the 2008 presidential campaign, GOP candidate John McCain's daughter wrote a book about him and then went on a book tour promoting the book and her father. Here as well, the books serve multiple functions, both as vehicles for issue investigation and as personality promotion. In these cases, however, the personality being promoted is not necessarily the author's.

Politicians have learned that the path from book publication to book promotion on radio and television is one that is both lucrative for the publishing house and advantageous for their own needs as well. By going on television programs such as *The Late Show with David Letterman*, *Oprah*, and *The Daily Show* to publicize their books, they can sell books at the same time they sell themselves to millions of American voters. It is now de rigueur for politicians to write books that tell their emotional stories (such as triumph over a poor upbringing, military heroism, or victory over personal tribulations) in order to pull readers towards them at the same time they make money for themselves and the major companies that publish the book.

Publishing houses themselves tend to be nonpartisan, selecting titles for their lists based on factors other than the political leanings of the author. There are obvious exceptions to this, most notably Regnery, Sentinel, and Encounter Books, all of which are conservative. Regnery, which calls itself "the nation's leading conservative publisher," has published titles from Newt Gingrich, Bernard Goldberg, and others. For conservative political writers, publishing with Regnery or one of its competitors gives them the advantage of promotional connections within the conservative media establishment: access to Fox News, *The Washington Times*, and popular talk radio programs. Additionally, conservative book clubs have sprouted around the country, which helps add a level of publicity to these titles. The "Book of the Month Club" added a conservative book club in 2003.[49] This interconnectedness has proven to be so successful and lucrative for the publishing houses that several of them have added conservative imprints to their company. One example is Sentinel Books, created in 2003 as a "dedicated conservative imprint" for Penguin U.S.A. Books.

If the intention of these conservative presses is to provide balance against liberal publishers, it is working far too well since there are very few specifically left-leaning publishing houses. Those that do exist are very small presses and include The New Press and Nation Books. However, conservatives argue that the publishing establishment is so inherently biased that, in the words of Steve Ross, publisher of Crown and its new rightward imprint, Crown Forum, a liberal publishing imprint would be "redundant."[50] This means, however, that there is a dedicated conservative press operating in a media system without a dedicated ideological counterpart. Although conservatives claim bias, there is not much hard evidence or data that back up this claim.

For those involved in politics without being an elected official—meaning mostly those in the political media—book publication is a good way to publicize oneself and cross-promote opinion. This phenomenon occurs across the ideological spectrum. Radio and television pundits such as Keith Olbermann, Bill O'Reilly, and Sean Hannity are authors of numerous books that help them advertise their broadcast endeavors while at the same time afford them the opportunity to advertise their books on their programs. These cross-promotion publications are meant to enhance the public image of a partisan who makes his or her money through outrage, and so in these cases the more attention-getting the book, the better.

Often, the best way to attract an audience is to incite emotion and feeling, and the queen of this trend has to be Ann Coulter. In 2006 Coulter, a conservative pundit prominently featured across all media, released her fifth book, titled *Godless: The Church of Liberalism*. While the title itself was provocative enough to sell thousands of copies of the book, the content proved to be even more confrontational. Coulter wrote that liberalism is "a comprehensive belief system denying the Christian belief in man's immortal soul" and that it is "the opposition party to God."[51] However, what earned her the most attention was what she wrote about the September 11th widows—the women who lost husbands in the attacks on the World Trade Center and the Pentagon. About these women, Coulter wrote:

> These self-obsessed women seemed genuinely unaware that 9/11 was an attack on our nation and acted as if the terrorist attacks happened only to them. . . . [T]hey believed the entire country was required to marinate in their exquisite personal agony. Apparently, denouncing Bush was an important part of their closure process. . . . These broads are millionaires, lionized on TV and in articles about them, reveling in their status as celebrities and stalked by grief-arazzis. I've never seen people enjoying their husbands' deaths so much.[52]

Coulter's incredible statements could not have surprised anyone even vaguely familiar with her work. The conservative magazine *The National Review* discontinued her column after she wrote of her ideal antiterrorism policy: "We should invade their countries, kill their leaders, and convert them all to Christianity."[53] Despite this cancellation, Coulter remains a popular, well-published, and powerful conservative voice in Washington. She has called Democratic presidential candidate John Edwards a "faggot," and instead of apologizing she later went on to say, "I'll just wish he had been killed in a terrorist assassination plot." Coulter wrote on her Web site, "Liberals want mass starvation and human devastation."[54] In a November 2006 syndicated column, Coulter wrote, "After the attacks of 9/11, profiling Muslims is more like profiling the Klan."[55] Two of her earlier books are titled *Treason: Liberal Treachery from the Cold War to the War on Terrorism* and *Slander: Liberal Lies about the American Right*. Her attitudes about the left in general, and liberalism in particular, have been well established. Nonetheless, these comments about the 9/11 widows garnered Coulter an immense amount of attention from media outlets of all stripes. She went on Larry King's show, the conservative radio talk shows, and NBC's *Today Show* to chat about her writings.

Coulter did not go on TV and radio programs to defend herself, because Coulter knew exactly what she was writing when she wrote it, and her editors at Crown knew exactly what she had written when they published it. Instead, Coulter went on TV and radio to reiterate her statements, give them more airtime, and broadcast her message most effectively. The reason to print something so inflammatory and hurtful is because everyone involved knew it would get attention, knowing full well that such attention-getting would lead to book sales and that book sales would lead to more money and fame for everyone involved. The point of discussing her actions on television and on the radio was to reap more attention for her book. Coulter was rewarded for her inciting statements with greater fame, a more recognized platform, and thus more attention. If she had softened her language just a bit, her book would not have garnered the immense free publicity that it gained. If she were more nuanced in her approach, her prominence as a conservative pundit, an ideological lightning rod, and agent provocateur would have been compromised. She would not have been heard above all of the media around today, nor would her publisher, Crown Publishing Group, reap the financial windfall from her publications. Coulter's example helps to illustrate how book publishing can present a variety of rewards for those who are successful at it. It offers financial compensation, personal fame, and ideological propagation.

Book publication is an effective way for politicians and political actors to double and triple their exposure, but as more readers go online this efficacy might lessen as well. As is the case with newspaper and magazine publication, the book publishing industry is facing challenges from the Internet, and many publishers are looking for innovative ways, beyond Google Book Search, to advance their own technology and go online as well. Audio books, or "books on tape," have been around for some time and are increasing their visibility on Web sites such as "Audible," where consumers can purchase MP3 versions of a book and download them to an iPod or other MP3 player. Thus, not only can you buy a book on CD (no one really uses tapes anymore) but you can find books on your computer and listen to them without reading.

Other ways computers are changing the face of publication is through so-called e-book technology. Electronic books are available now, and people can download entire texts to their computer or to e-book players designed specifically for readers to take with them, away from their PCs. The largest e-book publishing group, the International Digital Publishing Forum, reported e-book sales of $31.8 million in 2007.[56] To stay ahead of this curve, the Internet bookstore Amazon has launched its own e-book reader called *Kindle*, which weighs under a pound and can hold up to 200 books.[57] Looking at the unmitigated success of MP3 players for music, those in the publishing industry state, "The digitalization of personal book collections is certain to have its day soon."[58] The success of e-books has yet to be determined, but the success of the *Kindle* proves that there is a market for books in varying forms. At the present time, books still have paper pages and covers, but thanks to technology the future will undoubtedly bring significant change to this industry as well.

Conclusions

As print media change in format and structure, so do the ways politicians use them. Today, the print media are used as part of a broader media effort, where print, broadcast, and online media work together to provide news and advertise people or issues. However, the print industries are in such serious financial trouble that their future is uncertain. This then threatens the "surround sound" effort used by politicians that includes print media as one important component. Politicians will adapt to the declining importance of print media, but as fewer people read print material, there are consequences for the American electorate and for the news industry. One consequence is the loss of connectivity that a newspaper provides for a community. Newspapers have held an historic place in American life as the gatherers of information that is vital to democracy. As a city or town reads a common newspaper, the citizenry shares in a collective debate over issues and events because newspapers not only inform but also steer discussion in one direction or another. As fewer people read the newspaper— even if it an online newspaper—this communal exercise is lost. Lost also is knowledge of one's own community, the local politics and policies that drive our everyday lives. Without beat reporters watching town halls, this local news is gone. This is not a small problem since many of the issues that matter most to Americans transpire at the local level. Education, taxation, and zoning are all matters of great local import, and without local newspapers covering the town halls and borough council meetings, information about these matters cannot be communicated effectively to the citizenry. Deprived of this information, citizens cannot effectively participate in the political system.

Another consequence that will result from the loss of the print media concerns the news industry. As the print news media diminish in size and scope, the question remains: What happens to the journalists and staffers who helped to produce print journalism? Undoubtedly they will try to move on to other news outlets or to careers that use their skills. However, the news industry in general is faltering, and so while those with transferable skills, such as graphic artists and technical specialists, can shift industries it will be more difficult for the editors, reporters, and producers of the news to do the same. This can potentially be a time of great innovation in journalism, and certainly many print journalists will move online to collaborations with colleagues that bring new advances to their craft. Already, thanks to efforts such as *Congressional Quarterly Online*, *National Journal*, and *Politico*, we can observe Washington politics 24 hours a day, reported by expert, knowledgeable, and professional journalists. However, even these news online outlets are limited in number and cannot absorb every print journalist who wants to remain working in his profession.

There are many outlets that report on the news that has been gathered: Polling Web sites such as *Rasmussen Reports*, *FiveThirtyEight*, and *Pollster* provide citizens with as many polling numbers as they can handle. Political bloggers opine constantly about the events that shape our civic lives and allow readers to join the conversation through their online posts. These are important information channels, but their impact is limited without the proper context, which can only be provided by real journalists. Information is not in short supply, but actual news, sadly, is. John Naisbitt, in his 1988 book *Megatrends: Ten New Directions Transforming Our Lives*, wrote, "We are drowning in information but starved for knowledge." Without newspaper reporters investigating the news on their beats, drumming up facts and substance, there will be little actual news for other media to feed upon and little real news to inform the citizenry.

If the print industry fails there will be consequences for politicians too, since the newspaper endorsement, magazine profile, and autobiography have been so essential in American politicking. Politicians will adapt to the changing media landscape for the simple reason that they are forced to, but the public will be deprived of the valuable information that the print media provides. As the reading public moves online, so too will politicians because they understand the importance of electronic media in American society. According to *Time* magazine's James Poniewozik, this decreases the importance of print for those running for office: "The greater danger to a candidate is not from getting negative unsigned editorials about them from the *L.A. Times* and places like that, it's the controversy that bubbles up from out of nowhere online."[59] Electronic media allow fast information dissemination and easier access for a greater number of people. Yet at the same time, the shift away from print media bodes poorly for the electorate's understanding of complex issues and debates between actors that go beyond simple policy battles. The print form that tolerates longer, in-depth examinations and even encourages multifaceted analysis is sometimes found electronically—but not often. When the power of the print press is weakened irrevocably, so too will be journalism's watchdog function afforded to us by the First Amendment. Since print media are more tangibly substantive than broadcast media and generally more trustworthy than online media, the result will be an electorate that may be less informed than it once was.

NOTES

1. Bella Luscombe, "Killing the News to Save It," *Time*, August 17, 2009, 49.

2. Frank Luntz, *Words That Work: It's Not What You Say, It's What People Hear* (New York: Hyperion, 2007), 157.

3. Baldasty and Rutenbeck in Edwin C. Baker, "Advertising and a Democratic Press," *University of Pennsylvania Law Review*, Vol. 140, No. 6 (June 1992): 2129.

4. The State of the News Media 2008, The Project for Excellence in Journalism, http://www.journalism.org/ (accessed May 11, 2009).

5. The State of the News Media 2007, The Project for Excellence in Journalism, http://www.journalism.org/ (accessed July 12, 2008).

6. Bobbie Johnson, "Online-Only Newspapers May Lose More than They Gain," *Guardian UK*, April 16, 2009.

7. Marc Brownstein, "Stop Writing Those Obituaries for the Newspaper Industry," *Advertising Age*, October 29, 2007: 23.

8. "Newspapers: Economics," State of the News Media 2007, The Project for Excellence in Journalism, http://www.journalism.org/.

9. Zach Haberman, "Newsday Pleas: Execs Cop to Fraud for Fleecing Advertisers," *New York Post*, May 27, 2006.

10. State of the News Media 2007, The Project for Excellence in Journalism, http://www.journalism.org/.

11. Ibid.

12. Ibid.

13. Ibid.

14. Walter Isaacson, "How to Save Your Newspaper," *Time*, February 16, 2009, 30.

15. Ibid.

16. David Carr, "Let's Invent an iTunes for News," *New York Times*, January 11, 2009.

17. David Paletz, *The Media in American Politics* (New York: Longman Publications, 2002), 35.

18. Mark Shields, "Yahoo!'s Newspaper Consortium a Hit with Users," *Media Week*, July 30, 2008.

19. Ibid.

20. Brett Popplewell, "Organizing News of the World," *Toronto Star*, May 9, 2008, B04.

21. Richard Perez-Pena, "More Readers Trading Newspapers for Web Sites," *New York Times*, November 6, 2007, C9.

22. Arielle Emmett, "Handheld Headlines," *American Journalism Review* (August/September 2008): 1.

23. Howard Kurtz, "Winds of Change in Chicago News," *Washington Post*, April 1, 2009, C01.

24. Stephen Ansolabehere, Rebecca Lessem, and James M. Snyder, Jr. "The Political Orientation of Newspaper Endorsements in U.S. Elections, 1940–2002," *Quarterly Journal of Political Science*, Vol. 1, No. 4 (Fall 2006): 393–404.

25. Ibid.

26. Ibid.

27. Tim Porter, "What's the Point?" *American Journalism Review* (October/November 2004).

28. Ibid.

29. James Poniewozik, June 9, 2008, Personal interview with author.

30. President Barack Obama, White House Correspondent's Association dinner speech. Transcript, May 10, 2009, http://blogs.suntimes.com/sweet/2009/05/obama_at_the_white_house_corre.html (accessed May 11, 2009).

31. Randy Dotniga, "For a Magazine Industry, Less May Be More," *Christian Science Monitor*, May 14, 2007.

32. *Columbia Journalism Review: Who Owns What?* http://www.cjr.org/resources/ (accessed October 1, 2008).

33. David Paletz, *The Media in American Politics* (New York: Longman Publications, 2002), 37.

34. Callie Enlow, "Going Postal," *New York Review of Magazines*, http://74.125.93.132/search?q=cache:4Hj1SKOlxqYJ:www.nyrm.org/Features/FeatureEnlow.html+enlow+and+%22The+new+suggested+rate+system%22&cd=1&hl=en&ct=clnk&gl=us.

35. Ibid.

36. Ibid.

37. Randy Dotniga, "For a Magazine Industry, Less May Be More," *Christian Science Monitor*, May 14, 2007, 1.

38. Ibid.

39. Ibid.

40. State of the News Media 2007, The Project for Excellence in Journalism, http://www.journalism.org/.

41. "Barack Obama Celebrates Wedding Day with Roses," *FloraCulture International*, http://www.floracultureinternational.com/index.php?Itemid=116&id=640&option=com _content&task=view (accessed January 13, 2009).

42. David Paletz, *The Media in American Politics* (New York: Longman Publications, 2002), 39.

43. Motoko Rich, "Potter Was Still Magical, but Not All Books Rose," *New York Times*, May 30, 2008.

44. Ibid.

45. Ibid.

46. Vit Wagner, "Pinning Hopes on the Next Megaseller," *Toronto Star*, February 23, 2008, E01.

47. Karlin Lillington, "Reading between the Lines of Google Books Settlement," *Irish Times*, May 8, 2009, http://www.irishtimes.com/newspaper/finance/2009/0508/1224246114910.html (accessed May 11, 2009).

48. Paul Vallely, "The Big Question: Why Are So Many Political Memoirs Published, and Does Anyone Read Them?" *The Independent UK*, May 13, 2008, http://www.independent.co.uk/news/uk/politics/the-big-question-why-are-so-many-political-memoirs-published-and-does-anyone-read-them-827085.html (accessed June 13, 2008).

49. Jonathan Bing, "Left-Wing Authors Finding Their Niche," *Daily Variety*, July 1, 2003, http://www.variety.com/article/VR1117888775.html?categoryid=1064&cs=1 (accessed May 14, 2009).

50. Ibid.

51. Ann Coulter, *Godless: The Church of Liberalism* (New York: Three Rivers Press, 2006).

52. Ibid.

53. Howard Kurtz, "National Review Cans Columnist Ann Coulter," *Washington Post*, October 2, 2001, C.01.

54. Ann Coulter, *Godless: The Church of Liberalism* (New York: Three Rivers Press, 2007).

55. Dave Sidhu, "Media and Muslims," *Stanford Cyberlaw*, December 21, 2006, http://cyberlaw.stanford.edu/node/5074 (accessed July 28, 2008).

56. Peter Svensson, "Sony Opens Up e-Book Reader to Other Booksellers," *Associated Press*, July 24, 2008.

57. Randall Stross, "Freed from the Page, but a Book Nonetheless," *New York Times*, January 27, 2008, BU8.

58. Ibid.

59. James Poniewozik, June 9, 2008, Personal interview with author.

Chapter 3

RADIO: TALK, NEWS, AND MUSIC

This week, our friend Al Franken is launching a new all liberal radio network called Air America. They say the purpose of Air America will be to balance out all the conservatives in the media, except, of course for NPR, CNN, CBS, ABC, NBC, and the *New York Times*.

—Jay Leno

Radio may seem to be old fashioned and outdated, what with all of the new technology available for music listening, but a 2006 report issued by the radio ratings company Arbitron showed that 93.7 percent of those aged 12 and older listen to conventional AM/FM radio each week.[1] There are 318 broadcast markets in the United States today, with each market being an area that draws a "substantial audience."[2] Major cities such as New York, Los Angeles, and Chicago are considered to be the most important radio markets. Because of its history and because it manages to broadcast in our homes, offices, and cars to this day, radio remains an important player in American politics. Whether it is news reporting that interrupts music programming on the hour, or talk radio punditry that fills the day with opinion, most Americans hear some form of news on the radio at some point in their day. Since there are now so many ways for Americans to listen to the radio, there remain a few radio formats that stand out in their importance and significance. Talk radio, where a host interviews a policymaker or opines on the events of the day, remains hugely influential in political circles even as more and more Americans listen to their own music on iPods or subscribe to satellite radio.

It is because of this continued importance that politicians ignore radio at their own peril. Furthermore, the connection between entertainment and politics demands that politicians take seriously those who entertain on the radio, either the talk radio hosts who animatedly discuss politics or the popular musicians who sing about politics. As will be discussed, the financial imperatives of the media corporations that own radio stations and distribute programming profoundly affect the way politics is addressed on the radio. The extreme (but entertaining) language of talk radio hosts is rewarded with greater audience numbers, which translate to greater profit margins. This is one financial factor in political radio. Another part of the financial dynamic of political radio comes when musicians engage in political activity that offends the listening audience, and when this occurs the consequences for the artists can be quite harsh. There has been an immense amount of research done on politics and music,[3] on political advertising on the radio,[4] and on other aspects of political radio that are both current and important. This chapter, however, examines talk radio within the broader context of the technology of the medium, its financial imperatives, its political uses, and its political consequences.

TYPES OF RADIO PROGRAMMING

In the late nineteenth century, Italian Guglielmo Marconi was among the first to develop radio transmission through the system of wireless telegraphy. The *New York Times*, in an 1899 article titled "Future of Wireless Telegraphy," stated that because of radio transmission, "all the nations of the earth would be put upon terms of intimacy and men would be stunned by the tremendous volume of news and information that would ceaselessly pour in upon them." Because of its immediacy and the popularity of the medium, radio transmission has significantly increased the volume of news and information sent to the American public.

By the mid-twentieth century, radio had become the most important medium of its time, and there were two major corporations that controlled almost all of it: CBS and RCA. The latter organization ran NBC and what would later become ABC. The Federal Communications Commission (FCC) determined that having only two companies control the radio airwaves as they did constituted something close to a monopoly. Consequently, in the 1940s part of the NBC family within RCA was sold to Edward Noble, who renamed the formerly known "NBC Blue" company as the American Broadcasting Network (ABC). Today, the ABC, NBC, and CBS radio networks remain an integral part of the radio landscape, but they are joined by other major corporations such as Clear Channel and Infinity, which also own a significant number of radio stations around the country.

There are two types of conventional radio on the airwaves today: public and commercial. Public radio does not air commercials to fund its operations and programming, while commercial radio depends on the revenue from commercial airtime for its profits. Public radio relies instead on two sources: governmental aid appropriated by Congress and "listener support," a phrase familiar to anyone who has had to sit through pledge drives while waiting for *Morning Edition* or *Car Talk*. Public radio stations, many of which are housed in universities around the country, purchase programming from one of several sources, National Public Radio (NPR), American Public Radio, and Public Radio International (PRI) being among the biggest. Each network produces specific shows that have wide appeal. NPR's news shows include *Morning Edition* and *All Things Considered*, and PRI distributes *This American Life* with Ira Glass and economic programming on *Marketplace*. National Public Radio is based in

Washington, and the ratings of its news programming have increased to the point that NPR programs now reach an estimated 20.9 million listeners a week.[5] Public radio programs blend news, arts, and cultural information and are produced by the networks. NPR maintains 18 foreign bureaus, which allow the news organization to maintain strong international reporting.[6] Public radio's programming differs from talk radio in that it is news-oriented rather than opinion-driven, and while both have financial imperatives necessary to operate, NPR is not a commercial endeavor.

Studies have shown that public radio listeners are, on the whole, more educated, affluent, and politically active than their commercial radio counterparts. There is also an ideological difference between the listenership, with public radio listeners identifying themselves as Democrats more often than as Republicans. Many conservatives argue that this is because NPR leans liberal, while those on the left deny this claim vehemently. The government provides funding for public radio through assistance to the Corporation for Public Broadcasting (CPB). The CPB is a private corporation that was created by the federal government and does not produce its own programming; that is done by the public radio networks. In the 1990s, when the Republicans took control of the U.S. House of Representatives for the first time in 40 years, GOP leaders set their sights on the CPB, arguing that liberally biased programming on public radio and television should not receive taxpayer dollars. However, with a successful publicity campaign starring, among others, Big Bird from *Sesame Street*, the CPB was able to avoid total financial annihilation by Congress. The CPB still supports public radio.

Commercial radio stations, conversely, rely on ad revenue for their profit margin, and thus try to produce programming that will earn their stations the highest ratings. This means that within a format—be it country, rock, pop, or talk—it is in a station's best interest to play the songs that appeal to the most people and to feature on-air personalities who garner the most interest. The emphasis on popularity more often than not outweighs talent, resulting in commercial radio stations that sound an awful lot like one another, playing the same hit songs in a loop and featuring disc jockeys (DJs) who are provocative or funny, all to curry the favor of businesses that advertise on their stations. Radio broadcasting includes music, news, religious, and talk programming, and stations are structured around specific music genres or information styles. Radio is normally a 24-hour entity, with the most popular listening times being in the morning or afternoon during traffic rush hours. Deemed "drive time" by the industry, this is when the highest-profile DJs and talk radio hosts get to wax poetic and play music for the most listeners, who are, ostensibly, stuck in their cars. Other important broadcast times include noon, for lunchtime listeners, and also late at night when people are more likely to be listening at home.

Arbitron is the private media research firm that surveys the number of radio listeners to a specific radio program in a particular market and determines radio ratings. These ratings reveal how popular a station is at a specific time of the day, which then help the stations determine how much it can charge for advertising during specific shows: The show with the most listeners gets to charge the most money for a 15-, 30-, or 60-second advertisement. Arbitron reports on three basic estimates: person estimates, which are the estimated number of persons listening; ratings, which define the percentage of listeners in the measured area population; and the audience share, which is the percentage of one station's total estimated listening audience. Arbitron measures persons, ratings, and shares for quarter-hour averages, where estimations are gathered to show how many people listened to a station for a minimum of five minutes during any quarter-hour time period.[7] These are the numbers that help to determine ad rates for radio stations.

A radio station may produce its own programming with local DJs and on-air personalities, or it may buy syndicated shows from an outside production company far away from its own station. Before he went to satellite radio, for example, Howard Stern was the undisputed heavyweight of morning DJs, and he helped to popularize the "shock jock" sensation so prominent now. Stern broadcast his show in New York City, which was then distributed across the country by Infinity Radio, a company partially owned by Viacom, a major multinational media conglomerate. Infinity Radio sold and distributed his show to local radio stations across the nation, earning revenue on the national ads that it placed within the *Howard Stern Show*'s content. The local stations that broadcast Howard Stern benefitted as well from the local ad revenue they received from broadcasting such a popular show. This example helps to illustrate how profitable radio can be for different companies. It also helps to illustrate how confusing radio programming can be. There are companies that produce radio programs, other companies that distribute these radio programs, and different companies that broadcast the programs on the radio stations. Often, these companies do not overlap.

However, there are several major corporations that produce programming and distribute it to the radio stations they own. For example, Rush Limbaugh's talk radio program is distributed by Premier Broadcasting, which is owned by Clear Channel Communications. Clear Channel owns roughly 700 radio stations around the country, which means that Limbaugh's show will likely air on a Clear Channel-owned station. If this is the case, Clear Channel earns revenue from the production, distribution, and broadcast of the Rush Limbaugh Show. Yet while this synergy would maximize Clear Channel's profits, it is still possible that Limbaugh's show could air on a station that is owned by another company. Clear Channel would still profit from the distribution of the show thanks to revenue from national and local advertising.

Broadcast radio, like broadcast television, is regulated by the FCC, which regulates (among other things) station ownership and programming content. The 1996 Telecommunications Act limits the number of radio stations one person or company can own to eight stations in a market of 45 or more stations. In 2003, then-FCC Chairman Michael Powell argued that these ownership rules should be relaxed further to allow one person or company to own more radio stations than that, but he was constrained by the Senate, which passed a resolution by a vote of 55 to 40 that rolled back the FCC regulations Powell proposed. Today, one company is allowed to reach up to 35 percent of a market's audience.

The FCC also determines what can and cannot be said on broadcast radio and television, as best demonstrated by the late comedian George Carlin's 1978 "Seven Dirty Words" monologue. A New York radio station aired the monologue, warning its listeners in advance that the speech contained "sensitive language which might be regarded as offensive to some." A man, driving at the time with his son in the car, found the material to be so offensive that he complained to the FCC, which then sanctioned the station that aired Carlin's monologue. The case went to the Supreme Court, which determined that the FCC could level sanctions against a station that aired language not necessarily obscene, but instead was "patently offensive" to some listeners.[8] According to FCC guidelines:

> It is a violation of federal law to air obscene programming at any time. It is also a violation of federal law to air indecent programming or profane language during certain hours. Congress has given the Federal Communications Commission (FCC) the responsibility for administratively enforcing these laws. The FCC may revoke a station license, impose a monetary forfeiture, or issue a warning if a station airs obscene, indecent, or profane material.[9]

In recent years, the FCC has increased the amount of money it fines broadcast stations that violate its decency rules, but several legal cases have argued that these new fines are unconstitutional. At this writing, the constitutionality of these fines continues to be argued in federal court. Regardless of the legal outcome of the decency fine cases, radio and television stations watch carefully the content of their on-air product for fear of financial penalty by the government. However, this type of government regulation flies in the face of the incendiary (but ultimately profitable) material the shock-jocks are hired for. In 2004, Howard Stern was taken off the air for indecency, but afterwards his ratings improved in most markets, according to the "Friday Morning Quarterback Album Report," an organization that monitors radio content and ratings.[10] Thus, there is a delicate dance between DJs and station managers, where on-air talent is encouraged to act outrageous in order to raise ratings but not outrageous enough to get the radio stations sanctioned by the FCC.

Beyond government regulation, many of the major corporations that own stations on the airwaves have found it necessary to insist on their own standards of decency that go further than those defined by the FCC. Most of the time this is done to maintain audience levels and thus save station ratings from protests waged by angered (and ostensibly offended) groups. The country music group the Dixie Chicks, for example, famously criticized President Bush during a 2003 concert in London, which set off a storm of controversy. The Dixie Chicks received angry condemnation from not only the general public, but also fellow country music artists, and the group even received death threats from angry country music listeners. But the swiftest sword came from Clear Channel, the company that, at the time, owned almost 1,200 radio stations around the country and that pulled every Dixie Chicks song from its lineup. Gail Austin, Clear Channel's director of programming at two Jacksonville, Florida, radio stations, said, "Out of respect for our troops, our city and our listeners, [we] have taken the Dixie Chicks off our playlists."[11] In this case, it was not the government that levied penalties on the radio stations but the corporation that owned them. Corporate control in radio extends to music selection as well. Record companies are in business arrangements with station owners to play certain songs, which takes away from a DJ's autonomy or a program director's ability to experiment with new music. This kind of control by corporate media conglomerates over programming is attained in the name of minimizing risk and maximizing profits.[12]

Traditional broadcast radio technology is now being challenged by satellite radio, MP3 players, and Internet streaming radio. All of these technologies combine to test radio's limits and strengths. Satellite radio, represented by two merging companies (XM and Sirius), has grown its audience significantly in the past several years, although not as much as industry experts had predicted. One major advantage that satellite radio has over so-called "terrestrial" radio is freedom from FCC content regulation and the corporate demands of radio programming. Another is that you can listen to programs from coast to coast, something terrestrial radio does not allow. Several prominent DJs have moved from terrestrial radio to satellite radio (Howard Stern and Opie & Anthony included) in order to express themselves without filter. Satellite radio allows for more niche programming, which then lends itself to playing music beyond the Top 40. Together, XM and Sirius cater to around 14 million listeners, but the growth of the satellite radio audience is expected to slow, if not stop entirely, in the near future due to the enormous popularity of MP3 players as best exemplified by the iPod.

MP3 technology allows listeners to select music, news, and information content according to their own personal tastes for a fee, and listen without commercial interruption. According to the Pew Center, more than 22 million Americans own MP3 players, a significantly higher number than the 14 million who subscribe to satellite radio. News organizations are watching these numbers and have adapted their programming accordingly, offering "podcasts" of their programs to their readers and viewers. Podcasts allow a news organization to send streaming audio content over the Internet to anyone with an MP3 player. The virtues of MP3 players are that users can store a large amount of their own music, entertainment, and news shows and play them whenever they want to, wherever they want to. Apple's iPod was released in 2001 to little fanfare, but since then it has exploded to the point that by 2005, 8 out of 10 MP3 players owned by Americans were iPods. According to an article in *Time*, "There were MP3 players before the iPod. They just weren't very good."[13] Apple has expanded upon the iPod revolution with the iPhone, which combines a cell phone, an iPod, and Internet access in one handy gadget. As the price points on these MP3 devices become even more manageable for average Americans, these devices will become more ubiquitous.

Internet radio is another radio format that offers listeners a wider variety of listening options through music and news content that are streamed through a listener's computer. Both music and news stations have taken advantage of the Internet's audio capabilities. According to Artbitron, which now measures the ratings of online radio networks, about 5 million people listen to radio over the Internet each day, and that number is growing. Currently, the two major online radio networks are the AOL Radio Network and Clear Channel's Radio Network, each pulling in just over 1 million listeners daily.[14] These online radio stations combine traditional radio programming with on-demand services that allow the listeners to select specific musicians to either listen to or watch. This combination of traditional radio medium with the newer technology of MP3 music selection will only continue to grow as computer technology becomes even more sophisticated.

The new ways in which Americans listen to radio results from the growing technological developments in the media. Nevertheless, traditional radio remains important. Americans still listen to the radio in their homes, cars, and offices, and since conventional radio remains important, so too does talk radio.

TALK RADIO

Despite the fact that radio technology is more than a century old, the concept of talk radio is relatively new. Certainly, in the earliest days of radio there were talk radio shows, one of the most famous being Father Charles Coughlin's 1930s radio program, which was regarded as both financially successful and vehemently racist. Throughout the twentieth century, talk radio was isolated to specific shows that aired between music segments. In 1960, there were only two talk radio stations in the country, one in Los Angeles and the other in St. Louis.[15] Thirty-five years later, one in nine radio stations dedicated the majority of its programming to talk radio, meaning 1,130 stations had that format.[16] Political scientist David Barker defines political talk radio as "call-in shows that emphasize discussion of politicians, elections, and public policy issues,"[17] and the political focus of talk radio is normally centered on topical issues dominating the news and augmented by a great amount of opinion. Talk radio reaches an estimated 17 percent of the American public each day, and today there are about two dozen major talk radio hosts who dominate the vast majority of that audience.

In 1949, the FCC took the stand that the airwaves were a public trust, and therefore during the rapid rise of radio and television broadcast during the mid-twentieth century the government determined that content should be monitored. To prevent station owners from using their channels as exclusive outlets for their own opinions, the FCC mandated that political content on the airwaves reflect a diversity of positions. As a result, stations were forced to balance the content of opinion. This practice changed in 1985, when the Reagan administration took the first steps to end the Fairness Doctrine by issuing a "Fairness Report" that stated the doctrine had a "chilling effect" on political discourse and First Amendment freedoms. In 1987, the Supreme Court heard *Meredith Corp. v. FCC* and handed down the decision that declared that since the doctrine was not mandated by Congress, it was not enforceable by the bureaucracy. When Congress then passed the Fairness Doctrine into law, President Reagan vetoed the proposed legislation. Recent attempts by Congress to revive the Fairness Doctrine have fallen short of the support necessary to make it once again a part of the media landscape.

The end of the Fairness Doctrine directly led to the rise of talk radio. By removing the mandates of balance and evenhandedness on the airwaves, it opened the door to opinion talk as never before. The Equal Time provision remains in place, which mandates that non-news programs give equal time to all political candidates for a political office. However, news and information programming need not be ideologically balanced, and this helped give rise to talk radio. Once a smaller media force in the past, talk radio exploded in popularity and consequence during the 1990s, when Rush Limbaugh's radio show became the gold standard of conservative media. He was not the first, nor the last, conservative radio talk show host, but for a time he certainly was the most important. His ascent to media stardom coincided with the 1994 Republican takeover of Congress, and while it cannot be certain which came first—Limbaugh's popularity or the GOP revolution—certainly there was a symbiosis at play. "Rush Rooms" materialized in restaurants across the country, where listeners could eat lunch while listening to the show. Limbaugh became a force of his own as the semiofficial conduit of conservative political thought in America, and in doing so he managed to enrage his political opponents—which was precisely the point.

Although it reached its zenith in the 1990s, talk radio is still an important means by which conservatives disseminate their messages. These programs are so important that in the days before the 2006 midterm elections conservative radio talk-show hosts set up shop on the lawn of the White House and broadcast from the District of Columbia, interviewing heavyweight Republicans in an effort to rally the base of conservative voters while demonizing their Democratic counterparts.[18] Campaign strategists—and talk radio hosts—argued that the midterm elections were much closer than the "liberal" mainstream media would lead its viewers to believe. According to Sean Hannity, who spoke at a Republican rally in Ohio three weeks before the election, "the liberal media wants us to suppress the vote. They want to convince you that this race is over, they want you to go away, and they want us to lose. I'm here to tell you that you have the power [to prove them wrong]."[19] Hannity went on to argue that a

Republican election would not only be a boon for the electorate, but also a thumb in the eye of the left-wing media establishment: "If all of us go out to the polls and get every person to go out to the polls . . . the great thing that will happen on election day is that we will confuse and confound the pundits and confuse and confound the liberal media."[20]

Also in 2006, the White House invited more than three dozen talk radio hosts to the lawn of the White House to interview top administration officials. Two weeks before the midterm elections, talk radio hosts camped out to interview Vice President Dick Cheney and other stars of the GOP (including then-Secretary of State Condoleeza Rice and then-Secretary of Defense Donald Rumsfeld), and to address the matters most important to the party. According to the late Tony Snow, who as White House press secretary sat for 34 talk radio interviews in the tent that was set up to house all of the hosts: "The chief objective [was] to make our case as clearly as possible, to as many people as possible."[21] Since most talk radio hosts lean conservative, the vast majority of those who took part in the talk radio marathon session on the lawn of the White House were conservatives as well. In one of his magazine stories, Michael Harrison, the publisher of *Talkers Magazine*, evaluated a list of the 38 talk show hosts invited to the White House and wrote that a majority of them leaned conservative. He also noted there were others more moderate and liberal than the most vociferously conservative hosts who took part in the exercise.[22]

More recent kerfuffles between Rush Limbaugh and President Obama, Limbaugh and Colin Powell, and Limbaugh and GOP Chairman Mike Steele also prove this point. Shortly after President Obama's election in 2008, Limbaugh made headlines by openly hoping for Obama's failure. In the months that followed the election, Limbaugh filled the Republican power void with bomb-throwing missives and speeches aimed to both instigate and self-promote. One notable speech was the keynote address of the 2009 Conservative Political Action Committee (CPAC), a powerful group that meets annually to discuss the state of the Republican Party and advance the causes of conservatism. At the CPAC convention, Limbaugh rallied the crowd with a lengthy and aggressive speech that wrapped up the proceedings. That same night, Republican National Committee (RNC) Chair Mike Steele appeared on CNN's *DL Hughley Show*, where he was asked by Hughley to comment on Limbaugh's approach. Steele said that Limbaugh was an "entertainer" whose tactics were "incendiary" and "ugly."[23] Limbaugh responded on his radio show, stating that Steele was "off to a shaky start" as RNC chairman:

> You know who needs a little leadership? Michael Steele and those at the RNC. . . . I hope the RNC chairman will realize he's not a talking head pundit, that he is supposed to be working on the grassroots and rebuilding it and maybe doing something about our open primary system and fixing it so that Democrats don't nominate our candidates. It's time, Mr. Steele, for you to go behind the scenes

and start doing the work that you were elected to do instead of trying to be some talking head media star, which you're having a tough time pulling off. . . . I'm not in charge of the Republican Party, and I don't want to be. I would be embarrassed to say that I'm in charge of the Republican Party in the sad-sack state that it's in. If I were chairman of the Republican Party, given the state that it's in, I would quit. I might get out the hari-kari knife because I would have presided over a failure that is embarrassing to the Republicans and conservatives who have supported it and invested in it all these years.[24]

After Limbaugh's fans, Republican officials, and operatives all reacted aggressively against Steele, the RNC chair apologized to Limbaugh, calling him a "valuable conservative voice for our party. . . . He brings a very important message to the American people to wake up and pay attention to what the administration is doing."[25] The back and forth continued with Democrats and White House officials weighing in, arguing that this encounter proved that Limbaugh was, indeed, the head of the Republican Party. That he wields power is not in dispute. The question really is what the GOP will do with the power Limbaugh has—because not every member of the Republican Party is a fan. In a May 2009 speech, former Secretary of State Colin Powell weighed in on Limbaugh's prominence in the Grand Old Party: "I think what Rush does as an entertainer diminishes the party and intrudes or inserts into our public life a kind of nastiness that we would be better to do without."[26] Limbaugh, of course, reacted on his radio show: "What Colin Powell needs to do is close the loop and become a Democrat instead of claiming to be a Republican interested in reforming the Republican Party. . . . He's just mad at me because I'm the one person in the country who had the guts to explain his endorsement of Obama. It was purely and solely based on race."[27] This meant that Limbaugh had succeeded in keeping his name in the headlines and his power position solid, while at the same time dividing those in the Republican Party. Asked about Limbaugh on the CBS Sunday morning news program *Face the Nation*, former Vice President Dick Cheney said: "If I had to choose in terms of being a Republican, I'd go with Rush Limbaugh. My take on it was Colin had already left the party. I didn't know he was still a Republican."[28]

If Limbaugh is simply an entertainer, he's a very influential one, and his influence gives a great amount of power to conservatives and those on the right. While there are liberal talk radio hosts, the medium is disproportionately conservative, and several pieces of evidence prove the point. First, the top-five talk radio programs with the greatest listening audience are all hosted by conservative commentators. Second, the demographic breakdown of the listeners shows a definitive rightward lean. Third, the conservative institutions in Washington partner often with talk radio hosts and programs to help with political mobilization and issue advocacy.

According to *Talkers Magazine*, which compiles audience numbers according to national Arbitron ratings, the top-five talk radio hosts are Rush Limbaugh, Sean Hannity, Michael Savage, Dr. Laura Schlessinger, and Laura Ingraham. The undisputed heavyweight of talk radio is Rush Limbaugh, whose program serves up chat and information to more than 13 million listeners per week. According to *Talkers Magazine*, Rush Limbaugh calls the network that broadcasts his show the "Excellence in Broadcasting network (EIB)," but in reality it is Premier Radio Networks that transmits the show, and Premier is a subsidiary of Clear Channel Communications. Each day, Limbaugh addresses the issues and events that catch his eye, and he delves into the subjects without an ounce of objectivity or a pretense of impartiality. Quite the contrary, his goal is twofold: entertainment and influence. To this end, Limbaugh himself is unrepentant, saying once on his radio program: "I think you people can be persuaded. . . . I believe that the most effective way to persuade people is not to wag a finger in their face, but to speak to them in a way that makes them think that they reached certain conclusions on their own."[29] A 2006 study by the Pew Research Center for People and the Press stated that regular Limbaugh listeners identified themselves as conservative 78 percent of the time. Limbaugh not only secures speaking engagements at influential conservative meetings such as CPAC, but also lands big-time GOP guests on his show, including most of the high-ranking Bush administration officials during their tenure in office and almost the entire lineup of the Republican congressional leadership.

Scholar Kathleen Hall Jamieson, who studies political media as the director of the Annenberg Public Policy Center at the University of Pennsylvania, contends that Rush Limbaugh's radio show is one important part of the conservative "echo chamber" that serves to deliver and magnify Republican Party messages to the exclusion of their liberal counterpoints.[30] The result is a cohesive audience with a solitary and exclusionary opinion of the matters addressed by Limbaugh, which then hampers deliberation and debate. Limbaugh's outright hostility and contempt for those on the left are neither nuanced nor backed by data, but are instead visceral, clever, and occasionally far-fetched. For example, Limbaugh has repeatedly insinuated that Hillary Rodham Clinton murdered the late White House attorney Vince Foster, even though there is no evidence to support his contention. In March 1994, Limbaugh said on his radio program:

> OK, folks, I think I got enough information here to tell you about the contents of this fax that I got. Brace yourselves. This fax contains information that I have just been told will appear in a newsletter to Morgan Stanley sales personnel this afternoon. . . . What it is is a bit of news which says . . . there's a Washington consulting firm that has scheduled the release of a report that will appear, it will be published, that claims that Vince Foster was murdered in an apartment owned by Hillary Clinton, and the body was then taken to Fort Marcy Park.[31]

No such report was ever released. When he was questioned about this accusation Limbaugh denied having ever made it: "I don't know who's accusing her of murdering anybody."[32] Limbaugh's aggression against the Clintons was significant enough to register with the president, and in a 1996 interview on the C-SPAN program *Booknotes*, President Clinton described a "war of words in America where people are always bad-mouthing each other." Clinton said talk radio was "not serving the country well," and this was *before* the Lewinsky scandal hit.[33] President Clinton had good reason to be wary of the medium: it was effective. A 1997 study by political communications scholar Diana Owens demonstrated that talk radio "reinforced and perhaps enhanced" negative evaluations about President Clinton.[34] Even after Clinton left office, he and Hillary Clinton remained on Limbaugh's radar. During the 2008 Democratic primary season, Rush Limbaugh went after the Clintons again, organizing what he called "Operation Chaos." This was an effort to get Hillary Clinton selected as the Democratic presidential nominee, Limbaugh's assumption being that she would be easier to defeat than any of her rivals. His drumbeat against both Clintons was relentless and unforgiving and remains that way today, but with a new administration in office he has turned his attention to President Obama, his policies, and his staff. Limbaugh's unapologetic, bomb-throwing style is great entertainment, and he is rewarded for his style with ratings and prominent roles in American conservative politics. Limbaugh continues to be the most popular, well-known, and influential talk radio host in America today.

Although many correlate Rush Limbaugh directly with talk radio, there are other popular talk show hosts who come close to matching his audience numbers. The second most popular talk radio host is Sean Hannity, who brings in an audience of 12.5 million listeners weekly, which is right on Rush's heels. While Rush is still the bigger name, Hannity has comparable power within conservative circles, as demonstrated by his many appearances at conservative conferences, his cable show on Fox News Channel, his best-selling books, and his rock-star status within Republican circles. Broadcast by ABC Radio Networks, Hannity is paid an estimated $5 million per year to broadcast four hours a day. He also works for Fox News, headlining two different television shows. Broadcasting from more than 500 radio stations around the country, Hannity may lack Rush's talk radio fame but more than makes up for it with his Fox News presence. The guests who appear on his show are powerful and predominantly conservative, and the popularity of his show has been attractive to politicians eager for Hannity's limelight.

An article from CNN/Money online characterizes Hannity's style as thus: "If you agree with his conservative world view you are deemed a 'great American.' If you don't you're a pusillanimous blame-America firster who might as well pledge allegiance to France."[35] Hannity compared a Muslim congressman's swearing in on the Koran to being sworn into office pledging allegiance to Hitler's *Mein Kampf*. His obvious loathing of liberalism is evident from the titles of his two books: *Deliver Us from Evil: Defeating Terrorism, Despotism and Liberalism*, and *Let Freedom Ring: Winning the War of Liberty over Liberalism*. In the first book, Hannity writes: "Indeed, the greatest threat to our resolve today in the War on Terror is the political liberalism—and selfish opportunism—of the Democrats."[36] In his radio show, he uses the same style of language towards those whom he sees as sinners, moral relativists, and anti-American liberals out to destroy the fabric of our nation. His widespread appeal is evidenced by the immense amount of attention paid to him by the liberal press, most of whom laud him for his ratings.

Like Limbaugh, Hannity's ratings are enhanced by booking important guests, most of whom are Republican and conservative. During the 2008 campaign, Hannity was able to interview most of the Republican presidential candidates on either his radio or television show, and he interviewed both John McCain and Sarah Palin in the final days of the campaign. What makes Sean Hannity's radio program most convenient for politicians is the fact that they can phone in an interview rather than spend the time to come to a studio and wait in a Green Room to go on the air. This means that Hannity has interviewed Republicans heavyweights and former administration officials such as Secretary of Defense Donald Rumsfeld, Secretary of State Condoleeza Rice, and Vice President Dick Cheney. He even interviewed former President George W. Bush. Other guests on his show included then-House Speaker Dennis Hastert and Republican congressional leaders like John Boehner and Mitch McConnell. Hannity's ability to interview important conservative guests provides a platform for Republican politicians and a power position for himself.

With his multifaceted approach to punditry, Hannity is able to make an immense amount of money for several different corporations. His radio show is broadcast by ABC, which is owned by Disney. His television shows are on Fox News, which is owned by News Corp, as is HarperCollins, the company that publishes his books. While one company would undoubtedly like to control all of Hannity's offerings, they all benefit from his success with the others. Thus, it is in Disney's best interest for Hannity's Fox News show to succeed, for its success adds strength to his radio show. As is the case with Rush Limbaugh, Hannity's partisanship makes for strong adherents to his philosophy and for good, entertaining fighting. For a time, Hannity was pitted against a liberal counterpart, Alan Colmes, which allowed Hannity to fight aggressively against an ideological dupe. This was not necessarily illuminating, but it was certainly entertaining. Now Hannity hosts his show on his own.

Michael Savage, who comes in third in the talk radio popularity contest with 8.25 million listeners a week, is also well known for the ferocity of his attacks. Named Michael Alan Weiner, Savage took on the pseudonym to more accurately reflect his political linguistic style. Savage is based in San Francisco and uses the catchphrase "I can't take this anymore!" to illustrate his annoyance with the left. Lest anyone think he is simply a lunatic, Michael Savage has attracted powerful political guests to his show, including former Vice President Dick Cheney. Fired from MSNBC in 2003 for making antigay remarks, Savage returned to the airwaves. His radio show is broadcast by the Salem Communications Network, which also distributes *Focus on the Family*, the religious radio show hosted by Reverend James Dobson, contemporary Christian music programming, and Oliver North's conservative political radio show.

Savage has been outspoken in his antipathy towards a culture he sees as permissive or excessive. He eschews the tenets of liberalism and takes sharp aim at those who appear to oppose him on any front, even those who are not liberals themselves. One such fight pitted Savage against the conservative Republican Senator from Mississippi, Trent Lott, who criticized talk radio hosts for their vociferous opposition to an immigration bill. Another attack set Savage against Brian Lamb, the kind and soft-spoken CEO of C-SPAN, the cable network that covers Congress and public affairs. When *Talkers Magazine* gave Savage an award, C-SPAN covered the event. When Savage sent a DVD of his speech instead of delivering the remarks himself, however, C-SPAN declined to air it. Savage reacted antagonistically, saying the reliably unbiased network was "left-wing," that it banned his speech, and that his audience should contact C-SPAN by e-mail or phone to complain. Savage's listeners wrote in to call Lamb a Nazi, a Stalinist, a homosexual, and an enemy of the republic. Lamb responded by reading some of the more salacious comments on the air to show how extreme they were. The whole brouhaha brought Savage even more attention, which was perhaps more beneficial than C-SPAN simply airing the speech in the first place. C-SPAN CEO Brian Lamb spoke with me about this event and took it in stride, despite the personal invectives aimed at him, stating: "There's no question that these talk show hosts, in order to keep an audience, stir it up on purpose."[37]

In fourth place in the top-five talk radio audience list is Dr. Laura Schlessinger, who dispenses personal advice and (in the main) avoids political debate. An avowed conservative, Dr. Laura reaches more than 8 million listeners weekly. Because she does not engage specifically in politics, Dr. Laura's show will not be examined here except to say that she was syndicated in 1994 and makes public appearances on numerous media programs hawking her many books on fidelity and marriage. After the not-so-political Dr. Laura, in fifth place is the very political Laura Ingraham, whose show was launched in 2001. In addition to her radio work, the pundit appears on cable television and is the author of several books, including *Shut Up & Sing: How the Elites in Hollywood, Politics, and the UN Are Subverting America*. Ingraham has been awarded by the Conservative Political Action Conference for her work on conservative issues. Less blustery than some of her talk radio counterparts, Ms. Ingraham has spoken out often on the topics of liberals (she is opposed to them), the war in Iraq (she supports it), and immigration reform (she is happy that the 2007 bill was killed, but perhaps wished the legislation would have died a more violent death than it had). Ingraham said in a 2003 interview with *Media Week* magazine: "Politics is the anchor of my show, but entertainment and the media are the other two pillars."[38] With this style, she is able to cover the most amusing stories of the day, attracting an audience perhaps wider than if she had simply stuck to politics. Ingraham appears on other pundit shows, often with Sean Hannity and Bill O'Reilly. Using her conservative bona fides to increase her platform while pulling in 5 million listeners a week, Ingraham is seen as a force on the rise; and as the only female talk show host addressing politics in the top 10, she garners significant attention.

After the big five, the numbers drop to audiences of little over 3 million. All of the most popular talk radio hosts are affirmed conservatives, and their listeners are conservatives as well. According to the Talk Radio Research Project, a study undertaken by *Talkers Magazine*, the demographics of talk radio listeners show the majority to be between the ages of 35 and 54 (52%), male (55%), and politically active voters who call themselves some brand of conservative: either ultraconservative (12%), conservative (20%), or moderate conservative (23%). Of those polled, only 14 percent (total) called themselves either "liberal" or "ultraliberal."[39] The Pew Center for People and the Press released a study that supported the *Talkers* evidence: "The talk radio audience remains a distinct group. It is mostly male, middle-aged, well educated, and conservative. Among those who regularly listen to talk radio, 49 percent are Republican and 28 percent are Democrats."[40]

The question may be asked of cause and effect: Does listening to these shows make one conservative or does the self-selection that Cass Sunstein wrote of mean that conservatives are more inclined to listen to this programming? Political Scientist David Barker asked similar questions in two papers on political talk radio and voter choice. What Barker found was that listening to Rush Limbaugh in particular in the mid-1990s was influential for his audience: "Limbaugh's inflammatory rhetoric probably persuaded all but the most ardently liberal listeners (of which there are not that many) to spurn the president [meaning Bill Clinton]."[41] In other words, while a certain amount of self-selection is in place, the ferocity of the message had an effect on the attitudes of the listeners. This hypothesis was reinforced by Barker and Kathleen Knight in 2000, who argued that talk radio is most effective in message dissemination when the message is negative. When talk show hosts endorse a policy or politician, the impact of the endorsement is less significant than the influence of a negative message.[42] It is evident, then, that talk radio's power is strongest when its hosts are rallying against something, angrily ranting in opposition to a policy or engaged in name calling against a politician.

As for talk radio hosts assisting in the policymaking process, a case study can be used to effectively show the medium's effect on policy. In the summer of 2007, President Bush proposed a bill that would address the issue of illegal immigration in America. Garnering support from some Democrats and some Republicans on Capitol Hill, the bipartisan immigration reform bill had two important characteristics: it strengthened border enforcement measures and encouraged citizenship measures for the 12 million illegal immigrants living in the United States at the time. President Bush supported the bill and pushed hard for its passage, as did moderates from both parties. However, a few liberal lawmakers and a large portion of the conservative right had serious problems with the citizenship measures, and so this group of predominantly conservative politicians, with the assistance of talk radio hosts, aimed their guns squarely at the legislation and pulled the trigger. In a Pew Research Center study from June 2007 titled "Did Talk Show Hosts Help Derail the Immigration Bill?" author Mark Jurkowitz explored the amount of coverage and its effect. Most talk show hosts called it an "amnesty bill" that would allow illegals to stay in the country without penalty. Limbaugh and Hannity each devoted 15 percent of their air time to the topic during the weeks leading up to the bill's final demise. Savage claimed the bill "threatened the sovereignty of America," and Laura Ingraham stated that the Democrats were in favor of the bill to allow more immigrants into the country "because this electorate is not as liberal as the Democrats need it to be to get all their social policies enacted—So they need a new electorate."[43] With all of the firepower aimed at the legislation, it was not surprising that lawmakers in support of the legislation were flooded with hate mail, angry phone calls, and even death threats. The bill died in the Senate. The talk radio community called it a victory.

While President Bush may not have appreciated the defeat of his immigration bill, he did appreciate the power of the conservative talk radio hosts who helped to trounce it. Shortly after the loss of the immigration legislation, President Bush met for an off-the-record meeting at the White House with 10 of the nation's most popular talk radio hosts. At this meeting—his second in a year with conservative talk radio hosts—he discussed "the conservative talk radio audience's feeling about issues and policies."[44] This gave talk radio the political credibility it felt it deserved, and talk radio feels it deserves a tremendous amount of credibility because it is, after all, a very big business. The stars of talk radio make tremendous amounts of money for the major corporations that produce and distribute their shows across the country, and thus it is in the talk show host's best interest to keep his or her show lively, loud, and attention-getting.

There have been very few truly successful left-leaning talk radio hosts. There have been numerous attempts by those on the left to emulate the success of conservative talk radio programming, from such well-known liberals as Former Democratic Governors Mario Cuomo (NY), Lowell Weicker (CT), Jerry Brown (CA), and Doug Wilder (VA). All were talk radio failures. Former New York City Mayor Ed Koch and Harvard Law professor Alan Dershowitz both tried to host talk radio shows—and both were unsuccessful, as was Air America, a radio network antidote to conservative talk radio that was launched in 2004. But in the two years that Air America broadcast, it never reached profitability, losing money throughout its entire life span before the company finally declared bankruptcy in 2006. The most successful liberal radio talk show hosts are Randi

Rhodes, Ed Schultz, and Alan Colmes, but none of them are in the top 10 of *Talkers Magazine*'s list of the industry's most influential.

Therefore, scholars and observers of the industry have asked the important question: "Why does talk radio skew so conservative?" There are several answers from both sides of the ideological spectrum. The left argues that talk radio is an arm of the large corporate ownership machine that produces it, which, because of its affinity with big business, leans rightward. Certainly there is the case to be made that talk radio equals big money; and with the enormous number of listeners to talk radio, the parent companies that produce and distribute the shows are raking in significant profits. If that were entirely the case, however, then any successful liberal talk radio host would be shut down as a result of his or her ideological leanings. One moderate-liberal local host from Hartford, Connecticut was replaced by Laura Schlessinger's syndicated show, and he assumed his firing was for political reasons. When he spoke with his former bosses, he realized it was not the case: "It turned out my bosses' politics weren't that different from mine. All they cared about was the ratings. If Noam Chomsky playing the kazoo on air got them an 11 share, they would have put him on."[45] Therefore, corporate bias may not play the dominant role here.

Conservatives, meanwhile, argue that they espouse a better ideology and that there are more conservatives in America than there are liberals. Were this necessarily true, the Democrats would not have won such victories in the 2006 and 2008 elections. Despite the efforts by the White House and political strategists to use talk radio to get out the vote, Democrats took control of both houses of Congress in fairly wide margins in the 2006 midterm elections, and 2008 ushered in even more Democrats to congress and a Democratic White House victory. Why the disparity if these arguments from the left and the right do not explain the dominance of conservatism in talk radio?

One possibility is that the right's fondness for simplistic arguments lends itself more towards talk radio than the left's affinity for nuance and deliberate discourse. Former Democratic senator and presidential candidate Gary Hart made this case when he stated, "Progressive politics in this country has failed to compress the message, and I'm not sure that it can. Because, by definition, the reformer, the progressive, the liberal, whatever you want to call it, doesn't see the world in blacks and whites, but in plaids and grays. There never is a single answer. It is always a set of interrelated policies."[46] Many of the arguments waged on the right can be boiled down to a more uncomplicated judgment call of right and wrong. For example, the hot-button topics of abortion, gay rights, and gun control can be compressed to one- or two-word oppositions: Murder. Unbiblical. Second Amendment. Talented talk radio hosts are able to boil down even issues that are too complex to allow easy answers, and so questions about the length of the war in Iraq turn into an opposition to the Democrats' "cut and run" policies. The health care reform debate becomes about "death panels." In reducing complicated questions into simple, angry declarations against an identified opponent, right wing radio talk show hosts elicit a visceral response from their audience. In the process, they entertain listeners with heated remarks and garner ratings revenue for themselves.

Another explanation could be found in the coordination between talk radio hosts and conservative politicians who afford talk radio both the access to major stories and newsmakers as well as the talking points necessary to fight a well-rehearsed and well-coordinated fight. Because of this coordination, conservatives will gravitate towards talk radio to hear the stories they will believe to be true and that will reaffirm their existing beliefs. If the mainstream media are alleged to be liberally biased (and this book contends that those accusations are inaccurate), then it makes sense that conservatives will seek out a medium that not only supports their belief system, but that also gives them the news that they suspect they are missing from the liberally biased mainstream media.

One example to support this argument took place in 1997, when then-Assistant Secretary of the Army Sara Lister was eviscerated by talk radio to such a degree that her personal safety was threatened and her career ended prematurely. Ms. Lister was due to retire from her political appointment at the end of November of that year, but just before her retirement in late October she spoke at an academic conference hosted by the Olin Institute, a national security think tank affiliated with Harvard University. While on a panel discussing the military's relationship with the greater community, Ms. Lister stated, "I think the Army is much more connected to society than the Marines are. The Marines are extremists. Wherever you have extremists, you've got some risks of total disconnections with society. And that's a little dangerous." Also on the panel was Kate O'Beirne, the Washington editor of *National Review* who brought Lister's remarks to the attention of the *Washington Times*. The *Times* went on to run a story about the remarks almost a month after the fact. The gist of the story was that the assistant secretary of the Army called the Marines "extremists," casting aspersions on their character and their fealty to the United States of America. And that was when the whole situation became very messy. I corresponded with Sara Lister about these events, and she wrote eloquently about her treatment by talk radio.

On their individual talk radio shows, Rush Limbaugh, G. Gordon Liddy, and retired Marine Lieutenant Colonel Oliver North railed against Lister, calling her names and demanding her firing by the Clinton administration. In addition to their invectives, they announced ways to contact Ms. Lister, who wrote to me that: "Oliver North and Liddy . . . gave out the phone number of my office. . . . They said I lived in D.C., and of course we were in the phone book. Folks were so worried they had my Sergeants escort me home that night (along with all my stuff!)."[47] It should not have been surprising, then, that according to the *Washington Times*, the Pentagon received nearly 500 telephone calls from angry citizens who had heard the talk radio programs and were incited to action. Nor should it have been surprising that Ms. Lister received so many death threats, she had to be escorted home from the building. The talk radio effort to highlight a story that was written in a local (albeit conservative) newspaper helped add fuel to a fire that grew into a major conflagration. Republican House members took to the floor of Congress and demanded her firing. Despite her previously scheduled retirement the very next day, the White House forced Sara Lister to resign and issue apologies to the Marine Corps. According to the *Washington Times*, talk radio host North stated about Lister's resignation: "This great victory for America's armed forces would not have been possible without talk radio hosts . . . who would not let this pass."[48]

Why was such a big deal made about a statement from a retiring government official at an academic conference? Most likely it was because Sara Lister's name had been floated as a possible replacement for then-Army Secretary Togo West, who was leaving that post to become Secretary of Veterans Affairs. According to an article written in *Newsweek* magazine: "Lister would have been the obvious choice" to replace West as Army Secretary.[49] The *Washington Times* wrote about Lister in a news article:

> Her resignation comes amid an intense struggle inside the ranks. Some leaders want a more "feminized" force as more women move into nontraditional roles and train and deploy side by side with men. Other commanders, perhaps best symbolized by those in the tradition-minded Marine Corps, want to retain a masculine culture that, they say, is needed to bond and fight effectively. Mrs. Lister was the Pentagon's most vigorous supporter of expanding roles for women, including combat missions.[50]

The story was one that made for good talk radio, where there was an obvious enemy (Lister) to rail against and an obvious solution to her mistake (public humiliation and firing). Talk radio hosts were able to conduct interviews with then-House Speaker Newt Gingrich and other high-ranking Republicans who helped push the story along. Lister wrote to me: "Rush Limbaugh, among others, talked about me for quite some time. I remember a plumber who came to the house told me he was a Marine but I was okay."[51] Lister herself remains surprised that she was the target of such an effort. I asked her whether she thought the media coverage of her was coordinated by Republican lawmakers, and she responded: "Clearly the effort was coordinated, and I was viewed by some as much too liberal. . . . To be honest, I'm not sure why they went after me except for the rumors about SecArmy. . . ."[52]

The Lister example helps prove two things. The first is that talk radio is used in conjunction with other media outlets to effect political action, and the second is that talk radio hosts can incite their listeners, provoking them to the point of possible violence. That talk radio hosts and their listeners found Ms. Lister's comments objectionable is one thing. For the hosts to inflame their listeners' passions to the point of death threats is quite another. Talk radio remains an impressive political force today and plays an important role in conservative messaging.

Certainly, talk radio is a haven for provocative and occasionally rebellious speech, and with so much time to fill and the need to garner the large audiences that help keep ratings high, it is dubious that talk radio's language will become more moderate in the coming years. As long as it remains profitable it will remain a powerhouse in American political media.

The question, of course, is how profitable the medium will remain as other types of information technology become increasingly popular, and how radio will transform itself given the new technological hardware options available for its programming. For the meantime, talk radio remains a vital part of the American political landscape, as it helps politicians publicize their message, lambast the opposition, and appeal for their own support.

CONCLUSIONS

Radio has dramatically changed the way it broadcasts thanks to the technological developments that have made the medium more accessible, and thus radio remains important in American politics today. Political radio programming, in the form of talk shows, campaign advertising, or political music, reaches the American public even if it is not seeking it out. During campaign seasons, ads permeate the airwaves on music stations. Political songs crop up on rock, rap, or country music playlists. Talk radio hosts make the national news well beyond their own shows. The American public still listens to the radio and still hears radio content. So although politicians tend to use radio in conjunction with other media formats, they still pay attention to it. More than just relevant, political radio can be quite powerful due to the characteristics of radio itself. The medium is intimate and constant, and the combination of these qualities makes radio formidable. When the aggression that characterizes talk radio is added, the medium becomes extraordinarily influential.

Radio is an intimate medium. Radio programmer Rick Sklar wrote about radio: "[I]t reaches people through only one of their senses—hearing. It was this singularity that gave radio the unique ability to entertain, inform, sell, and motivate. Sound, imaginatively used, stimulated a listener to create in his or her mind a picture.... Every listener 'saw' a different show, but each show was perfect."[53] It is this intimacy that gives political campaign ads on the radio their strength, allowing listeners to feel personally connected to a politician who is asking them for their vote. The same idea follows for political music, allowing an audience to sing along with a tune, feeling the emotion of the lyrics, connecting with a song. Intimacy is especially important in talk radio, since the closeness of the connection between host and listener encourages a kind of relationship that gives a talk radio host a great deal of power. Because a radio show can be exclusively one-sided, a host can opine without acknowledging another point of view. Additionally, since talk radio hosts are rewarded for extreme language that entertains and inflames, the affect of talk radio on a listener can be very powerful. Three hours of loud, angry opinion, emanating from a host so intimately connected to a listener, can be politically influential.

Today, talk radio airs constantly, both over the airwaves and from personal computers where listeners can listen to shows online. As the *Washington Post's* Howard Kurtz wrote in his book *Hot Air*, "America is awash in talk. Loud talk. Angry talk. Conspiratorial talk. Raunchy talk, smug talk, self-serving talk, funny talk, rumor-mongering talk. A cacophony of chat fills the airwaves from coast to coast, from dusk to dawn and beyond, all talk all the time."[54] The popularity of talk radio and the ease with which it is distributed means that listeners can move seamlessly from program to program, from host to host, and never take a break from the chatter. Additionally, because so many talk radio hosts move between radio and television, and because so many prominent talk radio hosts write books to espouse their ideologies, the presence of the most influential hosts is comprehensive. The competition for attention, fame, and ratings among talk radio hosts is particularly strong, which means that there is incentive to coarsen the discourse and make the messages more vigorous, animated, and forceful than they might ordinarily be.

Aggression on the radio is viewed as entertainment, but when rooted within this intimate climate, this aggression becomes dangerous, able to enrage or even incite listeners to threats of violence. The arguments have become more simplified and angrier, which has an effect on the national discourse. As Howard Kurtz writes, "[T]he national conversation has been coarsened, cheapened, reduced to name-calling and finger-pointing and bumper-sticker sloganeering. . . . Outlandish opinion mongers on the left and right tend to drown out everyone else. Extremism in the pursuit of ratings is no vice."[55] Kurtz is correct in his assessment that those on the fringes of the ideological spectrum are verbally drowning out the middle, but most of the voices heard on talk radio emanate from the right.

As Rush Limbaugh's recurring role as agent provocateur and conservative activist proves, talk radio is an important political media tool. Because political talk radio leans so clearly to the right, the medium will continue to broadcast a wholly lopsided and angry view of the American political system. That the talk show hosts are often vicious, erroneous, or hypocritical is practically irrelevant because their ability to echo one another and reify their political goals at the same time make them an invaluable source of political power. Courting talk radio's favor is important to a politician who can see very clearly the effects of their displeasure. If a few talk radio hosts can garner enough outrage to inspire death threats, then they are not to be trifled with. This means that the political stands of a talk show host can be crucial to the success of a political campaign, and the support or opposition of these players is vital in electioneering and policymaking.

The American public is not served by such discourse. Talk radio exemplifies not so much a debate as a diatribe, and without careful consideration of an opposing view there is not much to gain from the "insight" delivered by a single source. The tendency of talk radio hosts to cultivate questions into two polarizing sides, those being "good versus evil" or "right versus wrong," detracts from the complexity of the issues that face us. The intricate and complicated political system in which politicians operate is also poorly served by these false dichotomies. By ignoring nuance and casting each issue or candidate in black-and-white terms, talk radio hosts demean the political system in their reach for ratings and their own popularity. Political discourse is hindered in the process.

Notes

1. State of the News Media 2007, The Project for Excellence in Journalism, http://www.journalism.org/.

2. Doris Graber, *Mass Media and American Politics*, 6th edition (Washington, D.C.: CQ Press, 2002), 41.

3. There has been such a wealth of information and research done on protest music, and I urge readers with a great interest in the topic to examine one of the many scholarly books written on the subject, including Ian Peddie's *The Resisting Muse: Popular Music and Social Protest* (2006), Courtney Brown's *Politics in Music: Music and Political Transformation from Beethoven to Hip-Hop* (2007), and Reebee Garofalo's *Rockin' the Boat: Mass Music and Mass Movements* (1999) among many others.

4. For more information on the use of radio advertising in American campaigns, please see Marvin Overby and Jay Barth's "Radio Advertising in American Political Campaigns," *American Political Research*, Vol. 34, No. 4 (2006): 451–478.

5. Paul Farhi, "Consider This: NPR Achieves Record Ratings," *Washington Post*, March 24, 2009, C01.

6. Ibid.

7. Arbitron Radio Market Report Reference Guide 2.1, http://www.arbitron.com/downloads/purplebook.pdf (accessed October 16, 2007).

8. *FCC v. Pacifica Foundation*, 438 U.S. 726 (1978).

9. "FCC Consumer Facts," http://www.fcc.gov/cgb/consumerfacts/obscene.html.

10. Stern Ratings Effect Continues, *Friday Morning Quarterback Album Report* (April 29, 2004), http://www.fmqb.com/Article.asp?id=23831.

11. Michael Fitzgerald, "Dixie Chicks Axed by Clear Channel," *Jacksonville Business Journal*, March 18, 2003.

12. An expert in this area is Robert McChesney, a communications professor at the University of Illinois. McChesney has authored several texts on the market forces that drive media competition and the lack of creativity that results from this.

13. Jeremy Caplan and Brendan Lowe, "Most Influential Gadgets and Gizmos," *Time*, June 29, 2007.

14. Arbitron Radio Market Report Reference Guide 2.1, http://www.arbitron.com/downloads/purplebook.pdf (accessed October 16, 2007).

15. Louis Bolce, Gerald DeMayo, and Douglas Muzzio, "Dial-In Democracy: Talk Radio and the 1994 Election," *Political Science Quarterly* 111 (1996): 457–481.

16. Ibid.

17. David Barker, "Rushed Decisions: Political Talk Radio and Vote Choice, 1994–1996," *Journal of Politics* 61 (1999): 527–539.

18. Andrea Hopkins, "Republicans Turning to Radio to Get Out the Vote: Medium Remains Predominantly Conservative," *National Post* (Canada), October 26, 2006, A13.

19. Ibid.

20. Ibid.

21. David Jackson, "White House Hosts Mass Talk Radio Event; Airwave Celebrities Gather under Tent on Front Lawn as Cheney, Others in Administration Appeal to GOP Base," *USA Today*, October 25, 2006.

22. Ibid.

23. Paul Bedard, "Washington Whispers," *US News and World Report*, March 2, 2009, http://www.usnews.com/blogs/washington-whispers/2009/03/03/gop-to-michael-steele-quiet-about-rush-limbaugh-or-youre-fired.html (accessed May 15, 2009).

24. Jonathan Martin, "Limbaugh Blasts Steele, the RNC," *Politico*, March 2, 2009, http://www.politico.com/news/stories/0309/19498.html (accessed May 15, 2009).

25. Mike Allen, "Steele to Rush: I'm Sorry," *Politico*, March 2, 2009, http://www.politico.com/news/stories/0309/19517.html (accessed May 15, 2009).

26. David Knowles, "Colin Powell/Rush Limbaugh War Rages On," *Politics Daily*, May 7, 2009, http://www.politicsdaily.com/2009/05/07/colin-powell-rush-limbaugh-war-rages-on/ (accessed May 15, 2009).

27. Ibid.

28. Michael O'Brien, "Cheney Picks Limbaugh's Version of the GOP," *The Hill*, May 10, 2009, http://thehill.com/leading-the-news/cheney-picks-limbaughs-version-of-the-gop-2009-05-10.html (accessed May 15, 2009).

29. David Barker and Kathleen Knight, "Political Talk Radio and Public Opinion," *Public Opinion Quarterly* 64 (2000): 149–170.

30. This theory is developed and quantified in Jamieson Hall and Kathleen and Joseph Cappella, *Echo Chamber: Rush Limbaugh and the Conservative Media Establishment* (New York: Oxford University Press, 2008).

31. "Limbaugh's Faulty Memory: 'I Don't Know Who's Accusing [Hillary Clinton] of Murdering Anybody,' " *Media Matters for America* (July 9, 2007), http://mediamatters.org/mmtv/200707090007.

32. Ibid.

33. Allison Mitchell, "Clinton Takes Aim at Critics on 'Right-Wing' Talk Radio," *New York Times*, December 16, 1996.

34. Diana Owen, "Talk Radio and Evaluations of President Clinton," *Political Communication*, Vol. 14, No. 3 (January 1997): 333–353.

35. Reed Tucker, "The 25 People We Envy Most," *CNNMoney.com* (October 17, 2005), http://money.cnn.com/magazines/fortune/fortune_archive/2005/10/17/8358072/index.htm (accessed September 23, 2009).

36. Sean Hannity, *Deliver Us from Evil: Defeating Terrorism, Despotism, and Liberalism* (New York: Harper, 2005), 4.

37. Brian Lamb, October 17, 2007, Personal interview with author.

38. Katy Bachman, "Talk Radio Network Expands Ingraham's Reach in Top 10," *Media Week* (September 1, 2003): 31.

39. "Talk Radio Research Project 2008," *Talkers Magazine*, 2008, http://talkers.com/online/?p=98 (accessed February 21, 2009).

40. "Attitudes Towards News Organizations," The Pew Research Center for People and the Press, http://people-press.org/report/19891113/attitudes-toward-news-organization (accessed May 15, 2009).

41. David Barker, "Rushed Decisions: Political Talk Radio and Vote Choice, 1994–1996," *Journal of Politics* 61 (1999): 536.

42. David Barker and Kathleen Knight, "Political Talk Radio and Public Opinion," *Public Opinion Quarterly* 64 (2000): 149–170.

43. Laura Ingraham, Fox News Interview, *Hannity & Colmes*, June 27, 2007.

44. David Hinckley, "Bush Welcomes Right-Wing Talkers to the West Wing," *New York Daily News*, August 2, 2007, http://www.nydailynews.com/entertainment/tv/2007/08/02/2007-08-02_bush_welcomes_rightwing_talkers_to_the_w-2.html (accessed May 15, 2009).

45. William Mayer, "The Myth of a Conservative Media," Paper presented at the American Political Science Association Annual Conference, Chicago, August 28–September 1, 2004.

46. Ibid.

47. Sara Lister, July 2008, Personal interview with author.

48. Rowan Scarborough, "Top Army Woman Quits after Uproar; She Said Marines Are 'Extremists,'" *Washington Times*, November 15, 1997, A1.

49. Gregory Vistica and Evan Thomas, "At War in the Pentagon," *Newsweek*, December 8, 1997, 44.

50. Rowan Scarborough, "Top Army Woman Quits after Uproar; She Said Marines Are 'Extremists,'" *Washington Times*, November 15, 1997, A1.

51. Sara Lister, July 2008, Personal interview with author.

52. Ibid.

53. Rick Sklar, *Rocking America: How the All-Hit Radio Stations Took Over* (New York: St. Martin's Press, 1984).

54. Howard Kurtz, *Hot Air: All Talk All the Time* (New York: Times Books, 1996), 3.

55. Ibid., 4.

Chapter 4

TELEVISION: NICHE PROGRAMMING ON BROADCAST AND CABLE

A lie can travel halfway around the world while the truth is putting on its shoes.

—Mark Twain

It is safe to say that television is the dominant media force in America today. According to Nielsen Media Research, the organization that monitors American television viewing, in 2009 98.9 percent of American households had televisions.[1] Cable and satellite companies now provide more than 300 channels of news, sports, and entertainment programming, with an additional 100 channels designated for music broadcast. One reason for the success of television is that it is a visual medium, able to capture the attention of the viewers completely. Another reason has to do with choice. Thanks to cable satellite technology, the number of television viewing options has increased significantly in the past several decades. This affords viewers the option to watch niche programming (e.g., sports, home decor, animal behavior) that appeals to specific tastes. In the near future the Internet may overtake TV in popularity and accessibility, but for now television remains the prevailing medium for news and entertainment broadcasting.

Politicians rely on TV to advertise themselves and their issue positions during election seasons and beyond. News programming is an obvious place to find politicians and policy discussions, but other television formats provide a multitude of ways for politicians to communicate as well. Politicians use television because of its popularity and also because the niche programming allows politicians to address certain demographics through particular shows. If a politician is campaigning for office, it now makes sense to diversify television undertakings in order to reach the largest number of potential voters or political supporters. He can reach rural voters by appearing on Country Music Television, he can reach young voters through MTV, he can reach male voters through ESPN, and he can reach female voters through HGTV. Because of this, and because 98.9 percent of American households have TV sets, politicians use television a great deal.

It is always in a politician's best interest to control his or her own message, and certain television formats accommodate this control better than others. Television appearances where a politician knows exactly what will happen is the most coveted by those doing the campaigning. This kind of control can transpire when politicians obtain script approval, vet interview questions in advance, and select the atmosphere in which they will appear. As desirable as this kind of control is, it is also hard to maintain for several reasons. First, programs do not often allow a politician to approve a script or control interview questions, as it is not in the interest of the media organizations to forfeit this power. Second, television is now completely tied in with other media, which means that a politician may end up on TV without intending to. For example, anything that appears on a Web site is now fodder for television coverage as well. With the ubiquity of camera phones and video recording devices, video can originate in a number of different places and end up on television eventually. This means that politicians must be extremely careful not only about the television coverage they plan on, but also the coverage they don't. For not only is TV a 300-channel behemoth, it both magnifies and feeds Internet and video distribution so that content is spread with alarming alacrity well beyond its confines.

This chapter examines broadcast and cable television and their emphasis on entertainment and diversion programming. It also explains how politicians use this medium to their advantage, and how sometimes TV coverage can be politically damaging.

TELEVISION FORMS: BROADCAST AND CABLE

In the early days of television, there was both trepidation and hope for the new medium's effect on the electorate, and debates ensued between those who thought it to be an "idiot box" that would encourage us to (in the words of the late scholar Neil Postman) "amuse ourselves to death," and those who hoped TV would spark a great information wave that would wash over the masses.[2] In the early days of television, however, there were only three channels and viewing options were limited. The situation changed when cable satellite technology emerged in the 1970s, and now there exists a glut of information—and entertainment, sports, and so forth—available on television. Broadcast and cable media channels differ from one another, their styles reflecting the varying natures of their histories, missions, and formats. Both entities are part of the larger media system, and both must meet the financial demands of their corporate owners, but that's where the similarities end. Broadcast television has a longer history with the American public than cable does and compared to their cable colleagues must provide a wide variety of programming. For example, while ESPN focuses solely on sports, ABC has a sports division, a news division, an entertainment division, and a daytime division to contend with programs like soap operas. Additionally, the rigidity of the broadcast network news schedule puts broadcast news in a reactive mode more often than cable news, which is hungry for stories all the time.[3] Further, because it needs to fill 24 hours with news, cable can focus more intently and for longer periods of time than broadcast TV. This focus is not without drawbacks, since constant attention to a topic can sometimes overemphasize the importance of a relatively minor story.[4]

Today, politicians running for high office strive for positive coverage on both news programs and on entertainment shows in order to appeal to a wide variety of demographics, and they routinely spread their attention between the broadcast and cable networks because of the strengths each can provide for them.

THE BROADCAST NETWORKS

Each of the big three broadcast networks is owned by a major corporation, all of which have considerable and diverse corporate holdings. When broadcasting became a lucrative and influential business in the early twentieth century, there were two major corporations that controlled the airwaves: The Columbia Broadcasting System (CBS) and the Radio Corporation of America (RCA). In the 1940s the two radio networks were CBS and NBC, the latter of which belonged within the RCA corporate family. NBC's radio network system was divided into two, named "NBC Blue" and "NBC Red." In 1943, the FCC determined that such a system constituted a monopoly and forced RCA to sell NBC Blue in an effort to encourage ownership diversity. The network was bought by businessman Edward Noble, who renamed it the American Broadcasting Company (ABC), and this sale set the stage for the competition between ABC, NBC, and CBS.

ABC. By the mid-1950s, ABC began to broadcast on television, but it remained in last place against its other "big three" competitors. ABC's last-place position changed as its entertainment offerings became increasingly popular, and the 1970s were particularly profitable for the network, thanks to the *Love Boat*, *Fantasy Island*, and *Dynasty*. In 1985, ABC was sold to the Capital Cities Corporation, and almost 10 years later it was sold again to Disney. Disney's network division includes ABC, ESPN, the Disney Channel, and 72 radio stations.

CBS. CBS was founded by William Paley in 1928, and for the next seven decades the Paley family controlled the network. From the earliest days of radio, CBS has been a media powerhouse, and it expanded its broadcast interests to include television in the 1940s. In 1995, the CBS Company was on the auction block and was acquired by the Westinghouse Corporation. Only five years later, in 2000, CBS was purchased by Viacom. In 2005, CBS and Viacom split into separate corporate entities, and Sumner Redstone is the chairman of both. Today the CBS Corporation controls not only CBS, but also television and radio stations, and Simon & Schuster publications.

NBC. The last of the big three is NBC, which began within RCA as "NBC Red" before RCA's divorcement of its two radio networks. Until recently, the network was owned by General Electric and Vivendi International. Within the

NBC family are Universal Studios, and this gives NBC its corporate name: NBC Universal. NBC Universal also owns 14 local television stations and Telemundo, the Spanish-language television network with its own 14 Spanish-language stations. In 2009, the cable company Comcast announced plans to take over NBC Universal but this deal will face a "lengthy regulatory review."[5]

Vertical integration, as defined in the Introduction, occurs within all three of the major broadcast television networks due to their corporate structures. This integration allows each of the corporate owners of the broadcast networks to make more money from their media enterprises. For example, within ABC there are news and entertainment divisions that produce such shows as the *ABC Nightly News*, *The View*, *Good Morning America*, *Nightline*, *This Week*, and *Jimmy Kimmel Live*. Because these programs fall under the same corporate umbrella, the opportunities for vertical integration within the Disney family are plentiful. George Stephanopoulos, host of ABC's Sunday morning newsmaker program *This Week*, appears on *The View*. The Disney film *Wall-E* was rated "4 Stars!" on the *ABC News* Web site, and the movie's robot application developer appeared on *Nightline*. Another example exists on NBC. The broadcast network and its cable companion MSNBC now share office space in midtown Manhattan, share content on their networks and Internet sites, and share hosts who bounce between these two entities as the need arises. As they share content and credit, NBC and MSNBC also help to illustrate the cross-marketing potential so valuable with vertical integration.

The effects of corporate ownership can be negative, as evidenced by a case involving the investigative news show *60 Minutes*. In the 1990s the executive producers of *60 Minutes* were told not to air a story on the tobacco industry for fear of a lawsuit that would harm CBS's sale to the Westinghouse Corporation. This type of corporate pressure to change or weaken the news may not be widespread, but it exists and helps to illustrate how this corporate control can affect the news we receive.

The Big Three broadcast television companies provide much of the news and entertainment that Americans enjoy each day, and their reach extends to the smaller affiliate stations around the country. In every major television market there are local affiliate stations that air programming from the Big Three networks, plus their own local newscasts, plus syndicated programming sprinkled in for good measure. Local news rarely focuses on hard news, opting instead to report on weather, traffic, and human interest stories that most appeal to a local audience. Affiliate stations determine their entertainment programming as well, selecting syndicated programming (such as sitcom repeats and talk shows) to air during the day and network programming to run in the evenings. Local stations are not necessarily owned by their broadcasting parent company. Local affiliates may be independently owned and operated, choosing to (or choosing *not* to) air broadcast network programming. This independence affects the relationship between broadcast networks and local affiliates and can cause tension between the managements of the two entities.

For example, on one occasion a network news program was removed by a company that owned a number of local affiliate stations. In 2004, the Sinclair Broadcasting Group (SBG) owned or controlled 62 television stations around the country.[6] Sinclair tends to lean conservative, and on its nightly editorials lends a conservative spin to its local affiliate programming. In 2004, SBG pulled an episode of *Nightline* from its eight ABC affiliates because it deemed the show too liberal. The episode, titled *Rollcall*, featured host Ted Koppel reading the names of U.S. service personnel killed in Iraq and Afghanistan aloud while their pictures aired behind him. SBG decided the episode was antiwar, too liberal, and refused to air it.[7] Later in 2004, Sinclair made headlines again during the 2004 presidential campaign between incumbent Republican George W. Bush and his Democratic challenger John Kerry. SBG ordered its affiliate stations to run an anti-John Kerry telefilm called *Stolen Honor: Wounds That Never Heal.*[8] The movie, which was produced by a former *Washington Times* reporter, accused Kerry of harming American prisoners of war in Vietnam by protesting against the war. The film was considered "news content" by SBG and preempted prime time programming just days before the 2004 presidential election.

Most evident in these situations was that Sinclair Broadcasting used its power over affiliate stations to push its political agenda on the viewers. Conventional wisdom mandates local news programming appeal to as many viewers as possible in order to keep viewers happy. However, the success of SBG's ideologically biased programming decisions comes from the fact that many viewers are both unaware of their local affiliate station ownership and uncaring about the content of local news and programming. Since most programming originates from the big networks and not from the local affiliate stations, most viewers simply accept local programming choices without differentiating between the two. Thus, if ABC shows the highly rated *America's Got Talent*, then most viewers find little reason to closely examine their ABC affiliate station. This is why the Big Three networks work so hard beat the competition and why local programming decisions garner such little attention.

Profitability is the key to network television, found in ad revenue dollars generated by different types of news and entertainment programming. The evening news is only one segment of news programming generated by the big three television networks, although it is clearly the largest and most important component of network news. Other formats include the morning news seen on shows like *Today* and *Good Morning America*, newsmagazine shows like *Dateline* and *60 Minutes*, and finally in Sunday morning chat shows such as *Meet the Press* and *This Week*. These shows combine to fill the news divisions of the big three networks, all of which have had to reduce their staff in recent years due to budget shortfalls and other financial cutbacks. In the past two decades there have been massive staffing cuts in the news divisions of the network news organizations. Media Professor Joe Foote, currently dean of the Gaylord College of Journalism and Mass Communication at the University of Oklahoma, did a study on the workload of news correspondents. He found that the reporters filing on-air stories were working harder and appearing more often on air. The number of stories an average correspondent filed in 1985 was 31.4 a year, and in 2002 it was 40.9, an increase of 30 percent.[9] This means that budget cuts have forced the network news to do more with fewer people, putting a strain on the news organizations and their staff.

Network news divisions have to produce news for the morning and for the night, with the evening news being the major news program on any network. Morning news across all three major networks is delivered via a more chatty, softer morning show that may include the news, but emphasizes more lifestyle stories than hard news. Fewer people watch the morning programs since many Americans are leaving for work when the morning news airs. Despite decreasing audience numbers, the competition between the morning talk and news shows is fierce. Throughout the years, the networks have tried to stock their morning programming with heavy news talent, such as ABC's Diane Sawyer and Charlie Gibson—two highly respected journalists who have spent years on ABC's *Good Morning America* program. The morning news is so heavily integrated with entertainment and lifestyle stories that there is barely news available at all in the morning. The *Today Show* has made a concerted effort to stack the first half hour of its three-hour broadcast with serious national and international news, which has proven to be a successful move for that show. The morning shows average just under 6 million viewers each. Morning news shows garner a slightly more diverse audience than their evening news counterparts, which results in an audience that is slightly younger and more female for the morning news than for the evening.

News magazines, such as the highly rated *60 Minutes* and *Dateline*, form another component of broadcast news divisions and air in the evening during prime-time programming on the networks. Because they are integrated within the broadcast news divisions, news magazines are also feeling the financial pinch of networks with tight budgets and the pressure from their corporate parents to deliver highly rated programming. *Dateline* has hit upon a successful formula with its series titled "To Catch a Predator," which sets up would-be child molesters on camera, exposing and humiliating them for the pleasure of the audience. Even *60 Minutes*, arguably the archetype of investigative television journalism, softens the blow of its hard-hitting news segments with lifestyle features on musicians, actors, and celebrities. Because newsmagazines share resources with network news staff, these shows are cost-efficient and profitable. Their audience skews older than the desired 18- to 24-year-old demographic that is so financially rewarding for media outlets.

The nightly news airs when most Americans are home from work. According to the Project for Excellence in Journalism, the evening news audience is around 26 million viewers total, per night. This number, spread across the three networks, has dropped by 1 million viewers per year for the last 25 years. The evening news audience is older than the news audience in other media, with an average age of about 60. Younger Americans either get their news from another source or do not get news altogether. As technology changes, more people are leaving TV for other news formats, including the Internet, radio, and cable news shows. Each format delivers news differently, and consumers make their choices based on their desire for immediacy or schedule regularity and their taste for ideological slant or opinion-heavy programming. The strength and size of the boomer generation, the group that watches the nightly news the most, indicates that these news programs will most likely maintain their lion's share of the news ratings, even as audience numbers continue to drop. Still, evening news production staffs are unwilling to rely solely on an aging audience for their entire viewership. Because their audience numbers are dropping, network executives have made assertive efforts to expand their news content availability to other outlets, such as their online Web sites or their cable-partner networks.[10] For example, NBC's Web site includes a blog from *NBC Nightly News* anchor Brian Williams. Often, the anchors jump back and forth between NBC and MSNBC for more in-depth coverage of topical events or current issues. This blending of media modes to disseminate the same news content to different audiences seems to be one efficient way to produce and distribute the news to the largest audience possible. Younger Americans are simply less likely than their older colleagues to pay attention to hard news, according to the Pew Center, which found that 25 percent of those aged 18 to 24 are completely disengaged from hard news. Therefore, in order to lure younger viewers to the news, broadcast news divisions have had to reshape themselves. Oftentimes, this means incorporating online content with broadcast news distribution to attract an Internet-focused younger audience. The move online poses problems for the news divisions that are already stretched thin by budget cutbacks. According to the *New York Times*:

> CBS and NBC are, for the moment, mainly using the Web to repackage their regular nightly news shows. . . . But the ABC Webcast is an entirely different animal, sometimes resembling a younger, more technologically advanced version of the traditional 6:30 report. It is intended in part for people who view Web pages on iPods and cell phones, and ABC executives say they are deliberately aiming to please the 25- to 54-year olds whom every news organization covets.[11]

The benefits of Webcasting a news program are numerous, as the Webcast presents another outlet for the work of the journalists already filing their reports. Online, the time constrictions are practically nonexistent, unlike the time pressures of television broadcast. However, the key to ABC's Webcast is the appeal to a younger audience, something that the Nightly News desperately wants. Over on NBC, the partnership between NBC, MSNBC, and their Web site components means that the larger media organization has more content to share. The network's online presence includes information content from *NBC Nightly News* or opinion pieces from MSNBC's Keith Olbermann. Since the broadcast news organizations have to compete so vigorously with cable channels, greater synchronization between television and the Internet is likely to increase. According to one study conducted by ComScore, a research firm based outside Washington, D.C., "Online video viewing increased 42 percent [in 2008], about 10 times the growth rate of TV viewing."[12] As technology improves, this trend will continue, and it is feeding into an emerging cultural shift to on-demand programming. According to Jeffery Cole from the Center for the Digital Future: "Teenagers today barely understand the idea of watching TV on someone else's schedule."[13] The effects of this on broadcast news programming are obvious. When a citizenry becomes accustomed to constant media on their own timetable there will be little appetite for the inflexibility of the evening news.

Broadcast news producers are fighting such a loss through the synchronization between broadcast and online media. They also try to appeal to the largest number of viewers as possible. The financial drive to lure large numbers of viewers leads them to soften the news to make it more accessible, interesting, or entertaining. As already defined, so-called "soft news" presents information in a way to make it easily understandable, which is attractive to producers who are striving for higher ratings through the draw of engaging stories. The problem with soft news is fairly obvious. By emphasizing the amusing at the expense of depth, little real knowledge about an issue, event, or conflict can be discerned. What a viewer is left with is only a partial understanding of something quite complicated, which leads to an exhaustively uninformed electorate.

Clearly, the confines of network news vary dramatically from those of their brothers and sisters on cable. For starters, network news divisions produce at most only a few hours of news each day. They adhere to a fairly strict formula of anchor person in New York who steers the news to different stories that occur around the country and around the world. The network news anchor is now a celebrity in his or her own right. For example, in 2006 Katie Couric took over the *CBS Evening News* with much excitement and attention. She was initially paid $15 million per year, shocking industry insiders and chagrining many at CBS News who knew their own budgets would be cut to accommodate such a salary. Despite poor ratings performance for her news program, Ms. Couric has been treated not as a journalist but as a celebrity—a star of such proportions that when she attends major news events, she garners as much attention as the news on which she is reporting. To prove this, the newscast is now called *CBS News with Katie Couric*. Placing the anchor in the title illustrates the importance and weight of the personality during the programming. In 2009, ABC News announced that it would move morning news host Diane Sawyer to the evening news, placing another big-name journalist in the anchor seat in order to compete with Katie Couric. This trend fits in with the emphasis on entertainment, since the hiring of a personality to be in charge of the news desk serves to make the news compelling as well.

Another trend found in the evening news is seen in the increasing emphasis on news found closer to home. Due to budget cutbacks, the number of foreign correspondents has dwindled significantly in past years and as a result the total number of minutes devoted to stories filed by reporters with a foreign dateline fell by almost one third in the past 20 years.[14] At the same time, the number of minutes devoted to stories about U.S. foreign policy increased by 25 percent in the same time period, having much to do with the wars in Iraq and Afghanistan.[15] Broadcast news is focusing on America, even as Americans operate internationally. This severely limits the kind of information that broadcast news consumers acquire when they watch the evening news. Not only is their news more entertaining, it is less extensive than it used to be.

On June 12, 2009, Congress mandated that analog television convert to digital broadcast, which means that in the United States television no longer broadcasts "over the air." The analog-to-digital TV conversion had only a slight impact on the popularity of television since 97.5 percent of the television market was already using cable and satellite.[16] Even though it is all digital, however, the distinction between broadcast and cable television persists because of history, structure, and content. Broadcast television, while still an important part of American media, is fighting for its life.

Technological changes are hampering broadcast television's profitability, and broadcast TV executives are looking for ways to survive. According to Rupert Murdoch, who spoke to News Corp investors in 2009: "Good programming is expensive. . . . It can no longer be supported solely by advertising revenues."[17] According to media analyst Craig Moffett, this means that broadcast television will soon begin to not only seek the traditional ad revenue, but also will look to the cable model for financial support: "The broadcast networks are really struggling to find a viable business model. . . . They're looking at the cable networks that make money both on advertising and the money that the cable operators pay them and saying, 'We need a dual revenue stream to survive, too.' "[18] To accomplish this, in 2010 cable company Time Warner announced that it will pay News Corp for its broadcast content. News Corp produces such broadcast hits as *The Simpsons* and *American Idol*. This is going to alter how the American public receives broadcast content, but it is too early to tell how. The move towards a cable-style system for broadcast television has the potential to save broadcast news, or the possibility of destroying it entirely. This would leave more room for cable news to flourish.

CABLE NEWS

Contrary to broadcast news, cable news networks can devote more resources and much more time to the news they deliver because they have the time and the money to do so. Starting in the 1970s, satellite technology increased the number of TV channels exponentially when the number grew first from three channels to 24, and then to more than 60 channels. Once media owners and investors saw the profitability of niche programming, that number increased even more, and now most satellite and cable providers deliver around 400 channels that generate news, entertainment, information, and music. As the number of choices increases on TV, so too does the ability for viewers to change channels on a whim, constantly self-selecting their ideal form of entertainment. Previously, in order to get to the sport or leisure part of the news, a television viewer had to sit through a newscast. Today, one need never watch the news or read about politics because there are so many entertainment options available. As political scientist Markus Prior has noted, this is at one time a boon for political junkies who now have numerous television options where they can get their fix, and at the same time a windfall for those who wish to avoid news and politics at all cost.[19] Thus, the abundance of choice allows political junkies the ability to pick their favorite flavor of politics at the same time it allows many Americans to avoid the news entirely and focus instead on entertainment that is easier to consume. For those who are interested in the news there are a multitude of choices on TV. Viewers might get their daily dose on broadcast television each night, they might catch nuggets of information on the morning chat shows, they might watch late-night comedy and garner news from the monologue, or they might immerse themselves in cable coverage. Even within these larger options, there are more choices to make. For the viewers who lean to the left of the ideological spectrum, they can watch MSNBC and rarely hear conservative voices; and the opposite goes for conservatives who watch Fox News Channel. This affords an exclusivity of thought that discourages debate and only serves to strengthen the divide between ideological sides. Add to television the multitude of radio programs and Web sites that cater exclusively to one side or another and this polarization becomes even more problematic.

Cable was in its infancy in 1979 when Brian Lamb founded the very first all-news network, the Cable Satellite Public Affairs Network (C-SPAN). The network's goal was to provide uninterrupted coverage of the legislative process, and its mission remains the same to this day. C-SPAN was a relatively inexpensive proposition. C-SPAN is a nonprofit company considered by the cable industry to be a public service, and as a result the network has no ratings imperatives that force it to stray from its mission. In the early days of cable and long before the Internet became a household technology, C-SPAN was the sole source of uninterrupted and unfiltered political information. Savvy politicians like Newt Gingrich figured out that virtually unlimited (and free) airtime was a priceless gift for politicians in Washington. When Gingrich was a young Republican congressman and then Speaker of the House, he made the most of "Special Order" time at the end of the legislative day when House lawmakers could speak for up to an hour, uninterrupted, on any topic. This vast amount of TV exposure served his political purposes quite well, and his use of C-SPAN helped him and members of the Conservative Opportunity Society (of which he was a founding member) succeed in their efforts to gain Republican control of the House in 1994. I spoke with Brian Lamb about how C-SPAN played such an integral role in American politics in these early days of cable television:

> If you go back to Gingrich and how he used us, back in the early '80s, and knowingly so, told the world he was using us, they don't do that anymore like they did— You can go another route now, you can go to an Internet site. But in that brief time period, we were the one place you could go to be heard all the time—They've picked other venues where they can totally control the message. And I don't blame them—why would they want to leave it to chance?—We fit in at a magic time and it made a difference; and now it's there, it's a staple, it's a tradition, but it's nothing unique anymore.[20]

Because C-SPAN set the stage for cable news to come, and because the Internet allows so much unfiltered information, it is not the unique entity it was 30 years ago. Yet it maintains a unique reputation in Washington and beyond the Beltway as the most balanced and intelligent public affairs information available due to its dedication to its mission, its strict policy of ideological balance, and its consistency of purpose. In 2007, Brian Lamb was awarded the Presidential Medal of Freedom by President Bush.

In 1980, Ted Turner founded the Cable News Network (CNN) based on C-SPAN's principle that nonstop news and information could be provided to the American public at a relatively low cost. The difference was the profit margin: CNN had one. Unlike C-SPAN, CNN is a commercial enterprise, which explains the difference between the two in terms of focus, pacing, and flash. CNN became so profitable, especially following the 1991 Persian Gulf War, that it gave rise to other all-news networks because Turner was able to prove that providing news to the public could be a lucrative endeavor. Turner went on to add CNN Headline News to his empire in 1982. Soon there were CNBC, MSNBC, Fox News, and Fox Business Channels, all of which provide nonstop news and information to the American public. CNBC, the Consumer News Business Channel, is owned by NBC Universal and was started in 1989 as a business off-shoot of the larger news organization. MSNBC was launched in 1996 and was owned by both NBC Universal and Microsoft until Microsoft left the organization in 2005. Originally envisioned as a news channel with a high-tech emphasis, MSNBC eventually became more like CNN: it transformed into a news channel focusing on general news and punditry. All of these cable news channels fight each other—and broadcast news divisions—for audience attention. This can be quite challenging, which is why they have tried to create their own brand of news by dedicating their channel to a certain personality and type of news.

The personality of a cable news channel is constructed through its ideological slant, emotion. energy levels, issue attention, graphics placement, and celebrities. For example, MSNBC and CNBC are both within the NBC corporate umbrella, but the two have distinctly different "personalities": MSNBC pays attention to general news and CNBC focuses on business news. CNBC covers Wall Street and the stock markets while MSNBC covers domestic and foreign news, politics, business, sports, entertainment, health, science, and travel. The loud and angry CNBC pundits—such as Jim Cramer—rail against the Obama administration while MSNBC's Keith Olbermann roars against the Republican Party. According to *Time* magazine's James Poniewozik: "It is as if—between MSNBC and CNBC—NBC News is trying to own the liberal and conservative voices of cable news. But CNBC's is a much different strain of conservative from Sarah Palin's or Bill O'Reilly's—It's an ideology not exclusively beholden to a party—but it's an ideology nonetheless."[21] The personalities of these networks are carefully constructed to draw in audiences, ratings revenue, and attention. Cable news must also pay attention to the type of news they broadcast.

There are three different types of news on cable, according to the Project for Excellence in Journalism. These types include news on demand, crisis coverage, and prime time personality. Each network strives for harmonization between these differing typologies, but each news type demands different conditions and requirements, and so often the cable news networks excel in certain areas and falter in others. There is evidence that the three types are evolving into one personality-driven news format.

News on demand is what *CNN Headline News* aims for. This type focuses on the latest headlines, and it changes when the news does. *Headline News* used to be 24 hours of constant news updates, but it has now adjusted to include programming much like its competitors. The mornings begin with a four-hour news show called *Morning Express with Robin Meade!*, and in the evening, pundit shows are hosted by Glenn Beck and Nancy Grace. Regardless of this format change, the mission of *Headline News* is to supply the "news on demand" type of news, and it stays true to this effort most of the time. The second type, crisis coverage, is the exclusive coverage of one crisis or important event, and all channel attention is concentrated on an unfolding emergency. CNN dominates with this type of news. Because of its CNN international partner, *CNN International*, CNN has ready access to video of both domestic occurrences and international upheaval more quickly than its competitors. The news organization made its name for itself during the first Persian Gulf War, and it kept providing thorough coverage of such tragedies as the Columbine shootings, the September 11th terrorist attacks, and the Hurricane Katrina disaster in the Gulf states. Again, because of its association and shared resources with NBC News, MSNBC also does well covering crises and major events such as national elections. The two networks pool resources and talent to provide comprehensive coverage of a crisis or important event, so it is able to begin coverage on network and continue this coverage on cable. Finally, prime time personality programming fills the air each night with the pundits who analyze the news and give it their own spin. Such programs include MSNBC's *Countdown with Keith Olbermann* and *Live with Dan Abrams*, but it is Fox News Channel that has consistently won this ratings race. With such programs as *The O'Reilly Factor*, Glenn Beck's evening program, and *Hannity*, Fox News Channel viewers are treated to a wealth of attitude and belief, most of it firmly in conjunction with the goals of the Republican Party and the ideals of conservatism. The primary benefit of prime time personality programming is that it clearly defines a network, giving it a brand and a direction. Once Fox News Channel gained a significant conservative audience with its personality-driven pundit programming, the rest of Fox News programming followed suit to create the brand we see today. By asserting a liberal bias in the rest of the mainstream media, Fox News has carved for itself a niche audience of conservative viewers. It is in Fox's best interest to maintain this audience through consistently conservative programming.

News can be slow, repetitive, and complicated, and so pundit shows were created to fill the hours and attract the widest audience possible. Pundits are commentators who may (or may not) have journalistic experience. They opine on the news of the day and provide criticism and praise on politicians, events, and institutions. Their analysis varies wildly in depth and substance, but across the board the most popular and observable pundits are those who make angry or outrageous statements that stand out from the rest. Cable news relies on punditry for two main reasons: to fill the abundance of airtime and to draw an audience to their network. In an election year, punditry is especially prominent. From the preprimary period (when pundits guess candidacy announcements) to the primaries (when pundits bet on victories) until election day (at which time pundits analyze every nuance of a heated campaign), these men and women are there to hypothesize and argue rather than report the news. According to *Washington Post* media critic Paul Farhi: "During the week of Super Tuesday 2008, 75 percent of available airtime on MSNBC, CNN, and Fox News was dedicated to dissecting the campaign."[22] On Super Tuesday itself, MSNBC's Keith Olbermann and Chris Matthews—pundits both—stayed on the air for eight straight hours.

Pundits do not have to be journalists, but they do have to be entertaining. An engaging or recognizable figure on the air helps generate ratings. Many pundits are political insiders who have experience on a campaign, working for an elected official, or in the military. It is lucrative to be a pundit, which is why so many D.C. insiders want the title; and with 24 hours a day of television time to fill, pundits are in demand. Pundits are not only in demand from cable news channels, but also from weekend news shows on broadcast TV, talk radio, and foreign networks with international news divisions in Washington. This gives pundits a significant variety of outlets on which to opine. Because there are so many pundits, however, the competition between them for airtime is also fierce. Thus, those pundits who are most successful often say things that are exaggerated or extreme in order to be heard and noticed. During the 2008 presidential campaign, two MSNBC pundits made comments that were so extreme that they had to apologize after the fact. The first instance occurred when Chris Matthews said about Hillary Clinton: "The reason Hillary Clinton may be a front-runner is her husband messed around." The second instance occurred when David Shuster said the Clintons were "pimping out" their daughter Chelsea for the sake of the campaign.[23] In both of these cases, the pundits were trying hard to be entertaining by inserting entertaining language into their commentary, but in both cases their verbiage crossed the line of decorum.

This decorum line is a difficult one to determine since mores and standards vary on each channel. This is exemplified by two popular pundits from different networks: Fox News's Glenn Beck and MSNBC's Chris Matthews. Beck hosts a talk radio program and an eponymous 5 p.m. pundit show on Fox News. Beck has characterized his style as a "fusion of entertainment and enlightenment,"[24] and his radio and television shows emphasize a libertarian-style apprehension of government. Beck said the following about the as-yet incomplete "Freedom Tower" monument marking the September 11th attacks on the World Trade Center: "I believe if it were up to you or me, just regular schmoes in America, the Freedom Tower would have been done years ago. . . . I believe the only reason we haven't built it isn't because of Americans. It's because we're being held back. And who is holding us back? Politicians. Special-interest groups. Political correctness. You name it—everybody but you."[25] Beck helped promote a 2009 march on Washington commemorating the day after the 2001 terrorist attacks, calling the effort the "9/12 Project." Claiming the Washington political establishment was ignoring the needs of the average American, thousands protested against President Obama in specific, and Democratic Party policies in general. Fox News provided live coverage of the event, as did all of the television news channels. However, the day after the rally Fox News ran an ad in the *Washington Post* asking: "How did ABC, CBS, NBC, MSNBC, and CNN miss this story?"[26] Since all of the media organizations carried the story of the protest, the premise of the advertisement was faulty, but it helps to prove a point: Fox News alleges liberal media bias where there might not be any, and in doing so brand themselves as the only legitimate news source.

MSNBC has tried to follow the example of Fox News and offers pundit programming with a more liberal bend. MSNBC's evening pundit line-up includes Keith Olbermann and Rachel Maddow, both of whom wage verbal war against their ideological opponents. One MSNBC pundit who tries for bipartisanship is Chris Matthews, who lets loose with an onslaught against politicians of all stripes but makes sure his tone is outrageous and provocative. He acknowledges this himself: "I am for the chalk line. You try to keep it in. If it hits the chalk line, that's perfect. People have that little gasp and say, '*I can't believe he said that.*' "[27] Because Matthews is purposely provocative, on occasion he offends someone. During the 2008 presidential campaign, he acknowledged that Hillary Clinton "drives some of us absolutely nuts" and compared her to Nurse Ratched (the evil authority figure from Ken Kesey's book *One Flew over the Cuckoo's Nest*) and Evita Peron (the evil authority figure from Argentina).[28] This makes for good television, but for bad journalism. Since Matthews appears on both his eponymous cable show *and* NBC News, this raises one important question: Can Matthews the pundit act as an objective journalist when called to NBC duty?

This question was highlighted during the 2008 political season when NBC pulled Matthews and fellow-pundit Keith Olbermann from their election news coverage, keeping them on the networks as analysts instead. According to MSNBC President Phil Griffin: "The channel made the decision [on September 4] after re-evaluating the wisdom of having the two of them anchoring the coverage while at the same time giving opinions."[29] This is evidence in itself that in today's television environment some viewers will have difficulty distinguishing between punditry and real news. Because the cable news channels are often part and parcel of larger news organizations, even if punditry stays mostly on cable it doesn't mean the pundit stays away from broadcast news. When pundits on MSNBC move between their home network and the *NBC Nightly News* to analyze politics, the news becomes a vehicle for punditry. This means that the news blurs the line of its mission, and opinion becomes a more integrated part of information dissemination. Analysis is an important part of politics, but because pundits are rewarded for loud behavior, and entertainment wins over substance, punditry outside the confines of a pundit show has the potential to taint the "real" news and make it something quite different.

A survey conducted by the Pew Center for People and the Press found that fewer Americans admire journalists than they did 20 years ago, and those who are admired are sometimes not journalists at all. While in 1985 Dan Rather and Walter Cronkite received favorable polling approval ratings with 11 percent and 6 percent, respectively, today CBS's Katie Couric is the winner of the approval race with a mere 5 percent and is followed closely at 4 percent by Fox News pundit Bill O'Reilly, who isn't even a journalist. In this same poll, both NBC's Brian Williams and *The Daily Show*'s Jon Stewart received 2 percent favorable ratings.[30] That Jon Stewart, who isn't a journalist at all, received favorable journalism ratings is not necessarily surprising. In July 2009, *Time* magazine conducted a poll asking its readers who, in the post-Cronkite era, was the most trusted newsperson in America. Jon Stewart was the clear favorite with 44 percent approval ratings, beating NBC News Anchor Brian Williams, who came in second with 29 percent.[31] The obvious significance of this poll is that a comedian is now viewed as a journalist, and one who is perceived as more reliable and truthful than those who are trained members of the press. One possible reason for Stewart's popularity may be the increasingly polarized nature of the cable news networks.

Fox News won its success by branding itself as the alternative to the so-called "liberal media" and puts a significant number of conservatives on its pundit programs. To combat this, MSNBC has carved its own niche as an alternative to Fox News, placing a considerable number of liberals on its lineup. The ideological leanings of these two networks have significant political impact. Democrats have boycotted Fox News, claiming they can't get a fair shake on the network.

Conversely, Republicans have called MSNBC an "organ of the Democratic National Committee."[32] Both cases serve to illustrate the effects of ideologically directed programming. Cable punditry, and the shouting that occurs when ideological opposites are pitted against one another, is theater. As noted by Fox News host Bill O'Reilly himself: "If a producer can find someone who eggs on conservative listeners to spout off and prods liberals into shouting back, he's got a hit show. The best host is the guy or gal who can get the most listeners extremely annoyed over and over again."[33]

The American public is the willing (and lucrative) audience of this theater. The partisan divisions seen in pundit programming is another consequence of entertainment overemphasis, where the stress is placed on conflict. When politicians fight with one another on television, the conflict makes for what many consider to be "good TV," meaning it is interesting and entertaining enough to attract viewers. However, this discord—filled with tension, provocative language, and ferocity—serves to discourage political activity that results from negative attitudes towards politicians and the policymaking process. The show *Crossfire* on CNN was an early staple of pundit programming and stayed on the air for more than two decades, pitting two ideological opponents against one another and allowing them to duke it out.[34] *Crossfire* began in 1982 as one of the first shows on CNN, pitting Tom Braden, a liberal, against conservative Pat Buchanan. Braden and Buchanan began with a radio program, moved to local D.C. television, and then was picked up by CNN as the cable network expanded its lineup and sought to fill the 24-hour news programming requirements. According to an interview with Braden in Howard Kurtz's book *Hot Air*, even in the early 1980s the program was bordering on the out-of-control: "You had too many guys who were interested only in what's going to make raw meat for the audience—It got to be a matter of one-liners rather than serious discussion. It was two guys who came pretty close to swearing at each other. It became just a game, more theater than rational argument."[35] *Crossfire* continued on CNN, changing hosts every few years, and was successful just for the reasons Braden didn't like it: not because it explored politics and policymaking in any kind of informative way, but rather because it featured so-called "experts" screaming at each other. Jon Stewart appeared as a guest on the show in January 2006, and to the hosts (conservative Tucker Carlson and liberal Paul Begala) he referred to the show as "theater instead of debate," begging them to "stop, stop, stop, stop hurting America." In these shout-fest shows, since the conflict is overemphasized in lieu of substance, viewers are not compelled to action since they don't know enough about a topic to feel engaged. Whether Stewart was correct in his assessment that the show hurt America is up for debate—but *Crossfire* was cancelled shortly after his appearance.

Politicians and candidates for high office understand the ideological boundaries of the cable networks and work within these confines. By vigilantly choosing one media outlet over all others, candidates do two things: They "preach to the political choir," while at the same time they are "shielded from especially aggressive questioning."[36] The increasing ideological slant of the media allows politicians to pick and choose their venues. According to C-SPAN's Lamb, this is not new as much as it is so newly expansive: "It's always been the case, it's just that today with all these new platforms around and ideological platforms, people will often go only to that platform that will serve them."[37] Lamb discussed an interview he did with Supreme Court Justice Clarence Thomas as Justice Thomas was promoting his book *My Grandfather's Son*: "It's a complicated process right now because if you're somebody like Thomas and there are many others like him, you can figure out that if I write a book I can only go to my people. I can take a chance with *60 Minutes* or take a chance with us (although that's not much of a chance), then I go to Limbaugh and Hannity and Laura Ingraham and friendly people and I can get my word out now."[38] The allure of a friendly audience, combined with the ability to control much of the message, is what drives politicians to pick and choose their media venues, which then leads to an increasingly divided media in accordance with a politicized nation.

Politicians try to control the media coverage they receive, and this is easier in the entertainment media than in the news media. Since most journalists pride themselves on their tenacity and hard-hitting questions, politicians who consent to interviews know that they will be aggressively tested and prepare for such an inquisition. Occasionally, however, landing an important interview may lead certain news organizations and newsmen to soften their approach, or promise a politician a friendly forum. When this happens, interview subjects can place stipulations on the interview that prevent journalists from asking certain questions. According to the *Los Angeles Times*, "With so much competition, publicists and other image handlers of celebrities and politicians alike often place restrictions upon the interview. They frequently request questions beforehand or try to set certain potentially embarrassing topics off-limits. Some outlets, desperate for access, concede."[39] This acquiescence serves to weaken the news, and more often than not journalists do not accept conditions placed on their interviews. Since media attention is so important, and since politicians still must try to reach voters who avoid the news, politicians will adapt their messages to fit the design of entertainment programs.

These entertainment programs fall into three general categories: entertainment talk shows, strictly nonpolitical programming, and political satire shows. Entertainment talk shows include daytime fare such as *Oprah* and nighttime programming like *The Tonight Show* and *Late Night with David Letterman*. As Matthew Baum writes about presidential candidates who appear on talk shows: "Many Americans who might otherwise have ignored the presidential campaign entirely were, as a result of candidate appearances on a variety of E-talk shows, exposed to at least *some* information about the candidates prior to the election."[40] These entertainment talk shows do provide some information, as they afford a politician or candidate a venue or a platform on which they can advertise themselves. These shows provide a friendly interviewer, since talk show hosts are generally uninterested in "gotcha" journalism, and they allow a politician to show he is funny, self-deprecating, and engaging.

The second type is pure entertainment programming with no political content whatsoever. These shows cater exclusively to Americans seeking escape from politics and reality, and their main attraction for a politician is that they are immensely popular. By associating themselves with such a show, politicians are able to convey that they too have tapped into the zeitgeist, that they understand "real" America, and that they have similar tastes to the majority of the American public. The last type includes political satire shows, programs that are witty and amusing yet at the same time political in nature. *The Daily Show* mocks a newscast, *Colbert Report* mocks a pundit show, and *Saturday Night Live* mocks politicians in general. These shows are successful because the American public is overloaded with news content about current events and politics and often are in search of authenticity in an atmosphere of construction and artifice. The humorists who write on these satire shows appear to provide the reality, peeling back the facade of politicians and exposing the truth underneath. The more distrusting the public is of politicians, the more trusting they are of those who mock them. Alex Baze, head writer for *Saturday Night Live's Weekend Update*, satirizes the political system for a living; and when I asked him about the current state of political satire, he responded:

> I think this is a very strong time for political humor. The deeper public dissatisfaction runs, the greater the need and desire for satire. Satire always thrives and grows when the nation is in trouble. I think comedy or humor, whichever you want to call it, is the language of revolt—We couch in comedy those sentiments that no one seems to be saying anywhere else. If everything is great, there is no need for comedy. We use it to escape what's happening, yes, but more importantly, we use it to address what's happening. Jon Stewart can say things that "straight" newsmen can't. You can sense when you're not being told everything and that is when people tend to turn to the comedians. I don't know how much comedy influences people's opinions. I think it's more of a place to find your opinions, your fears and concerns, crystallized.[41]

Because so many Americans—younger Americans in particular—turn to these shows for entertainment and sometimes the news itself, politicians have begun to turn to them, too. With the knowledge that most Americans—especially young Americans—do not watch the nightly news, most candidates see that they have no choice. Even Jon Stewart, host of Comedy Central's *The Daily Show*, acknowledged this, admitting that political candidates "flock to his show to attract his much sought-after younger audience."[42] And so John McCain and Hillary Rodham Clinton appeared on *Saturday Night Live*, McCain and Obama (and Edwards and Huckabee, etc.) appeared on *The Daily Show* and *Colbert Report* in order to prove they have the ability to seem droll and amusing, and to garner an audience.

Baze agrees: "I think appearing funny and hip is important, but I think when politicians come by SNL or similar shows, it's more about just being seen as much as possible."[43] Furthermore, when politicians appear on these shows, often they make fun of themselves both to prove they have a sense of humor and also to get in front of the joke already existing about them. Again Baze:

> It does seem to serve [politicians] when they get in on the joke. Once John McCain himself started doing "John McCain is old" jokes—how can the comedians really go back to them? When the punch line is sitting there doing a joke, it kills that joke. Oh, we'll still do them, but it won't be the same. So it's a great way for them to defuse a meme. And getting in on the joke does serve to make them seem hipper. John McCain's oldness would be a different issue if he didn't know he was old or insisted he wasn't that old. But there he is doing old jokes, so I guess that story's over.[44]

Since these shows are popular with younger audiences, they will continue to be magnets for politicians who are trying to construct themselves as hip and connected. They also provide that entertainment allure that so many Americans are interested in. To prove this point, one of CNN's main anchors from the 1980s and 1990s, Bobbie Battista, now reports for ONN: The Onion News Network. *The Onion* began in 1988 at the University of Wisconsin, Madison as a satirical newspaper and then launched a very successful Web site that now broadcasts a fake news channel. *The Onion* now partners with the *Washington Post* and its Web site features a real former cable news anchor presenting the fake news.[45] The line between real and unreal is becoming increasingly difficult to ascertain.

Not only do candidates appear on entertainment programs, but now they court entertainment endorsements as well. Oprah Winfrey endorsed Barack Obama in the 2008 presidential race, kicking off a flurry of celebrity endorsements for the different candidates on both sides of the aisle. While most Americans stated that they were not influenced by these celebrity endorsements, this didn't stop the candidates from both pursuing them and widely advertising them to the public. This connection between candidate and celebrity is mutually beneficial, because the celebrity gets to advertise himself or herself at the same time the candidate gets to share some of the spotlight. Oprah's endorsement of Obama paid off because now she is considered a friend of the President of the United States, but even if the candidate doesn't win there are benefits for a celebrity to endorse a candidate. The stories about Oprah's endorsement gave her more attention at the same time they gave Obama attention. Additionally, when celebrities share their spotlight with a candidate the politician becomes a celebrity himself and is also able to connect with the American public via an established and beloved figure. One humorous television campaign ad for GOP presidential candidate Mike Huckabee featured western/martial arts star Chuck Norris. Connecting himself to Norris served to bolster Huckabee's street credibility as a tough guy at the same time it proved Huckabee's sense of humor and ability to poke fun at himself. Celebrity endorsements of political candidates are one connection between entertainment figures and elected officials, and it is an important connection in our current celebrity culture.

News and entertainment appearances on television are important for politicians who need to reach the American public. However, politicians need to be careful about the television exposure they receive. As television news increasingly turns entertaining, and as TV viewers can narrow their viewing focus to specific types of programming, politicians will (by necessity) focus more on the amusing than the informative. Television has financial imperatives that demand the medium be engaging and enjoyable. When politicians use television for their own purposes, they fall into these demands as well. If television becomes a medium that is devoid of substance, political uses of the medium will become just as frivolous.

CONCLUSIONS

Television can be smart, amusing, and fun, but most of the time the medium does not provide the kind of substance necessary to truly understand complex issues because the profit motives of the industry mandate entertainment. Even on cable news channels that supposedly devote their time to information, in order to fill the 24 hours of each day the producers turn to diversion in order to acquire and hold an audience. The visual medium emphasizes the superficial. Depth is considered boring. The hard truth is that Americans are woefully ignorant of not only the politics of their own country, but also of the world around them, and television contributes to this ignorance. Political scientist Rick Shenkman, the author of *Just How Stupid Are We? Facing the Truth about the American Voter*, wrote of this problem in an editorial published in the *Boston Globe* and placed much of the blame squarely on television: "Once television replaced newspapers as the chief source of news, this happened around 1965, shallowness was inescapable as Americans began judging politicians by how they looked and acted."[46] Many Americans seem not to be bothered by their lack of knowledge, opting instead to take cover with the attitude that all politicians are untrustworthy. This message is reinforced by the television comedians and satirists who are so talented at mocking those in office. The hard part is that even as intelligent as television writing is—and political satire shows such as *Saturday Night Live* and *The Daily Show* are brilliant because of their talented writing staff—television still does not serve to inform as much as it diverts and amuses.

Television coverage today is part of what the *Wall Street Journal*'s Washington editor Gerald Seib calls a "complex media ecosystem involving reactions and counter-reactions among Internet (text and video) sources, broadcast and cable TV and print."[47] Digital cable makes this even more complex since cable companies are now utilizing their "on demand" function to bring political news to the voting public at their convenience. Television's part within this ecosystem is crucial because it is so prevailing in our society, but the way television operates today does not bode well for more sophisticated use. The financial imperatives of the news mandate what Jon Stewart called a "false sense of urgency" that has ramped up language and attention in the effort to draw audiences to interesting events.[48] These imperatives have also led to a greater emphasis on entertainment, which first leads viewers away from news and then finds politicians chasing after viewers by trying to be entertaining themselves. At the end of the day, more people are viewing television than any other medium, smiling and amused but perhaps not as knowledgeable about our political system or as well-versed in the important issues that most affect us.

Because there are so many television channels, the ability for niche programming has led to an ideologically specific news type, where pundits from one channel lean right while those on a competing channel lean left. In 2009, White House Communications Director Anita Dunn called Fox News Channel "the research arm or the communications arm of the Republican Party,"[49] and a great outcry was heard from those arguing that Fox was, as it calls itself, "fair and balanced." The problem is not that Fox pundits espouse conservative philosophies, but rather that viewers of all news channels rarely see the distinction between punditry and journalism. The line has blurred between opinion and fact so much that real information tends to fall through the cracks of TV entertainment. For example, a 2009 poll conducted by NBC and the *Wall Street Journal* found that "72 percent of self-identified Fox News viewers believe the [Obama] health care plan [would] give coverage to illegal immigrants,"[50] an assertion that was proven to be categorically untrue. The way that television approaches politics, through entertaining punditry, leads to this kind of ignorance. As television continues to entertain more than to inform, the part it plays in the "media ecosystem" will amplify screed at the cost of informed debate.

Notes

1. "TV Basics: Number of Households," Media Trends Track, http://www.tvb.org/rcentral/mediatrendstrack/tvbasics/02_TVHouseholds.asp (accessed October 3, 2009).

2. Neil Postman is well regarded as one of the best media critics of the modern age, and I urge readers to examine *Technopoly: The Surrender of Culture to Technology* (1993) and *Amusing Ourselves to Death: Public Discourse in the Age of Showbusiness* (2005 reissue).

3. Much has been written on the news: See Todd Gitlin's *Inside Prime Time*, Bonnie Anderson's *News Flash: Journalism, Infotainment and the Bottom-Line Business of Broadcast News*, and Debora Halpern Wenger and Deborah Potter's *Advancing the Story: Broadcast Journalism in a Multimedia World*.

4. See Paul Fahri's *Cable Clout* for a discussion of Anna Nicole Smith's death coverage during a time of war.

5. Cecilia Kang, "Merger Plans for Comcast, NBC Ignite Battle over Television Access," *Washington Post*, December 4, 2009.

6. Elizabeth Jensen, "Sinclair's Shadow: Canned News and Conservative Commentary," *Columbia Journalism Review* (May/June 2005), http://cjrarchives.org/issues/2005/3/jensen.asp (accessed May 12, 2008).

7. Elizabeth Jensen, "Conservative TV Group to Air Anti-Kerry Film," *Los Angeles Times*, October 9, 2004, http://articles.latimes.com/2004/oct/09/nation/na-sinclair9 (accessed October 5, 2009).

8. Ibid.

9. State of the News Media 2007, The Project for Excellence in Journalism, http://www.journalism.org/.

10. Larry Dobrow, "Weary of 'Old' Label, Nets Take Snooze Out of News," *Advertising Age*, May 8, 2006, S-28.

11. Brian Stelter, "ABC Reshapes the Evening News for the Web," *New York Times*, October 12, 2007.

12. Paul Farhi, "Click. Change: The Traditional Tube Is Getting Squeezed Out of the Picture," *Washington Post*, May 17, 2009.

13. Ibid.

14. Matthew Baum, *Soft News Goes to War* (New Jersey: Princeton University Press, 2003), 92.

15. Ibid.

16. Kathryn Darden, "Analog to Digital TV Conversion: Approximately 2.8 Million Americans Now without Television," *Associated Content*, http://www.associated content.com/article/1864451/analog_to_digital_tv_conversion_approximately.html (accessed October 3, 2009).

17. Andrew Vanacore, "Broadcasters' Woes Could Spell Trouble for Free TV," *Washington Post*, December 29, 2009.

18. Kelly Riddell, "Fox-Time Warner Cable Deal Could Mean Billions for Broadcasters," *Washington Post*, January 2, 2010.

19. Markus Prior, "The Real Media Divide," *Washington Post*, July 16, 2007, A15.

20. Brian Lamb, October 17, 2007, Personal interview with author.

21. James Poniewozik, "CNBC's Bull Market," *Time*, March 23, 2009, 28.

22. Paul Farhi, "Political Pundits, Overpopulating the News Networks," *Washington Post*, February 19, 2008, C01.

23. Ibid.

24. David Von Drehle, "Mad Man: Is Glenn Beck Bad for America?" *Time*, September 17, 2009, 23.

25. Ibid.

26. Ad: "How Did ABC . . . " *Washington Post*, September 13, 2009, A9.

27. Howard Kurtz, "Hardbrawl: Candid Talker Chris Matthews Pulls No Punches," *Washington Post*, February 14, 2008, C01.

28. Ibid.

29. Paul J. Gough, "MSNBC Votes Off Feuding Anchors," *Washington Post*, September 8, 2008, http://www.washingtonpost.com/wpdyn/content/article/2008/09/08/AR200809 0802835.html.

30. "Today's Journalists Less Prominent," *The Pew Research Center for People and the Press*, released March 8, 2007, http://people-press.org/report/309/todays-journalists-less-prominent (accessed November 2, 2009).

31. "Now That Walter Cronkite Has Passed on, Who Is America's Most Trusted Newscaster?" *Time Magazine Online*, http://www.timepolls.com/hppolls/archive/poll_results_417.html (accessed September 23, 2009).

32. Howard Kurtz, "MSNBC Leaning Left and Getting Flak from Both Sides," *Washington Post*, May 28, 2008, http://www.washingtonpost.com/wp-dyn/content/article/2008.

33. Diana C. Mutz and Byron Reeves, "The New Videomalaise: The Effects of Televised Incivility on Political Trust," *American Political Science Review* 99 (1): 1–15.

34. There has been a great deal written about the rise of the pundit class in American political media. Please see Howard Kurtz's *Hot Air: All Talk All the Time* and Jeff Cohen and Norman Solomon's *Adventures in Medialand: Behind the News, Behind the Pundits*.

35. Howard Kurtz, *Hot Air: All Talk All the Time* (New York: Basic Books, 1996), 107.

36. Howard Kurtz, "For the Candidates, Not Just Any Brand of Soapbox Will Do," *Washington Post*, August 13, 2007, C01.

37. Brian Lamb, October 17, 2007, Personal interview with author.

38. Ibid.

39. Martin Miller, "No Hard Questions We Promise," *Los Angeles Times*, November 12, 2004, E27.

40. Matthew Baum, "Talking the Vote: Why Presidential Candidates Hit the Talk Show Circuit," *American Journal of Political Science* 49 (2005): 213–234.

41. Alex Baze, September 2008, Personal interview with author.

42. Sasha Johnson, "Jon Stewart Lectures Reporters on Coverage," http://politicalticker.blogs.cnn.com/2008/08/25/jon-stewart-lectures-reporters-on-coverage/ (accessed August 25, 2008).

43. Alex Baze, September 2008, Personal interview with author.

44. Ibid.

45. Robert Mackey, "Former CNN Anchor Moves to the Onion," *New York Times*, March 25, 2009.

46. Rick Shenkman, "The Dumbing Down of Voters," *Boston Globe*, June 15, 2008.

47. Paul Farhi, "Cable's Clout," *American Journalism Review* (August/September 2008), http://www.ajr.org/Article.asp?id=4574.

48. Sasha Johnson, "Jon Stewart Lectures Reporters on Coverage," http://politicalticker.blogs.cnn.com/2008/08/25/jon-stewart-lectures-reporters-on-coverage/ (accessed August 25, 2008).

49. David Bauder, "Picking a Fight: White House vs. Fox News," *Washington Post*, October 18, 2009.

50. Gene Lyons, "Fox News Isn't Even Pretending Any More," *Salon.com*, October 15, 2009, http://www.salon.com/opinion/feature/2009/10/15/fox_news/ (accessed October 19, 2009).

Chapter 5

THE INTERNET: A SERIES OF TUBES

If at first you don't succeed; call it version 1.0.

—Internet Joke

The Pew Center estimates that in 1995 only about 5 million Americans went online for their news at least three days a week, but by 2005 about 50 million Americans got their news online on any given day. This tremendous expansion was possible because of broadband, wi-fi, and other technological developments that increased speed and access for Internet users. The Internet revolution has changed so much about American life that it is hard to quantify the most important shifts in our society today. We now shop, talk, mingle, and game instantaneously from our computers without ever having to face another person. The Internet has also had an important impact on the news, and it has served to change the very definition of journalism. In addition to Internet-only news sites such as *Slate* and *Salon*, nearly every newspaper, magazine, television channel, and radio station has their own Web site to accompany their primary content. These news sites range in focus, seriousness of purpose, and scale. The multitude of news Web sites available allows readers an even greater ability to pick niche information catered to specific tastes and ideologies.

Additionally, Internet technology has given rise to the "blog" phenomenon: Web-logs (blogs) are Web sites where the organizer updates news and headlines and links itself to other news outlets and other blogs. This platform affords bloggers (the people who write and stock their blog with content) the ability to comment on the news of the day without having their own cable TV show, their own newspaper column, or even any journalistic training. Because creating a blog is inexpensive and relatively easy to do, the number of bloggers has increased significantly in recent years, and so the amount of opinion in the zeitgeist has increased as well. Finally, the Internet has changed the way American politics is conducted. Politicians can now instantaneously reach their constituents and communicate their policy stands with ease. However, politicians must also contend with an omnipresent media force that is accessible to everyone and is thus constantly scrutinizing them. It is obvious that the Internet has revolutionized American life and, along with it, American politics.

The sheer size of the Internet and the ubiquity of computers give the medium its greatest advantage: unrestricted openness that allows unfettered participation. Computers used to be cost-prohibitive, limiting Internet users to those affluent enough to own a computer, but technological developments have made personal computers more affordable, and as a result almost everyone in the United States has access to the online world. As a universal norm, Internet access is now a requirement in schools, homes, offices, hotels, and even restaurants. Thus, the potential for democracy amidst all of the voices is a tempting and positive promise of the technology. The Internet can accommodate any taste and persuasion, and access can be affordable. These two factors make the Internet feel very democratizing, and indeed the Internet opens the world to its users. The term *netizen* is a hybrid of "Internet" and "citizen" and suggests: "As the Internet became a center of power it would confer a new sociopolitical identity in its users, as the city did for citizens."[1] In this manner, the Internet has made politics at all levels more accessible to Americans, which in turn makes politicians more accessible to the voters. For all the access the Internet affords, however, there are serious problems with it as well. In 1999 when the Internet was still very young, Roger Hurwitz from the Massachusetts Institute of Technology (MIT) Artificial Intelligence lab wrote of the "ironies of democracy in cyberspace" and argued that the medium brought with it certain predicaments. These problems included the anonymity of Internet discourse that encourages extreme language use, the individualistic nature of online discourse that excludes real debate, the potentially obstructing of laws regarding Internet content, and the often surveillance nature of the Internet that makes everyone feel somewhat scrutinized in their computer use.[2] These problematic qualities limit the Internet in its political use.

The immediacy and connectivity that the Internet affords are also among its most important qualities. Internet users can instantly connect to one another or are able to upload visual information and make it widely available. Thanks to tiny cameras that can broadcast from anywhere, thanks to documents that can be scanned and posted without filter, and thanks to an influx of opinion, the Internet offers a deluge of information, judgment, and lies. The sheer amount of information available allows us to feel we are seeing the "truth" that perhaps other media outlets ignore. However, the "truth" that the Internet delivers may be far from truthful, and there have been relatively few times that Internet content has been fact-checked for accuracy. Another problem with the Internet is the cacophony of voices it supports that forces some people to make extreme statements online in order to be heard above everyone else. Because of the size of the Internet, Web sites or blogs must make as much "noise" as possible to be noticed, so that others will link to them, send their pages to their friends, and otherwise get them noticed.

It is within these contradictions and dilemmas that the public surfs the vastness of the Internet, and politicians use the technology to advance themselves and their causes. This chapter examines exactly how politicians use the Internet and the ways the Internet has changed politicking and journalism in the modern era.

POLITICAL USES OF INTERNET

American politics can be found all over the Internet, either on sites that originate from politicians, sites that analyze politics, or sites that spread political news. Jeremiah Owyang, a political blogger, addressed the reasons for an increased political Internet presence: "Why the Web? The Web is faster, cheaper, national, and most importantly where many voters spend their days and nights."[3] Savvy political candidates have used the Internet to great success, reaching millions of Americans and asking them to channel their energy into a campaign. Less savvy politicians have been stung by the pervasive scrutiny that the Internet now affords. All politicians, however, are able to use Internet technology for a wide variety of functions, including fundraising, message dissemination, and voter mobilization.

Fundraising is crucial to a campaign, and the 2000 presidential election marked the first major Internet presence in presidential campaigns. In 2000, Senator Bill Bradley became the first presidential candidate to raise $1 million online, and Senator John McCain became the first Republican to reach the same goal.[4] But the medium was very new then and dial-up access did not afford the campaigns the speed they needed to fully exploit the medium. Thus, 2004 was the first presidential election when the Internet played a serious role in election-eering thanks to Howard Dean, whose campaign team was led by Joe Trippi. Dean failed in his effort to become the Democratic candidate in the 2004 presidential election.

Howard Dean's campaign became revolutionary in opening up the campaign's Internet site to his supporters, making it an "open source" site where there was an "open invitation to improve, to innovate, to make better," which meant the site was constructed and updated by the users—and not by the campaign.[5] This effort mandated the trust of the campaign over its supporters, but that trust manifested itself in a groundswell of support that made the Internet campaign successful. For Dean's Internet campaign, the 2004 election year fundraising payoffs were immense. According to Trippi: "By summer [2004] more than half our contributions were coming in over the Internet."[6] However, again the Internet proved to be contradictory in that reaping the benefits of an open-source Internet campaign also meant suffering new and unexpected problems, because open source meant anyone could tamper with the site and wreak havoc: "Suddenly we faced problems no one ever encountered before—The attack we worried about could come from a 14-year-old kid in Thailand. Some guy in his garage in Oakland could take out a presidential campaign with nothing more than his $500 laptop."[7] But the innovation of Dean supporters led to some truly innovative campaign tactics, none of which were created by political consultants. It was a genuine grassroots campaign.

Despite the great advances of Internet campaigning in 2004, it was the 2008 presidential election that brought out the big money via the Internet.

During the 2008 primary season, Republican candidate Ron Paul raised a record $3.5 million in 20 hours through intense Internet fundraising. The contributions came from more than 22,000 online donors in commemoration of Guy Fawkes Day.[8] Ron Paul's 2008 presidential campaign is another example of how the Internet can rally millions of passionate Americans to a cause without actually succeeding, since Paul lost his bid for the presidency. His supporters, however, were devout and unyielding, and they became well known as ferocious in their devotion to Paul and vicious in their attacks against his opponents. According to *Wired* magazine:

> To many immersed in the political blogosphere, Paul's passionate supporters seem to be everywhere at once. Editors of political websites are inundated with angry e-mails demanding they devote more coverage to Paul. Blog posts that criticize Paul are often followed by hundreds of livid comments from his fans. Most frustrating to those not on board the Ron Paul bandwagon, he routinely ranks first in online presidential polls on sites ranging from CNN.com to niche political blogs. Conversely, Paul rates in the low single digits in scientific telephone polls and few political pundits afford him any chance of winning the nomination. When the editors at *National Journal*'s The Hotline compiled their well-respected White House 2008 Rankings in May, they put Paul in last place among the 12 Republicans running, tacking on a fed-up message to his fans: "Just please stop e-mailing us."[9]

Paul's immense success online did not translate to electoral success, but it gave a dark-horse candidate more traction—and a great deal more money than he received when he previously ran for president in 1988.

Politicians are able to raise substantial amounts of money online because it is so easy for Americans to contribute from their computers. Ron Paul's success aside, Republicans have been less successful than their Democratic counterparts in this effort. Barack Obama raised more than $28 million online in January 2008 alone. To put this into perspective, Howard Dean raised $27 million online during his entire campaign.[10] From January to June 2008 during the primary season, Democratic candidate Barack Obama raised at least $130 million online. By the time the campaign was over, the Obama campaign had raised more money over the Internet in donations of $200 or less than Hillary Clinton or John McCain raised from all other sources combined.[11] Fifty-three percent of Obama's primary donations were in $200-or-less category, and during the general campaign 46 percent of individual contributions were less than $200 as well.[12] The specific amount donated over the Internet is not accessible since neither the Federal Election Commission nor campaign finance watchdog groups specifically monitor the types of donations—online versus standard—contributed. Herein lies one problem with online donations. Since the current campaign finance laws do not mandate donor information disclosure for these smaller contributions, the campaigns do not need to keep specific track of their acquisition type. This fact opens the door to other potential problems, such as fraud, illegal contributions, and abuse. There is campaign finance reform legislation pending in both the House and the Senate that tries to address the imperfections in the current system. However, since future Internet fundraising innovations are all but inevitable, it is doubtful the campaign finance laws can keep up with the technology. Additionally, since Obama broke so many records in 2008 it is also likely that online fundraising will continue to play a major role in American politics.

Another way politicians use the Internet is to spread messages. The standard technique is to send mass e-mails to constituents or advertise on an official Web site; but once again the technology is generating very creative ways to get a message to constituents or supporters. For example, the 2008 Obama campaign used text messaging very effectively. The 34-year-old behind the texting effort was Obama campaign worker Scott Goodstein, who said about the natural progression from Internet to text message: "To me, texting is the most personal form of communication. Your phone is with you almost all the time. You're texting with your girlfriend. You're texting with your friends. Now you're texting with Barack."[13] The major benefit to texting is that it is a two-way medium that allows a text recipient to reply back—which then provides the campaign even more information about a potential donor or supporter. Once someone registered with the campaign, their information was logged into the campaign's database, which stored an immense amount of voter data. The Obama campaign officials amassed an extremely large voter database, which he used to mobilize voters long after election day had passed:

> By the end of the general election campaign the [Obama] campaign had 13 million addressed on its campaign's e-mail list. The campaign's integrated social networking tools became the engine of its voter mobilization campaign. . . . The Obama staff built a structure *within the campaign* that previously had been handled by ongoing organizations with more permanence than a candidate's campaign committee. . . . Because these resources belonged to the candidate, the same tools that helped Obama raise more money than Clinton or McCain also helped him out-organize them.[14]

This system worked well for the most part, but in today's highly mediated political environment no single medium operates in a vacuum. One example helps to make this point: In the summer of 2008, before the selection of a vice presidential running mate had been announced, the Obama campaign used an innovative technique to attract support. The campaign sent out e-mails and texts to registered Democrats promising an early vice presidential selection announcement if these party members provided the Obama campaign with their contact information. Anyone who registered with the campaign would get the vice president announcement via text message before the press did. It was a great gimmick, but the wheels fell off the train, thanks to the mainstream media. At the time

Obama's selection choice was nothing more than a guessing contest (something the mainstream press loves to enter, since such a guessing game is entertaining and involves little intellectual heavy lifting) between Indiana Senator Evan Bayh, Delaware Senator Joe Biden, and former candidate Hillary Rodham Clinton. The press camped out in front of all three homes, trying to solve the Veep-Stakes puzzle, and when it became clear that there was virtually nothing happening at the Bayh and Clinton homes while the entire Biden extended family quickly arrived in Delaware, the jig was up. The press began to crow about Biden's selection *before* the Obama campaign had sent out the promised e-mail and text messages giving their valued supporters the exclusive information. In the words of one political insider: "Sure, the campaign could wait to send the message minutes before the nominee took the stage at the Old State Capitol in Springfield, Illinois. But that ignored the fact that the nominee had to get to Springfield. And with the media camped out in front of each of their houses, how exactly were they going to do that without getting noticed?" This conundrum forced Obama's campaign to send its supporters the promised text message—at 3 a.m. Eastern time—which served to wake up a number of journalists, pundits, and supporters in a panic, fearing the dreaded 3 a.m. emergency wake-up call. The technologically-savvy campaign strategy proved to be inventive and novel, but it simply did not work because the technology does not operate in a vacuum: it has to work in conjunction with the rest of the American media.

A third way the Internet is used in campaigns and for political purposes is to rally supporters and ignite a level of excitement for the general public. This began in 2004 through what were called "Meetups," in which Howard Dean supporters would register their names and locations online in order to connect with supporters at the grassroots level. MeetUp.com is a Web site where people with similar interests meet online to arrange personal encounters. Trippi used MeetUp.com to rally supporters, and was surprised when shortly thereafter there were more than 2,000 supporters registered. This number then exploded to 190,000, proving MeetUp's efficacy in blending online technology with old-fashioned boots on the ground politicking.[15] Dean's use of MeetUp technology has been translated into a political tool that most of the candidates use, connecting people within close geographic distances based on their support for the candidate. Incumbent politicians use MeetUps now as a way to gather constituents for close-knit gatherings or to bring people together for "house parties" where donations may be solicited. The use of the Internet in this process has evolved as the technology has become more sophisticated. According to Trippi, the difference in just four years of political Internet activity is staggering: "Four years ago we had pretty primitive tools. . . . Folks on MeetUp got together across the country, but we at headquarters didn't know what they did. Now, with Google-Maps, people can pinpoint where they are. They pinpoint their polling places. They can go online, get voting lists, and hit the ground. And their campaign can know all of this."[16] This provides even more data and information for the campaigns, which can use it to pinpoint donation solicitation and Get Out The Vote efforts.

Use of the Internet to build excitement for a cause, a politician, or a candidate is increasingly attractive in a society where most young Americans seem to be constantly in touch, always on line, or continually texting their friends. During the 2008 presidential campaign, the Obama advisors made even more use of the Internet in an effort to mobilize his supporters. This made sense because the candidate himself was very tech-savvy and was constantly plugged into his BlackBerry. According to one article about Obama's Internet use from the British newspaper, the *Telegraph*: "The Internet has been central to his candidacy, allowing him to establish a network of grassroots activists and attract small donations."[17] Obama's GOP challenger John McCain was not nearly so savvy: "Senator John McCain, the Republican presidential candidate, has admitted that he never uses e-mail and that his staff has to show him websites because he is only just 'learning to get online myself,' " which explains why the Internet was not as much a part of his campaign as his Democratic rival.[18]

INTERNET MEDIUM

There is a wide variety of Internet formats especially designed for political purposes. These include Web sites officially affiliated with existing news organizations such as newspapers, television channels, and radio stations and podcasting from these news organizations; Internet-only news sites such as Yahoo! News or Slate; information sites formally associated with elected officials, candidates for office, or governmental agencies; user-generated Web sites such as YouTube or DIGG that provide political content; social networking sites such as BlackPlanet, Facebook, or MySpace; political blogs and Twitter. All of these combine to create a tangle of news and information available all the time. Obviously, given this vast amount of online data, there will be sites far more reliable than others, with this reliability measured in fact versus opinion, verity versus fiction. The Web sites that are formally attached to existing news organizations are typically trustworthy sites.

Practically every American news outlet has a Web site attached to it now, and most major news organizations have dedicated a sizable amount of staff and financial support to their online endeavors. Online efforts differ between broadcast and print news organizations, since the content of each type of news media outlet is dramatically different in style. For example, CNN has a staff of 250 for its CNN.com Web site, and MSNBC has a staff of 175, according to the Project for Excellence in Journalism. Conversely, the *Washington Post* and *USA Today* each have online staffs of about 75 people, most likely because print content is more simply and easily transferred to an online format.[19] The Web sites of established print news organizations most often try to mimic the tone of the host company. For instance, the Web site of the *New York Times* looks very much like its newspaper, as does *USA Today*'s Web site. The difference, of course, is in the amount of content available on the Web site as opposed to the print edition. On a single Web site page, which can scroll down far longer than the broadsheet of a newspaper, content can be encapsulated to a single headline that sends readers to a longer article. This means all sections of a newspaper are somewhat featured on the "front page" of a newspaper's Web site, giving each section an appearance of importance and value, equalizing the significance and importance of entertainment news that shares front-page status with hard news. Placing a detailed newspaper table of contents on one page accomplishes two tasks: it allows readers to quickly sort through the material to pick what is most interesting to them and it also allows the news organization to use as much information as possible to lure potential readers with widely varying tastes.

Print newspapers are printed and distributed once daily, but their Web sites are constantly updated and refreshed, which allows newspapers to "break" news as often as their broadcast counterparts, starting out with banner headlines of major news events and expanding further as more information becomes available. In order to woo their readers to their Web sites when news breaks, most newspaper Web sites now send out electronic bulletins to their "subscribers," even when those subscribers do not spend money for their subscription. The benefit of having such online subscribers for newspapers is that they increase the number of hits their pages receive, which is akin to the ratings of a radio or television program.

The online components of television news channels generally maintain the same type of graphics as their broadcast hosts to maintain their visual brand. As is the case with newspapers, when a broadcast news entity goes online there is much more content available than on the original news source since they are trying to stock their Web site with as much content as possible to lure any potential visitor. A benefit for broadcast entities includes their ability to link their own video product to their Web site and distribute their television content to a wider audience. For local broadcast stations, this means linking not only their local content but also the content of their network parent channel. For network news sites, this can mean cross-content from their cable *and* affiliate partners. For cable channels, not only is content linked from their official partners, but it also links to amateur content from viewers who send in video for the network to use. Most broadcast channels are following in these footsteps. Also, television shows are now able to make TV an interactive event. You can vote for an American Idol or respond to ESPN sports questions, upload video taken from a cell phone, follow up on a news segment on the Internet, or take part in programming decisions in chat rooms and online focus groups. This makes television feel more democratic as it integrates its own technology with Internet technology to make viewers interact with the televised content.

Often, existing news organizations offer "podcasts" of their stories for their audience. Podcasts are digital audio files of interviews or news stories, and their production allows news organizations to broadcast even when their programming is not on the air. For example, National Public Radio issues podcasts of much of its programming for free, which means its listeners can listen to its programming any time that is convenient for them. Podcasting is not limited to broadcast news operations. The *New York Times* and other newspapers offer podcasts of their op-ed pieces and interviews for subscribers as well. Podcasts increase the "on-demand" quality of the news and add to the bottom line of the news organization that offers them.

Both print and broadcast news organization Web sites want to attract an audience, and therefore news stories often take second place to human interest stories or articles about celebrities or entertainment figures. Even within the most serious news organizations, the most popular stories are those about celebrity happenings or features that concern the lighter side of the news. This presents a conundrum for news editors and reporters, many of whom disapprove of soft news reporting in lieu of more hard-hitting coverage. News organization Web sites offer proof that not only does this battle between hard and soft news continue, but that the soft news side seems to be winning.

News sites that originate on the Internet and have no other outlet, such as Yahoo! News and AOL News, are reliable news sources and are successful in their own right, but their production and content are radically different from the sites affiliated with existing news companies. These sites do not offer original content like the established news organizations do, and instead link to news outlets or post stories from services such as the Associated Press (AP) or Reuters. This has raised some problems as well, since news services supply their stories to their paying customers—and not to online clearinghouses like Yahoo! and Google that turn around and distribute their stories for free. For instance, the AP is a subscription news service that sends its journalists out to cover major stories. Subscribers to the AP can access their stories and use them in their own publications. Now, because the Internet allows non-subscribers to access AP content, there are Web sites that disseminate AP news for free. The AP recently began an initiative to "affirm the value of original news reporting and protect the news industry's content from being misappropriated online,"[20] their argument being that at some point someone has to be paid for the journalism involved in gathering the news. As with the print and broadcast television industries, this is yet another area of new journalism that is in flux and that faces an uncertain future.

The real value of online news clearinghouse sites is their currency, since these sites are constantly updated and often post exactly how old the story is to the Web site. Since these news sites are small parts of larger search engine sites, it is possible that many search engine users do not read the news stories, or they glance through them in passing. Indeed, often these Internet news sites concentrate on oddball news (a whale falling in love with a cruise ship, for example) or news that is easy to understand (such as polling stories)—virtual sound-bites of news events without background or detail. However, some Internet news sites are dedicated especially to news and politics that provide substantive commentary and information for their subscribers. Such Web sites as *Slate, Salon,* and *Politico* are all staffed by experienced journalists, and although Slate has partnered with the *Washington Post,* each site maintains its content autonomy.

Political candidates across the ideological spectrum use the Internet to advertise themselves on their own homepages, which contain biographical information, issue and policy stands, and press releases. Some extend beyond this formula to include ads that the candidates are running, which gives these ads more visibility than those simply placed on television or radio, and some politician-originated Web sites include blog spots to communicate with constituents. Most politicians, however, realize that their official Web sites are good for several specific purposes, and making news is not one of them. The real purpose of official Web sites is to provide enough information to answer the easiest questions posed by the public and to put forth the best face of the politician who posts it. These official Web sites often lack creativity or elegance, but the news from these sites is reliable and completely controlled by the politician.

Unofficial political sites are created constantly, and both support and opposition sites appear in search engine listings when someone tries to find a candidate, which means an unsuspecting voter might be led to an incredibly hostile site *against* a candidate instead of a site that supports him or her. For example, several anti-Hillary Clinton Web sites were established by conservatives who have opposed her for years. If someone went to Google to search for "Hillary Clinton," the sites called "StopHerNow.com" and "AgainstHillary.Com" would come up in the search results. These unaffiliated and unsourced pages are sometimes humorous outlets for people's opinions, but at the same time they can serve misinformation to the general public, which is why official Web sites are the best place to find real information online. One exception to this rule of staid official Web sites is that of Democratic presidential candidate Barack Obama, whose 2008 presidential campaign Web site was widely regarded as innovative and groundbreaking. More than 1 million people signed up for "MyBarackObama," also known as "MyBO," to blog, meet up online, donate money, and help plan for the campaign. This site garnered not only support for Obama's candidacy, but also received rave reviews from political consultants for helping to push the Internet further along the campaign trail.

YouTube played a major role in the 2008 elections, allowing anyone to post video of just about anything, from music videos promoting candidates to television clips of candidate appearances to movies of politicians on the campaign trail or at work in Washington. The immediacy of YouTube helps make it one of the most effective methods of message dissemination on the Internet. Since anyone can create a video or a mash-up (a piece of media that combines two or more complementary sources) and post it on YouTube, the results can be impassioned, hilarious, or devastating. One YouTube example illustrates how the Internet spreads video content faster, cheaper, and even more effectively than mere television. In his bid for the presidency, former Arkansas Governor Mike Huckabee held a news conference to announce that his campaign would eschew negative ads. To illustrate the type of ad he would never run, Huckabee played a negative ad attacking an opponent. The ad was posted on YouTube. Because the news organizations were able to obtain video content of the ad and link it to their own Web site, it spread around the blogosphere and into the in-boxes of American e-mail with lightning speed. Governor Huckabee did not have to pay a dime for it.

These are known as "vapor" or "ghost" ads, the goal of which is to "stir up news-media interest rather than to reach voters directly through the purchase of expensive TV time."[21] The Internet makes "vapor" ads so much more common now since an ad can be created without great expense and then sent around to personal computers via e-mail or links to YouTube. Both sides play the "vapor" game because it is so effective. According to Brooks Jackson from the Annenberg Center: "When [the campaigns] tell people that an ad is going to be seen and talked about by everyone, it becomes a self-fulfilling prophecy."[22] The process is completed without the candidate having to buy airtime and also without reporting by the mainstream news media.

Social networking sites, like Facebook or BlackPlanet, allow those with only a slight interest in politics to group with others about issues or candidates they support. These sites are meant to connect people from varying demographics and with varying interests, and users can form groups and ask their friends to join with them. These social networking groups can be silly or serious, and they can be politically oriented. Many social networking sites extend to different demographics, such as BlackPlanet, a networking site for African Americans, AsianAve for Asian Americans, and MiGente for Latinos. This social networking not only gives citizens of differing backgrounds the ability to connect with one another despite geographic distance, but also allows politicians and candidates to tap into differing demographics and constituencies via these sites. Although the primary purpose of these sites is social, they do encourage political activity, especially among the 18- to 30-year-old demographic. These social networking sites are being used today in American politics to mobilize voters, allowing people both far away and close to one another to connect and organize.

Once again, Democrat Howard Dean was at the forefront of this in 2004, when his adherents (known as the "Deaniacs") would organize "Meet Ups" via the Internet. Voter mobilization is also greatly assisted by the blog phenomenon. Since 2004, political candidates have used the Internet to help their supporters organize house parties to raise money and, on occasion, to meet the candidate himself or herself; yet the rise of the bloggers has added to the noise surrounding presidential politics in 2008. The end result is that the Internet has been extremely useful for average Americans to support the candidates of their choice. Since the medium is so user-friendly and does not require too much political knowledge, from the outset novices to American politics are becoming more involved in the process. In fact, political scientists Caroline Tolbert and Romona

McNeal found that Internet access increased the probability of voting by 12 percent.[23]

Blogs are another online source of political information. They began as pages produced by individuals who took on mainstream journalism or politicians on their own. Bloggers often opine on current events or link to other blogs. Often, bloggers try to act as a gadfly for the so-called "mainstream media," catching errors and exposing the biases of the established news media. One such watchdog occurrence happened during the 2008 campaign when Town Hall blogger Amanda Carpenter found a number of significant discrepancies in a *Washington Post* front-page article about John McCain campaign supporters. The article alleged improprieties without offering substantiating evidence. When Carpenter did some digging herself, she found the article to be false, which then resulted in its retraction and a black eye for the *Post*. Another more famous example of the watchdog function of the blogosphere occurred in 2004 when Dan Rather on *60 Minutes II* reported on President Bush's military record, accusing the president of falsifying his record and avoiding his military service in the Texas Air National Guard. When the documents used to support this story were found by bloggers to be falsified, not only was the story retracted, but Dan Rather quit CBS amidst a flurry of scandal, and his producer, Mary Mapes, was fired from the network.

An important function of blogging is to catch politicians off their guard. A common argument made by bloggers is that the mainstream media do not perform their watchdog function as the guardians of truth, and so many bloggers take it upon themselves to act as "citizen journalists." Since bloggers and their workforce are everyday citizens, often they have access to politicians and events that the official press does not. The previously mentioned Mayhill Fowler, the *Huffington Post* blogger who caught both President Clinton and then-candidate Obama off guard during the 2008 campaign, helps to illustrate how bloggers can access important political figures when accredited members of the press cannot. The political consequence of blogging is impressive: No matter how distant the press, a politician's actions are always on the record. Conservative blogger Mary Katherine Hamm said, "Politicians need to learn that anyone can break news, and citizens who run into you—even if you're not writing for the Huffington Post—can post it anywhere."[24] This means that constant and extreme caution is imperative for politicians in the Internet age. *The Huffington Post*'s Fowler has stated that her existence and that of the bloggers who dog politicians "flummoxes some longtime journalists—because suddenly here I am, unpaid but as a consequence with much more freedom to find out what's going on out there, and writing for a new and encroaching media that is a Wild West of lawlessness."[25]

This brings up the issue of tensions between "old" and "new" journalists demanding attention and respect from one another. The bad news for the so-called "old" journalists is that the old ways are pretty much gone. Nicholas Carr from *The Atlantic Monthly* wrote an article about the effects of the Internet:

The Net's influence doesn't end at the edges of a computer screen, either. As people's minds become attuned to the crazy quilt of Internet media, traditional media have had to adapt to the audience's new expectations. Television programs add text crawls and pop-up ads, and magazines and newspapers shorten their articles, introduce capsule summaries and crowd their pages with easy-to-browse info-snippets.[26]

The "old" style journalists have to adapt to the constantly changing landscape of information dissemination, even as they gain information from their online colleagues and adapt to their methodology. One traditional journalist who has made the move to blogging is Andrew Sullivan, a writer who has worked for the *New Republic* and the *Atlantic Monthly*. Sullivan wrote an article for the *Atlantic Monthly* called "Why I Blog" in which he explained several arguments that support blogging. Blogging, argues Sullivan, is personal, conversational, immediate, and engaging: "Blogging is to writing what extreme sports are to athletics: more free-form, more accident-prone, less formal, more alive. Blogging is writing out loud."[27] Matt Drudge, creator of *The Drudge Report*, was one of the first political bloggers to make a name for himself, breaking such stories as Jack Kemp's selection as Bob Dole's running mate in 1996. He was among the first to report the Monica Lewinsky scandal in the 1990s, and his name became synonymous with the kind of muckraking Internet journalism that was often incorrect but always provocative and entertaining. In 1998, the magazine *Brill's Content* studied the Drudge Report between January and September and found that of the 31 exclusive Drudge stories that ran during this period, 32 percent were untrue, 36 percent were true, and the remaining 32 percent were questionable in authenticity.[28] Drudge does not hold himself to the same journalistic standards as those in the mainstream press, opting instead to act as a foil against the journalistic establishment. When asked about the inaccuracies of his stories, Drudge responded, "Screw journalism! The whole thing's a fraud anyway."[29] After Drudge opened the door to blogging, other bloggers became famous themselves and infamous in political circles.

Today there are many political blogs, and several have become politically important themselves. One of the most important ones is *Daily Kos*, which garners not only public attention but political attention as well. *Daily Kos* founder Markos Moulitsas Zúniga blogs himself and serves as an organizer for other liberal political bloggers. In 2006 Zúniga organized a meeting of liberal bloggers that he called "Yearly Kos," which has turned into a massive four-day conference that Zuniga renamed "Netroots Nation." In 2008, Netroots Nation hosted 2,000 attendees and four-star guests of honor, including House Speaker Nancy Pelosi and former Vice President Al Gore, who was treated to a lengthy standing ovation. The Netroots Nation conference was deemed so important among liberal and Democratic circles that most of the party's leadership came to the event. Conservatives began to host their own blogging conference to combat Netroots Nation. In the summer of 2008 this effort brought 500 conservative bloggers to Texas to talk about their own position in the blogosphere. Called "Right Online," the conservative conference was not as well-attended as Netroots Nation, nor did it hold the star-power of its liberal counterpart (unless you consider Grover Norquist a star), but it made the conservative online presence known. Conservative bloggers are becoming as well known and influential as their liberal counterparts as more and more Republicans turn online for their political messaging.

Blogging is not without problems, and the problems with blogging emerge from its strengths. Blogging circulates personal opinion, and the ability to espouse ones beliefs is a positive thing in a democracy. But blogging's emphasis on judgment over fact makes any criticism within the discussion instinctively a personal attack. Blogging can also be conversational, which allows a more causal and fun take on current events, but at the same time this relaxed attitude can lead to lethargic and sloppy copy. Colloquial conversation is fine in certain circumstances, but not in formal journalism (nor in book publishing). Blogging can be immediate and reactive, but at the same time it can also be primitive and careless. Even as Sullivan writes of the strengths of blogging, he also writes of the real strength of old-fashioned reporting and writing: "Each week, after a few hundred [blog] posts, I also write an actual newspaper column. It invariably turns out to be more considered, balanced and even handed than the blog."[30]

The speed of technological development has meant that blogging is now considered an old technology. The most recent Internet-based phenomenon to hit the nation is Twitter. According to PcMag.com, Twitter was launched in 2006 with the specific purpose of informing others about the user's "daily activity." The Twitter messages, called "tweets," are short, limited to 140 characters in length, and distributed only to those who elect to "follow" your Twitter updates. Politicians have started Twittering their supporters, sending short tweets to constituents or ideological adherents, keeping everyone up to date on the politician's thoughts. President Obama addressed a joint session of Congress when members of congress were seen Twittering messages on their Blackberries during the speech. This appallingly rude behavior aside, some of the messages that came from the House floor were graceless in their content. Rep. Joe Barton, a Republican from Texas, Twittered: "Aggie basketball game is about to start on espn2 for those of you that aren't going to bother watching pelosi smirk for the next hour," only to have his message removed shortly thereafter.[31] Thanks to Blackberries and iPhones, Twittering is now extremely popular. The national political party organizations Twitter, pundits Twitter, elected officials Twitter, and since each message is no longer than 140 characters they are easy to read— if not grammatically correct. According to WeFollow.com, which tracks Twitter use, the most followed political Twitterers are President Obama, former Vice President Al Gore, and Senator John McCain (in that order).

All of this political Internet use has sparked politicians from both sides of the aisle to use the technology as much as possible, but the left seems to have a stronghold on the Internet over conservatives. As long as the Internet has been around, the left has dominated it as a political medium in the areas of fundraising, message dissemination, and voter mobilization. It is evident that the use of the Internet is changing the landscape of political participation as it becomes more sophisticated. Political scientist Bruce Bimber found that prior to 2000 the political uses of the Internet were most often limited to financial donations.[32] Its utility has shifted remarkably in the past decade, giving rise to a new pundit class of bloggers and a new medium that expands the existing traditional mainstream media. According to one expert on the use of the Internet in modern American politics: "What the Web does so well is it picks up the early warning signals, the first glimmers of a movement. Think of the online world as kind of a more visceral connection to the zeitgeist."[33]

Not everyone is able to make this transition from old to new media, as demonstrated by the 2008 presidential campaign. During this campaign, the Democrats were far more successful with their Internet use than their Republican counterparts. The Democrats tried to prove in their 2008 campaigning that their most significant goal was a change from the traditional, established political system, and that an entirely new philosophy in Washington was necessary for progress. Their desired image of change, progressive politics, and diversity was circulated fastest and most effectively with the use of nontraditional media. On the other hand, Republicans used the traditional methods of political dissemination successfully, which matched their traditional philosophies. The GOP values and beliefs were dispersed through traditional means like talk radio and cable television pundit shows because through these mediums there tends to be a sole person of authority disseminating the message. Democrats banked on the Internet to assure themselves an electoral victory in 2008, and then a policy victory beyond that. There have been think tanks established to help Democrats take advantage of the Internet, such as the New Politics Institute.[34]

Political strategists argue that in 2008, a campaign year where fundraising was so crucial, the Republicans were not as savvy as Democrats in their online fundraising for three major reasons. The first is that for many months of the lengthy 2008 election cycle, there was no clear GOP frontrunner, which only changed at the exact time attention turned to the Obama-Clinton protracted primary race. The second is that the poor poll ratings of the president and weak public support of the war in Iraq drove voters away from Republicans during much of the fundraising period. The third is that besides McCain, few Republicans had used Internet fundraising before. According to Howard Dean's 2004 presidential campaign manager Joe Trippi, "On the Democratic side, a lot more people have already contributed to political campaigns on the net. Whereas on the Republican side, no one gave to George Bush on the net. Why? Because they never asked. Now they're sort of behind."[35]

Opinion diffusion is another area where Democrats and liberals beat their conservative counterparts in number and strength. The force of the liberal blogosphere crushes that of their ideological opponents in numbers of hits on Web sites, the political power of their readership, and the quality of their message. Liberal Web sites tend to contain commentary and opinion on a wider variety of topic than their conservative counterparts, and they certainly do not shy away from criticizing their own. Conversely, conservatives use the Internet as an arm of their existing media outlets to vilify their opponents: "[C]onservatives . . . skillfully use the Web to provide maximum benefit for their issues and candidates. They are generally less interested in examining every side of every issue and more focused on eliciting strong emotional responses."[36] Thus, unless the rest of the conservative media machine picks up on a blog's message, it is less likely to gain traction than a liberal blog in Democratic circles.

Dean strategist Trippi writes in his book *The Revolution Will Not Be Televised*: "The Internet . . . is a forward-thinking and forward moving medium, embracing change and pushing the envelope of technology and communication. I do think this gives the Democratic Party a leg up on the Internet ladder—as long as it continues to be the traditionally progressive party, intent on moving forward, trying to make the world better."[37]

DEMOCRACY ONLINE

Two of the most important qualities of the Internet are its ability to support an abundance of voices that afford a great deal of egalitarian democracy among its users and also the its ability to provide nonjournalists a forum to voice their opinions about politics. Cyber advocates argue that because anyone with a computer can create his or her own Web site and anyone who has logged onto a Web site can post anything (within certain limits of legal liability), the Web is therefore uniquely democratizing and encourages citizen participation. A. J. Liebling's statement that "Freedom of the press is guaranteed only to those who own one" no longer applies, since the Internet now allows anyone to voice his or her opinion on blogs or break news by uploading videos to YouTube. The egalitarian nature of the Internet is positive for civic engagement, but problematic for a few reasons. First, the vastness of the medium means that it is difficult to regulate, and as a result Internet content is sometimes fallacious or vindictive. This leads to a second problem, which is that some Internet content is either offensive or downright destructive. The third dilemma that results from Internet use is the ensuing lack of control and privacy that abounds, especially for those in the public eye. All of this means that politicians have to maneuver very, very carefully in this environment to prevent careless errors and gaffes that become uncontrollable and destructive. Politicians have figured out how to use the Internet in very creative ways, but they haven't quite mastered the ability to avoid all problematic Internet exposure.

As the medium develops, the number and scope of cyber-regulations increase to protect those who go online and those who are discussed online. Because of its sheer size and its constant expansion, the Internet remains largely unregulated by the government. Lawmakers and elected officials have agreed in principle to keep the Internet open, but in practice they have crafted policies and laws that aim to rein in the unruly nature of the Internet. The courts have also been leading the way in expanding Internet regulation. Current rules on Internet activity have to do with strict sanctions against child pornography, intellectual property protections, cyber-commerce taxation edicts, international jurisdiction over the Internet, and libel laws that protect the targets of Internet speech and also the hosts of Web sites that post unlawful material. These laws are thorough and can be very well administered, but the truth of the matter is that the Internet is a host for all sorts of nasty behavior because it is so big that the government cannot effectively monitor all aspects of the medium. Therefore, it is up to private citizens to monitor themselves.

The Electronic Frontier Foundation (EFF), a nonprofit dedicated to cyber independence, advocates a resolutely hands-off approach to the Internet. To that end, it lobbies fiercely against new regulations that will affect computer use. When regulations are instituted, the organization aims to assist technophiles in their compliance with the rules and policies of the medium. The perceived threat to the First Amendment freedoms makes many Internet users vehemently opposed to legislation that would limit their expression, which gives the online community a Wild West quality to it. It is this perceived lawlessness that makes Internet communication egalitarian at the same time it is unruly. Since everyone can say anything he or she wants, then anything can be said by anyone—be it profane or profound. The anonymous quality of cyberspace also contributes to the sense that an Internet surfer can post anything he or she wants without consequence. Psychologists have coined the term "deindividualization" to describe the loss of personal identity in crowd or group situations. Psychologists argue that in group settings people become anonymous, which can then lead people to "act aggressively or deviate from acceptable social behaviors."[38] In the case of the Internet, the group is so immeasurably large that people feel anonymous and this leads to the deindividualization addressed by psychologists. Put another way, when going online many feel the "keyboard courage" that pumps up the rhetoric and leads to some very vicious attacks. In a face-to-face contact situation, these invectives would seem to be insulting (at best), but in cyberspace anything goes.

Lack of accountability also leads to unsubstantiated rumors that get special traction for two important reasons. First, these rumors are spread easily via e-mail, and second, legitimate news organizations respond to the rumors as if they were facts. During the 2008 campaign, incredible Internet rumors spread so quickly it was difficult to keep up with what the truth actually was. Entire Web sites were devoted to debunking the myths that made their way around the country about Obama's heritage, his wife's language choice, McCain's anger management, and much more. One such example of rumors becoming real news came from the Web site called "Insight," which is owned by the Unification

Church (also owner of the *Washington Times*). In January 2007, Jeffrey T. Kuhner posted on Insightmag.com that then-candidate Barack Obama attended a radical Islamic school while living in Indonesia as a child. The report, according to Kuhner, had been leaked to the Web site directly from the Hillary Clinton presidential campaign. The two primary problems with the Insight article were that Obama did not attend such a school and the Clinton campaign did not leak this information. However, this did not stop the mainstream media from picking up the story and using it as fact and evidence of Clinton's campaign tactics and also of Obama's intentional mischaracterization of his background. In an interview with the *New York Times*, Kuhner stated that he stood by the veracity of the posting on his site, but he refused to name the "reporters" who gathered the information upon which the posting was based. This event prompted Ralph Whitehead, a journalism professor at the University of Massachusetts, to note: "If you want to talk about a business model that is designed to manufacture mischief in large volume, that would be it. . . . How do we know that Insight magazine actually exists? It could be performance art."[39] Despite this question, Fox News reported on the posting, which then gave it credence among other mainstream news organizations. Thus, a real story was born, even though it was fiction and even though there was no corroborating evidence. The *Columbia Journalism Review* reported on this story, and author Paul McLeary wrote: "It doesn't take a respected news organization to run a big-time smear campaign—all it takes is for the rest of the media to repeat the story, while neglecting to follow it up with their own reporting."[40]

In 2008, a scholar from Princeton University, Danielle Allen, tried to find the origination of an e-mailed rumor that Obama was a secret Muslim. She researched extensively and found that the Web site "FreeRepublic.com" posted a copy of an e-mail on its Web site a year before Allen received it that said: "ALSO, keep in mind that when he [Obama] was sworn into office he DID NOT use the Holy Bible, but instead the Kuran (Their equivalency to our Bible, but very different beliefs)." Through the spelling and factual errors, Allen found that the originator of the erroneous rumor was a man named Andy Martin, a former political opponent of Barack Obama.[41] When others began to write with certainty that Obama was, indeed, Muslim, many cited the Internet as their source of information, saying it was "more trustworthy than the mainstream media."[42] Another rumor that made its way around the Internet during the 2008 campaign was that Michelle Obama used the term *whitey* in a diatribe against Caucasians from the pulpit of a church. Spread by Rush Limbaugh on his radio program, the false rumor prompted the Obama campaign to establish its own Web site to combat the falsities being spread about the candidate and his family, called "FightTheSmears.com." Other Web sites offer fact checking for such rumors, like Snopes, PolitiFact, and FactCheck, all of which do the digging to ascertain the veracity of the rumors being spread. Even though these sites exist, however, very few people will check out the truth to a rumor they receive by e-mail. Instead, depending on their political views, they either delete the message or forward it to their friends, propagating the rumor by letting even more eyes view it.

Other false rumors from the 2008 campaign include the following: Michelle Obama wrote a paper in college that stated America was founded on "crime and hatred" and that whites in America are "ineradicably racist"; that Obama wrote in a book that he "found solace in nursing a pervasive sense of grievance and animosity against my mother's race"; that Obama would "stand with the Muslims should the political winds shift in an ugly direction"; and that Obama received "suspicious" contributions from Saudi Arabia and Iran. None of these statements proved to be true. The Internet remains a prolific source of false rumors, innuendo, and straight-up lies because of its ability to disseminate information quickly and anonymously. An entire movement called the "Birthers" erupted because of false Internet rumors that allege President Obama was born in Kenya. Although the Republican Secretary of State of Hawaii produced Obama's birth certificate, and the local newspaper produced his birth announcement from the day he was born, the rumors persisted and continued to spread. The "Birther" movement gained traction in the mainstream press when CNN's Lou Dobbs stated that President Obama had not supplied enough evidence to support his American citizenry. Said Dobbs on his broadcast: "There's a lot of questions remaining, and seemingly the questions won't go away because they haven't been dealt with."[43] The Internet rumor and the mainstream press that supported it gained so much traction that a bill was proposed in the U.S. House of Representatives, cosponsored by 11 Republican members, which would require future presidential candidates to produce a U.S. birth certificate before running for office.

During the 2009 debate over health care reform, a false rumor was spread alleging that President Obama wanted to install "death panels" that would euthanize senior citizens. While the rumor spread virally around the Internet, it was voiced as reality by Betsy McCaughey, the former lieutenant governor of New York and an opponent of health care reform who appeared on Fred Thompson's radio talk show:

> One of the most shocking things I found in this bill, and there were many, is on page 425, where the Congress would make it mandatory, absolutely require, that every five years, people in Medicare have a required counseling session that will tell them how to end their life sooner.[44]

Other news sources picked up McCaughey's claim, used it as fact, and propagated the rumor throughout the mainstream press, without questioning either its validity or its source. The rumor was referenced by Fox News, CNN, the *New York Post*, the *Wall Street Journal*, and the *Washington Post* as well as by House Republican Leader John Boehner in his efforts to defeat the reform proposal.[45]

The "death panel" rumor also never completely went away. The potent combination of the Internet and the 24-hour news cycle can help disseminate information, but the information may not necessarily be accurate. Fast is first today, and as a result news organizations are pressured to deliver information as quickly as possible, even when the content may not be correct. Politicians can use the swift and emotional qualities of the Internet for their own politicking purposes, knowing full well their messages will resonate and amplify throughout the American public.

The Internet is attractive not only because it is so immediate but because it is also free. As a society we have grown accustomed to obtaining Internet content without having to pay for it, and for this reason alone traditional news organizations are feeling the pressure to move online to attract an audience.

MONEY

The principal quandary for traditional news organizations that go online is that while it is expensive to produce the news, the Internet demands distribution for free. This means that news organizations have to find ways to make money while circulating their product in a culture that demands free or low-cost access. The *New York Times* tried a subscription-only service called "Times Select" that failed because so few people were willing to pay money for online newspaper content. Because of this culture of free online content, news organizations have to do what other online sites do, which is find innovative ways to advertise in order to earn a profit. Despite industry rumors that most newspapers and broadcast news outlets will join their news magazine colleagues in demanding subscription fees, there has not been any movement in this direction thus far. Instead these sites rely on online advertising. The Internet has only recently become a place for online news organizations to earn advertising revenue, and they are wary of disturbing their customer base. According to the Project for Excellence in Journalism: "Historically in journalism, audiences come for news and are exposed to advertising incidentally. Online, hunting through advertising is an activity unto itself."[46]

The ads on news Web sites fall into three general categories: search ads, classifieds, and display ads. Search ads are those that emerge when someone looks for a service or product on a search engine such as Yahoo! or Google. Since both of these search engines also host news sites, the advertising is an important part of their Web site and branding. For example, on the Yahoo! site there is a hyperlink next to a story about the housing crisis that leads directly to the mortgage company Lending Tree. This blends advertising in with the news the site produces, producing a synergy between information and marketing. Classified advertising on Web sites is another way news organizations can earn revenue for their online efforts, and this type closely mimics the classified ads seen in print, those individual advertising efforts for people trying to sell personal items. The last type is display ads, which are unique to the Internet. Display ads on the Internet are composed of banners that stretch along the top or on the side of an Internet page, containing static or flash graphics designed to attract attention. These ads are at one time the most effective and the most annoying because they distract a reader from the information for which he or she was looking. Online news organizations also use display ads that are more interactive, pulling in Internet users who answer poll questions or move onto different sites. There are also display ads that use audio or video content to make them more appealing to surfers already mesmerized by a television-like Internet.

According to the Newspaper Association of America (NAA), more newspapers are spending their advertising dollars on Internet ads than ever before, and this number continues to increase as the budget for standard advertising decreases:

> Advertising expenditures for newspaper websites in 2007 increased 18.8%, to $3.2 billion—accounting for 7.5% of all newspaper ad spending last year (up from 5.7% in 2006). . . . In the fourth quarter of 2007, advertising expenditures for newspaper websites increased to $847 million, up 13.6% compared with the same period a year earlier. That was the thirteenth consecutive quarter of double-digit growth for online newspaper advertising since NAA started reporting online ad spending in 2004.[47]

This portends a greater online emphasis for newspapers, and this trend of moving online does not seem to have an end in sight.

CONCLUSIONS

All of the types of Internet news and information coverage combine to create a massive online political presence. Within all of this data, information, fact, rumor, and gossip, there is a tremendous opportunity for citizens to learn about the politicians who run for office, the policies they make, and the effects of these policies on the nation. Additionally, because the Internet is the medium of the people, there is also a remarkable opportunity for more citizens to take part in the political conversations being held across the country, and also to reach out more effectively to political actors who are so important to the political process. Indeed, the Internet is a technology that is serving to smash the divide between politicians and their constituents, forcing our elected officials to reach out to the voting public more often and with more ingenuity than ever before. Between online instant chats with journalists, lawmakers, and bureaucrats, the public is now more able than ever to ask the tough questions first hand, joining the discussion and framing the debate in their own terms. This potential connectivity is immense and inspiring. But one can fairly ask the question: Will the reality of the Internet live up to this potential? With so much news and non-news available, what will the citizenry gravitate towards on the Internet? Will it be substantive debate or will it be the entertainment that amuses more than it educates? Does the Internet's potential lie in entertainment, following the other forms of the media? Why should the Internet be different?

As one could argue the dangers of the Internet are few and ultimately address-able, so too can it be argued that the Internet is not the panacea that many believe it to be. The technology cannot be used alone, because politics demands offline communication. Citizens can reach out to their elected officials online, but it remains more inspiring and effective to see politicians in person. Furthermore, while computers help connect people from all corners and allow anyone to take part in the process, the result can be that too many people join the conversation. For example, during the 2008 presidential campaign the public was allowed instant and informal access to the primary election debates via YouTube. Here, citizens flooded the site with thousands of questions, leaving the sorting to be done by the political insiders who were running the debate. The questions that were asked were those chosen because they were general enough or entertaining enough to entice viewers to watch the debate. The Internet can be a great politi-cal tool, but it must be used in conjunction with actual human activity.

The Internet has already changed the field of political journalism and prom-ises to continue this metamorphosis. As *Time* magazine's James Poniewozik notes, even the term *journalist* is something that is amorphous and historically recent, emerging during the mid-twentieth century when there was the push to professionalize the news industry: "There are reporters and there are writers, and there are opinion commentators and they all fall under the broad . . . canopy of what we call journalism."[48] The Internet throws these varying facets into a more jumbled stew of information, rumor, and buzz that is harder for the Ameri-can public to sort through. The enormity of the Internet means that some politi-cal journalism has lost the sheen of professionalism, and it is up to consumers to determine for themselves what is real and what is not.

Politicians will continue to adapt to an online political climate that is very fast and very public. According to Poniewozik: "There are more potential landmines for them to step on" in this new Internet era, which means politicians have to be very careful about everything they say, do, and emote. The difference this has made in political campaigning is in stark contrast from the way campaigns used to be conducted. For example, during the 2008 presidential campaign one-time candidate Hillary Rodham Clinton was preparing for her speech to the Democratic National Convention. Before the nightly proceedings began, she and her team brought a number of different colored blazers to test which one would look best on her that evening. She was trying to control her image, and yet someone took a picture of her holding up the jackets, sent the photo around the Internet, and she was mocked for caring so much about her appearance. This was exactly what John F. Kennedy did in 1960 before he appeared with Richard Nixon on the very first televised debate, but in 2008 Hillary looked too manufac-tured, which served as evidence that she was artificial and insincere. The instanta-neous connectivity of the Internet forces a rush to judgment.

The Internet helps to amplify political emotion since its sheer size allows so many different voices, many of whom link to one another. Since it is so quick to spread information, the Internet is not only important in message dissemination but is also crucial in opinion fortification. Ideological Web sites spread gossip or opinion, link to like-minded sites, and present a united opinion front. The ability for non-Internet sources to augment their presence online has served to magnify ideological screed. For example, the successful conservative magazine and Web site, Newsmax, features both news and propaganda, and has grown in its influence and prominence since the magazine went online. Newsmax reports on the Washington political scene at the same time it spreads false rumors about Democrats, spreading conspiracy theories about those in power. The collaborative efforts between Web sites and offline media make for a powerful resource. Writes *Slate.com*'s Joe Conason: "Everyday [Newsmax] blasts forth a barrage of supposed Obama scandals and embarrassments to be amplified by Limbaugh, Glenn Beck and the panoply of talk radio and cable megaphones, knowing that by sheer volume, some of it will stick."[49] That politicians use a combination of media is not new, but what is new is the speed and constancy with which this media is spread.

As more Americans turn online for their political news and information, there will be more truth available to the American public. Also available will be falsities, rumors, gossip, and vindictive lies aimed at those in power, but also serving to destroy trust within the electorate. Because of the collaboration between online and offline media sources, there is a new way to divide the public, leaving an angry and disaffected citizenry in the wake.

NOTES

1. Roger Hurwitz, "Who Needs Politics? Who Needs People? The Ironies of Democracy in Cyberspace," *Contemporary Sociology* 26 (November 1999): 655–661.

2. Ibid.

3. Jeremiah Owyang, "Web Strategies of the 2008 Presidential Candidates," http://www.web-strategist.com/blog/2007/04/05/web-strategies-of-the-2008-presidential-candidates/ (accessed June 11, 2008).

4. Thomas Hollihan, *Uncivil Wars: Political Campaigns in a Media Age*, 2nd edition (New York: Bedford/St. Martin's, 2008).

5. Joe Trippi, *The Revolution Will Not Be Televised: Democracy, the Internet, and the Overthrow of Everything* (New York: ReganBooks, 2004), 13.

6. Ibid., 137.

7. Ibid., 131.

8. Jim Kuhnenn, "Paul Raises More than 3.5 Million in One Day," *Fox News Online*, http://www.foxnews.com/wires/2007/Nov05/0,4670,PaulFundraising (accessed November 5, 2007).

9. Brendan Spiegel, *Ron Paul: How a Fringe Politician Took over the Web*, *Wired*, http://www.wired.com/politics/onlinerights/news/2007/06/ron_paul (accessed May 12, 2008).

10. Jose Antonio Vargas, "Campaigns Experimenting Online to See What Works," *Washington Post*, February 3, 2008.

11. Michael Malbin, "Small Donors, Large Donors and the Internet: The Case for Public Financing after Obama," *The Campaign Finance Institute*, April 2009, http://www.cfinst.org/president/pdf/PresidentialWorkingPaper_April09.pdf (accessed May 24, 2009), 14.

12. Ibid.

13. Jose Antonio Vargas, "Obama's Wide Web," *Washington Post*, August 20, 2008.

14. Michael Malbin, "Small Donors, Large Donors and the Internet: The Case for Public Financing after Obama," *The Campaign Finance Institute*, April 2009, http://www.cfinst.org/president/pdf/PresidentialWorkingPaper_April09.pdf (accessed May 24, 2009), 14.

15. Joe Trippi, *The Revolution Will Not Be Televised: Democracy, the Internet and the Overthrow of Everything* (New York: ReganBooks, 2004), 84.

16. Jose Antonio Vargas, "Campaigns Experimenting Online to See What Works," *Washington Post*, February 3, 2008.

17. Toby Harnden, "John McCain 'Technology Illiterate' Doesn't E-mail or Use Internet," *Guardian UK*, July 18, 2008, http://www.telegraph.co.uk/news/newstopics/uselection2008/johnmccain/2403704/John-McCain-technology-illiterate-doesnt-email-or-use-internet.html (accessed July 25, 2008).

18. Ibid.

19. Ibid.

20. "The Associated Press and Intellectual Property Protection," *Webwire*, April 13, 2009, http://www.webwire.com/ViewPressRel_print.asp?aId=92326 (accessed May 13, 2009).

21. Paul Farhi, "The Ads That Aren't," *Washington Post*, September 11, 2008, C01.

22. Ibid.

23. Caroline Tolbert and Romona S. McNeal, "Unraveling the Effects of the Internet on Political Participation?" *Political Science Quarterly* 56 (June 2003): 175–185.

24. Howard Kurtz, "Blogging Without Warning," *Washington Post*, June 19, 2008, www.washingtonpost.com/wp-dyn/context/article/2008.

25. Ibid.

26. Nicholas Carr, "Is Google Making Us Stupid?" *The Atlantic Monthly*, July/August 2008.

27. Andrew Sullivan, "Why I Blog," *The Atlantic Monthly*, November 2008, 108.

28. Howard Gardner, Mihaly Csiskzentmihalyi, and William Damon, *Good Work* (New York: Basic Books, 2001), 147.

29. Ibid.

30. Andrew Sullivan, "Why I Blog," *The Atlantic Monthly*, November 2008, 113.

31. Peter Hamby, "Members of Congress Twitter Through Obama's Big Speech," *CNN Political Ticker Online*, February 25, 2009, http://politicalticker.blogs.cnn.com/2009/02/25/members-of-congress-twitter-through-obamas-big-speech/ (accessed May 26, 2009).

32. Bruce Bimber, "Information and Political Engagement in America: The Search for Effects of Information Technology at the Individual Level," *Political Research Quarterly*, Vol. 54, No. 1, (2001): 53–67.

33. Jose Antonio Vargas, "For Candidates, Web Is Power and Poison," *Washington Post*, November 8, 2007, A01.

34. Ibid.

35. Michael Luo, "Democrats Take the Lead in Raising Money Online," *New York Times*, July 13, 2007, http://www.nytimes.com/2007/07/13/us/politics/13internet.html?_r=1&oref=slogin.

36. Michael Crowley, "Conservative Blogs Are More Effective," *New York Times*, December 11, 2005.

37. Joe Trippi, *The Revolution Will Not Be Televised: Democracy, the Internet and the Overthrow of Everything* (New York: ReganBooks, 2004).

38. Jenna Chang, "The Role of Anonymity in Deindividualized Behavior," *Undergraduate Journal of Baylor University*, Vol. 6, No. 1 (Fall 2008): 2.

39. David Kirkpatrick, "Feeding Frenzy for a Big Story, Even if It's False," *New York Times*, January 29, 2007, A2.

40. Paul McLeary, "Insightmag, a Must-Read," *Columbia Journalism Review* (January 29, 2007), http://www.cjr.org/politics/insightmag_a_mustread.php (accessed October 16, 2009).

41. Matthew Mosk, "An Attack That Came Out of the Ether," *Washington Post*, June 28, 2008, C01.

42. Ibid.

43. "The Origin of Rumors," *On the Media, National Public Radio*, July 31, 2009, http://www.onthemedia.org/transcripts/2009/07/31/01 (accessed August 17, 2009).

44. Ibid.

45. Ibid.

46. State of the News Media 2007, The Project for Excellence in Journalism, http://www.journalism.org/.

47. "Newspaper Online Advertising Spending Jumps 19 percent, Print Ads Down 9 percent," http://www.marketingcharts.com/print/newspaper-online-advertising-spending-jumps-19-print-ads-down-9-4024/ (accessed September 8, 2008).

48. James Poniewozik, June 9, 2008, Personal interview with author.

49. Joe Conason, "The Vast Right-Wing Conspiracy Is Back," *Slate.com*, October 5, 2009.

Chapter 6

CONCLUSIONS

I n 1987, scholar Judith Lichtenberg wrote: " 'Mass media space-time' is a very scarce commodity: Only so much news, analysis, and editorial opinion can be aired on the major channels of mass communication."[1] Now, barely more than 20 years later, that notion has been invalidated because the mass media are no longer confined by space and time. There are not only 100 times more television channels to watch than when Lichtenberg wrote this, there are now hundreds more radio stations to listen to and millions of Web sites to surf. There is so much information that one can be overwhelmed by the enormity of it all. Information comes to us so quickly that it is almost impossible to catch everything. And so it is within this vastness of media content that politicians must maneuver to get elected and reelected, to advertise and promote policy, and to take positions that will advance their careers. All of these efforts mandate much media use by American politicians. Politicians sit for interviews and appear on niche broadcasting channels to highlight their niche interests. They poke fun at themselves on late night television and bring in the ratings for shows that need to sell ad time. They use talk radio to reach specific audiences and the Internet to reach their constituencies. Politicians use all of these media carefully, scripting themselves to appear unscripted, all the while hoping they will not make the kind of "Macaca" mistake that took down Senator George Allen in 2006.

It takes time to plan a well-coordinated media campaign, but the payoffs in our heavily mediated society are significant. Today, politicians use print media in conjunction with other media forms to advertise themselves and their causes. Politicians write books about themselves (their histories, their triumphs over tragedy) and their policy stands (the "simple" solutions to national crises), and then go on to publicize these books through other media forms. Politicians coordinate interviews in magazines and newspapers to delve deeper into their personas and tell a more nuanced story about their lives, a story that cannot be communicated as effectively in the short-form electronic media styles. The future of the print media is uncertain, however, so more politicians are using electronic media in their campaigns. As this trend continues, the country will lose valuable and substantive journalism and with it a solid understanding of American politics.

Politicians use radio in their media ventures as well, and the intimacy of radio encourages it to broadcast big emotion. However, the talk radio hosts who are the most successful are thriving because they amplify discourse as they entertain, and with talk radio come extreme language and a certain amount of aggression that is contrary to deliberation and discourse. As talk radio hosts continue to rail against politicians and political opponents, they force a wedge into the electorate, separating us even more than we already are. Politicians also use television in their media efforts, and between the niche entertainment programming and the ideologically bifurcated news channeling there are many places for politicians to reach the American public. However, so much programming on cable news channels is occupied by punditry rather than actual news, which can be confusing to an audience that tunes in for information and instead gets opinion. Politicians use the Internet in innovative ways, mostly in conjunction with other media forms, and this new technology is helping to speed up political communication. Bloggers and online commentators put pressure on the mainstream media, on politicians, and on the citizenry to get involved in learning more about important issues and events. But the Internet brings with it some difficult problems, including an increasingly uncivil tone and falsities that are spread quickly and virally.

Today, politicians must sort through this rapidly expanding and increasingly tricky media system, learning which components to use when. At first blush it would seem that so much media would benefit these politicians inordinately, giving them the ability to advertise themselves where once only a few select politicians earned national media attention. However, the modern media have become inhospitable to politicians and public officials, rewarding them with great attention and at the same time punishing them with vicious overexposure and oversimplification. Partisan allegiance is neither new for media outlets, nor does it necessarily imply some sort of corruption on the part of the news industry. Since the modern media are not official house organs of the political parties, as they were in the Jacksonian era, there are other imperatives at stake that have led to this partisanship. The media's drive for profit makes the entire news system less about politics or policy and more about entertainment, which leads to an overemphasis on ideological battling: more for show, and less about true beliefs.

CHANGES FOR POLITICIANS, JOURNALISTS, AND CITIZENS

Politicians have to utilize this media for their own purposes, but today that represents a dangerous venture. They want to control their message, but the enormity of the American media makes it completely uncontrollable. The attention towards a political actor always seems to start out well enough, which is enormously tempting for anyone in politics, but after too much exposure the coverage turns ugly. Once the tide has turned, it is difficult to turn the coverage around to be positive once again, and politicians can become caricatures of themselves. Additionally, technology has sped up the media so much that it is hard to keep up with it all, and therefore it can be difficult for politicians to adapt to the changing news media norms. YouTube only emerged in political circles in the 2006 midterm elections, and now it is a standard tool for both parties. Texting is becoming ordinary; e-mails are seen as elderly communication; and Twittering will be old hat by the time President Obama runs for reelection. New media change everything so fast that it takes many smart people to stay on the cutting edge of the technological developments. Add to that the immense financial imperatives of the major corporations that control the mainstream media and the ensuing emphasis on entertainment, and you have a media system that is too large to navigate well and so deficient of substance that it actually has become harmful to democracy. The art of politicking is now rooted in rapid reaction and the emotional, both of which are plentiful in today's super-fast media age. Effective governing is rooted in fact, however, and facts are becoming much less common as America turns away from hard news and focuses instead on the diversion afforded to us by the short bursts of entertainment.

The abundance of media tilts towards the amusing and away from the substantive. This shift may be because our current political environment is so thorny and because people desire an escape from reality. It could also be because public affairs are complicated and messy and many do not want to engage in the complexity of the issues, or it could be because we are, as a society, far too busy. In today's media age there is much content, but not enough time to catch most of it. Despite our incredible control over our media consumption, most Americans do not have any time left in the day to explore anything new. A discerning public has to sort through the massive amount of information in a short period of time, which means that logically we take our cues for what to tune into by adhering to a specific type of media outlet. For those interested in right-wing news, there is Fox. For those interested in left-wing opinion, there are blogs. Yet the fact remains that people seek entertainment more than news, which makes it very appealing for the major media companies to provide entertaining content.

At the same time that there are many media options available, there is also an economic requirement for media companies to attract as many people as possible. This results in a "lowest common denominator" practice, where the entire American media system strives to be as accessible to the greatest number of people possible. This accessibility is the only thing that makes any financial sense because the larger the audience is, the more lucrative the program. These same monetary requisites result in an entertainment-driven news media as well in order to secure the highest audience ratings. As writer and humorist Adam McKay wrote in 2008: "Four corporations own all the TV channels. All of them. If they don't get ratings they get canceled or fired. All news is about sex, blame and anger, and fear. Exposing lies about amounts of money taken from lobbyists and votes cast for the agenda of the last eight years does not rate. The end."[2] Beyond television, the profit incentives stretch to radio, print, and the Internet as well, and so the very nature of the news has changed as the amount of money in the business has increased.

This change is evident in the journalism industry, in the kinds of stories that are covered by its practitioners, and in the practitioners themselves. The job of journalists now demands that as they investigate a story, they also look for friction points instead of substance, because tension has natural entertainment value. False rumors about lawmakers and the policies they propose abound on the Internet and are substantiated by the pundits on radio and television, who address them as if they were fact. This is then reported by journalists who see a controversy as entertaining news. Journalists flock to the stories that will capture the attention of their audience instead of those stories that will most inform the electorate. Since there are many journalists who are hired to fill the endless hours on television and radio and space on the Internet, these journalists are in competition with one another to file the most extraordinary story first. As a result, falsities abound. Reporting on a false story reported by CNBC and Fox Business Channel, the *Washington Post* wrote: "In the current media environment, where it's more important to have it first than to get it right, it won't be long until the next mix-up."[3]

The current media environment begs the question: Who actually *is* a journalist today? Is it only the Katie Courics of the world, those afforded television airtime? Or is it Mayhill Fowler, the Tennessee woman without any journalistic experience but with loads of moxie and access to a Web site? Both have achieved varying degrees of fame and prominence, but they operate under wildly dissimilar constraints. The lines distinguishing pundits, bloggers, reporters, and anchors have been blurred to the point that the word *journalist* today is virtually meaningless. In the new information age we are all potential journalists without a solid understanding what that actually means. Television news outlets beg their viewers for homemade video content of natural disasters and crime scenes, allowing everyday citizens to work as cameramen. Thanks to the Internet, anyone can be a pundit too, posting their opinion, responding to a news story, or spreading a rumor. All of this is now considered part of "the news."

A relatively new breed of news is found in the late-night shows that address politics and current events within the context of satire and humor. These shows are tremendously popular with the under-45 crowd, who look to them for their news and information. The hosts—comedians in real life—are considered journalists despite their protests to the contrary; and they interview politicians and candidates and opine on the news of the day just like "real" journalists and pundits do. It is not the fault of these programs that Americans view them as seriously as any real news source, but the American public has thrust upon these shows this duty. A *Time* magazine poll proved that the American public not only considers Jon Stewart to be a journalist, but they also rank him as the most trustworthy one.[4] If any of us can be journalists or pundits, then what happens to the quality of the news? These shows are terrific: They are funny and smart and often inform much more than straight news does. But there exists a disconnect between their ability to inform and their actual mission, which is simply to entertain. When politicians contort themselves by appearing on these shows in order to garner attention and approval, it seems at one time natural and at the same time very anomalous. Of course, politicians go on the programs for attention and to show they can give or take a joke, but the question has to be asked: Since when did it become important for our elected officials to be funny or cool? And truth be told, the politicians who appear on these shows almost never look particularly funny or cool. So says *Saturday Night Live*'s *Weekend Update* head writer Alex Baze about politicians who appear on *Saturday Night Live*:

> I don't know that they're trying to get big laughs. I think it's a way of angling for that "hey, he's cool for trying that" credit. None of the politicians that have come through the show in my memory really pulled down the laughs. When a politician does comedy, it gets a laugh because it's just so odd and unexpected. It's like seeing a dog wearing a sweater. It's not that the dog looks great in the sweater . . . it's just . . . Jesus, that dog's wearing a sweater!!![5]

And much like the dog in the sweater, a politician on a late night comedy show is an oddball combination that attracts attention. The politicians who appear on these shows do so to appeal to a certain demographic of voter, a group who is looking for something besides the construction of sound bites and the evening news. The evidence shows that politicians are successful in their wooing—but at what cost? These appearances might be mutually beneficial for the political actors and the comedy shows, but their consequence can be discourse that is flimsy and trivial.

CONSEQUENCES OF THESE CHANGES

The profusion of media creates the ability to gather an enormous amount of information to make us feel that we have all discovered the "truth." Following are several unintended consequences of this discovery:

Too Much Information

While the media allow Americans to move away from the construction of politicians, we are concomitantly uncovering far too much about who these politicians really are. Cell phone cameras, Web sites like Gawker, and a profusion of celebrity journalism across all media have allowed the American public to view politicians more candidly than before. Additionally, as social mores have changed so too has our national appetite for the salacious. The American press of 40 years ago would never have reported on the private dalliances of politicians, but today this is commonplace. We now believe that we have the right to know everything about our politicians, and thanks to technology this intimate knowledge is ultimately quite possible. Too much information, however, is not necessarily a good thing, and the scandalous details we now know about some of our politicians can disgust the voting public. It is up to each individual voter to decide whether a politician's values are up to their standards, but when all voters are treated to the dirty details, it deters political engagement.

An Abundance of the Same Information

Media coverage today tends to examine the same thing, opting to attract audiences with the same "hot" story as their competitors. Political scientist Larry Sabato wrote in his book *Feeding Frenzy* that since journalists "prefer to employ titillation rather than scrutiny," the political press will opt to cover a trivial matter more than a substantive one.[6] A rumor will lead to an allegation, which will then lead to a question about the allegation posed to a politician. The press reports on the question, giving credence to the rumor, and then the story becomes a self-feeding report, one lacking substance: a "feeding frenzy." We want to know as much as we can about an event or an issue, but when all the media outlets constantly cover the same thing, we tire of the topic and move on.

The Exclusion of Real Information

When everyone is talking about the economy, no one is talking about foreign policy. When the press reports on the war in Iraq, it neglects the war in Afghanistan. This is the nature of the news. However, when the attention moves from coverage of the economy and foreign policy to the sexual dalliances of an elected official, real information is excluded from our zeitgeist. The result is a widening knowledge gap among American voters.

Constructed Reality

The abundance of media outlets and the ubiquity of media in our society have forced politicians to construct for themselves an image that is universally appealing. A cynical public tries to peel back the layers of this construction in order to find the "truth," and they punish the people who are less than perfect. For example, during the 2008 presidential campaign, in order to appear "regular" and thus appeal to the most voters, then-candidate Barack Obama went bowling and played the game terribly, setting off a firestorm of criticism about his lack of bowling acumen. The construction of Obama as an "everyman" was completely false, but necessary for the campaign. Comedian Jon Stewart said that in recent campaigns politicians have been "animatronic" because "all the humanity has been managed out of campaigns."[7] Since no one is perfect, politicians will make mistakes, and now those mistakes are broadcast and rebroadcast until the next firework explodes. If a politician admits to making a mistake, then this admission is repeated too, serving as searing indictments and validations of incompetence or stupidity. This feeds on the existing cynicism about American politics and politicians.

American Partisanship Is Becoming Angrier

Partisanship is a natural occurrence in American government and in electoral politics. Indeed, party differences and allegiances help to organize our political system. Partisanship in itself is a healthy thing for a democracy, allowing our citizens to take sides in a debate and address the nuances of issues and events. Party politics encourage political participation at the grassroots levels, promoting civic engagement as it persuades Americans to take part in the political process. Partisanship in itself is not a negative thing, but through the media's lens it morphs into something more polarizing. Because of the entertainment value of political tension and vilifying rhetoric, partisanship is displayed most determinedly in the media. Left to opposing partisan pundits, partisanship is not a civil disagreement about policy but instead a signal of a broader ideological catastrophe. Media bias has become so commonplace that politicians use varying forms of the news and entertainment media as weapons in their fight against one another. This has been shown throughout this book, in the print media, on the radio, on television, and in cyberspace. Politicians go straight to the public to advertise themselves and their policies, thumping their opponents in the process when the need arises. This serves the attention needs of the politicians, and it also serves the financial purposes of the media in their efforts to attract an audience. It does not, however, serve the needs of the American public, which today is treated to a daily onslaught of angry posturing and extreme language. In lieu of a debate on policy differences, media partisanship takes the form of all-out loathing. This deters the public from engaging with one another or even considering an opposing viewpoint.

The Media Breed Cynicism

When the polarization in the media reaches the public, and when politicians are ferociously mocked, the outpouring of annoyance and distaste for politicians has a rippling effect over our citizenry and our political system. It is wise to examine policy with a critical eye, but when the national pastime involves insulting our elected officials, gone is the optimism that inspires civic engagement. To effect real change in society, you must maneuver through the public *and* the American political system, too. So if the assumption is that politicians are corrupt, then citizens are less likely to engage themselves and participate in the political process. Without this engagement, our democracy becomes more tenuous.

The Media Breed Incivility

The spiteful negativity in the media leads to a greater lack of civility within the general public. If it is acceptable to call a political opponent a "fascist" on TV, then it is reasonable to use this term in everyday discourse against those you do not like, regardless of one's understanding of the term. The same goes for "idiot," "asshole," "Nazi," "feminazi," and "murderer." What are we teaching our emerging leaders about civil discourse if criticism routinely devolves into name calling? In 2009, President Obama addressed a joint session of Congress to discuss his health care reform proposal. This public policy effort was met with great resistance from many Republicans in Congress, and as lawmakers sometimes do, the GOP members expressed their distaste for the plan by holding their applause during the speech and holding up anti-plan props for the cameras. Halfway through the president's speech, he was interrupted by South Carolina Republican Congressman Joe Wilson, who shouted "You lie!" Never, in the history of the House of Representatives, had a member of Congress interrupted a presidential speech in this manner. The event sparked a debate on the merits of free speech and the absence of civility in American politics. Wilson's outburst proved that the modern American public is far more tolerant of boorish behavior, for in the days immediately following the interruption, Wilson raised almost $2.7 million for his reelection campaign. There is not a direct correlation between the current media climate and Congressional rudeness, but there does exist a tolerance for anger that is new.

CONSEQUENCES FOR THE AMERICAN PUBLIC

The last several decades have provided a great expansion in media technology and an enormous increase in the number of American news media outlets. The Pew Research Center conducted a survey in 2007 that showed that even with this expansion, there has been "little impact on how much Americans know about national and international affairs."[8] We have more media, but we are not any more informed about American politics. The American media's emphasis on entertainment over information leads to both a pervasive ignorance of current affairs and political distrust. The Pew study found that in 1989, 74 percent of the American public could name the vice president. In 2007, 69 percent could answer the same question. The American media mercilessly mocked Vice President Cheney during the Bush Administration, but that did little for the public's knowledge of who he actually was. Along with our ignorance, there has been a significant increase of cynicism about American politics among the voting public. With political corruption being broadcast so relentlessly, it is understandable that Americans view the political system with a highly critical eye. However, encouraging this cynicism does not bode well for the future of the republic if you remember that today's media consumers are tomorrow's elected officials. We have become disillusioned about our political system, about our politicians, and about our role in the democratic process.

Politicians have adapted to the immensity of the media by trying to be everywhere and everything to all viewers, readers, listeners, and surfers. They appear on the niche cable channels, chat up talk radio hosts, write serious and heartfelt books about their family/military/service/policy efforts/love of animals, and generally try as hard as they can to make the people laugh and cry with them instead of at them. They must appear funny, smart, controlled—but not *too* controlled or else they look inauthentic—succinct, self-deprecating, eloquent, emotional, stoic, handsome, sober, witty, and normal. This is unreasonable to expect, and yet the American public expects it. We hold politicians accountable when the media show how they fall woefully short of these disproportionate standards. Citizens are lacking the knowledge necessary to make informed political decisions, and politicians are forced to operate under a media glare that rejects substance. The American political media system does not meet the needs of a democratic republic. Citizens and politicians should demand more from our "fourth branch" of government.

NOTES

1. Judith Lichtenberg, "Foundations and Limits of Freedom of the Press," *Philosophy and Public Affairs* 16 (1987): 329.

2. Adam McKay, "We're Gonna Frickin' Lose this Thing," *The Huffington Post Online* http://www.huffingtonpost.com/adam-mckay/were-gonna-frickin-lose-t_b_124772.html (accessed September 15, 2008).

3. "The News Is Broken," *Washington Post*, October 20, 2009, http://www .washingtonpost.com/wp-dyn/content/article/2009/10/19/AR2009101902988.html ?sid=ST2009101903583 (accessed October 20, 2009).

4. "Now That Walter Cronkite Has Passed On, Who Is America's Most Trusted Newscaster?" *Time* (July 22, 2009), http://www.timepolls.com/hppolls/archive/poll _results_417.html (accessed August 17, 2009).

5. Alex Baze, September 2008, Personal interview with author.

6. Larry Sabato, *Feeding Frenzy: How Attack Journalism Has Transformed American Politics* (New York: Free Press, 1991), 6.

7. Sasha Johnson, "Jon Stewart Lectures Reporters on Coverage," http://political ticker.blogs.cnn.com/2008/08/25/jon-stewart-lectures-reporters-on-coverage/ (accessed August 25, 2008).

8. "Public Knowledge of Current Affairs Little Changed by News and Information Revolutions, What Americans Know: 1989–2007," *Pew Research Center for People and the Press*, April 15, 2007, http://people-press.org/report/319/public-knowledge-of-current-affairs-little-changed-by-news-and-information-revolutions (accessed October 20, 2009).

BIBLIOGRAPHY

Abramowitz, Michael. "President Reaches Out to a Friendly Circle in New Media." *Washington Post*, September 16, 2007.

Allen, Mike. "Steele to Rush: I'm Sorry." *Politico*, March 2, 2009. http://www.politico .com/news/stories/0309/19517.html (accessed May 15, 2009).

Althaus, Scott L. "American News Consumption during Times of Nation Crisis." *PS Online*, September 2002. www.apsanet.org (accessed June 7, 2008).

Anderson, Kevin. "US Politicians Embrace Podcasts." *BBC News*, April 13, 2005. http:// news.bbc.co.uk/1/hi/world/americas/4441135.stm (accessed May 15, 2008).

Andrews, Edmund L. "ABC Pulls the Plug on a Populist's Radio Show." *New York Times*, October 9, 1995, 24.

Ansolabehere, Stephen, Rebecca Lessem, and James M. Snyder, Jr. "The Political Orientation of Newspaper Endorsements in U.S. Elections, 1940–2002." *Quarterly Journal of Political Science* 1, no. 4 (Fall 2006): 393–404.

Arbitron Radio Market Report Reference Guide 2.1. http://www.arbitron.com/ downloads/purplebook.pdf (accessed October 16, 2007).

"Attitudes Towards News Organizations." The Pew Research Center for People and the Press. http://people-press.org/report/19891113/attitudes-toward-news-organization (accessed May 15, 2009).

Bachman, Katy, "Talk Radio Network Expands Ingraham's Reach in Top 10." *Media Week* (September 1, 2003): 31.

Baker, Edwin C. "Advertising and a Democratic Press." *University of Pennsylvania Law Review* 140, no. 6 (June 1992): 2097–2243.

"Barack Obama Celebrates Wedding Day with Roses." *FloraCulture International*. http:// www.floracultureinternational.com/index.php?Itemid=116&id=640&option=com _content&task=view (accessed January 13, 2009).

Barker, David. "Rushed Decisions: Political Talk Radio and Vote Choice, 1994–1996." *Journal of Politics* 61 (1999): 527–539.

Barker, David, and Kathleen Knight. "Political Talk Radio and Public Opinion." *Public Opinion Quarterly* 64 (2000): 149–170.

Baum, Matthew. *Soft News Goes to War*. Princeton, NJ: Princeton University Press, 2003.
———. "Talking the Vote: Why Presidential Candidates Hit the Talk Show Circuit." *American Journal of Political Science* 49 (2005): 213–234.

Baze, Alex. September 2008. Personal interview with author.

Bedard, Paul. "Washington Whispers." *US News and World Report*, March 2, 2009. http://www.usnews.com/blogs/washington-whispers/2009/03/03/gop-to-michael -steele-quiet-about-rush-limbaugh-or-youre-fired.html (accessed May 15, 2009).

Bennett, W. Lance. *News: The Politics of Illusion*, 6th edition. New York: Pearson Longman, 2005.

Bing, Jonathan. "Left-Wing Authors Finding Their Niche." *Daily Variety*, July 1, 2003. http://www.variety.com/article/VR1117888775.html?categoryid=1064&cs=1 (accessed May 14, 2009).

Blumenthal v. Drudge, 992 F. Supp 44 D. D.C. 1998.

Bolce, Louis, Gerald DeMayo, and Douglas Muzzio. "Dial-In Democracy: Talk Radio and the 1994 Election." *Political Science Quarterly* 111 (1996): 457–481.

Brownstein, Marc. "Stop Writing Those Obituaries for the Newspaper Industry." *Advertising Age*, October 29, 2007, 23.

Caplan, Jeremy, and Brendan Lowe. "Most Influential Gadgets and Gizmos." *Time*, June 29, 2007.

Carpini, Michael X. Delli, and Scott Keeter. *What Americans Know about Politics and Why It Matters*. New Haven, CT: Yale University Press, 1997.

Carr, David. "Let's Invent an iTunes for News." *New York Times*, January 11, 2009.

Cavna, Michael. "Comedians of Clout." *Washington Post*, June 12, 2008.

Chaffee, Steven, and Stacey Frank. "How Americans Get Political Information: Print Versus Broadcast News." *Annals of the American Academy of Political and Social Science*, 546 Annals 48 (July 1996).

Chang, Jenna. "The Role of Anonymity in Deindividualized Behavior." *Undergraduate Journal of Baylor University* 6, no. 1 (Fall 2008): 1–8.

Chong, Dennis, and James N. Druckman. "Framing Theory." *Annual Review of Political Science* 10 (2007): 103–126.

Columbia Journalism Review: Who Owns What? http://www.cjr.org/resources/ (accessed October 1, 2008).

Coulter, Ann. *How to Talk to a Liberal (If You Must)*. New York: Crown Forum, 2004.

———. *Godless: The Church of Liberalism*. New York: Three Rivers Press, 2007.

"Coulter under Fire for Anti-gay Slur." *CNN.com*, March 4, 2007. http://www.cnn.com/2007/POLITICS/03/04/coulter.edwards/index.html (accessed May 1, 2007).

Craig, Tim. "Blog Comments Become Fodder for Attack Ads." *Washington Post*, September 22, 2007.

Craig, Tim, and Michael D. Shear. "Allen Quip Provokes Outrage, Apology: Name Insults Webb Volunteer." *Washington Post* (Washington, D.C.), August 15, 2006, A01.

Crowley, Michael. "Conservative Blogs Are More Effective." *New York Times*, December 11, 2005.

Davis, Richard. *The Press and American Politics*, 3rd edition. Saddle River, NJ: Prentice-Hall, 2001.

de Moraes, Lisa. "The Race for Comedian in Chief." *Washington Post*, August 5, 2008.

Dobrow, Larry. "Wear of 'Old' Label, Nets Take Snooze Out of News." *Advertising Age*, May 8, 2006, S-28.

Dolliver, Mark. "The 24-Hour Limit." *Ad Week*, December 11, 2006.

Dominiak, Mark. " 'Millennials' Defying the Old Models; Younger Online Consumers Leaning More Toward User-Generated Content." *Television Week*, May 7, 2007, 68.

Dotniga, Randy. "For a Magazine Industry, Less May Be More." *Christian Science Monitor*, May 14, 2007.

Druckman, James. "On the Limits of Framing Effects: Who Can Frame?" *Journal of Politics*, November 2001.

Drum, Kevin. "Political Animal." *Washington Monthly Online*, August 2006. http://www .washingtonmonthly.com/archives/individual/2006_08/009364.php (accessed November 11, 2007).

Dunn, Thomas. Personal interview with author. April 2007.

Eggan, Dan, and Paul Kane. "Justice Department Would Have Kept 'Loyal' Prosecutors." *Washington Post*, March 16, 2007, A02.

Eilperin, Juliet. "Fight Club Politics: How Partisanship Is Poisoning the House of Representatives." *Hoover Studies in Politics, Economics, and Society*. Rowman & Littlefield Publishers, Inc., May 25, 2007.

Emmett, Arielle. "Handheld Headlines." *American Journalism Review*, August/ September 2008.

Enlow, Callie. "Going Postal." *New York Review of Magazines*. http://74.125.93.132/ search?q=cache:4Hj1SKOlxqYJ:www.nyrm.org/Features/FeatureEnlow.html +enlow+and+%22The+new+suggested+rate+system%22&cd=1&hl=en&ct=clnk &gl=us.

Entman, Robert. *Democracy without Citizens: Media and the Decay of American Politics*. New York: Oxford University Press, 1989.

———. "How the Media Affect What People Think: An Information Processing Approach." *Journal of Politics* 51 (1989): 347–370.

Farhi, Paul. "Cable's Clout." *American Journalism Review*, August/September 2008. http://www.ajr.org/Article.asp?id=4574.

———. "Click. Change: The Traditional Tube Is Getting Squeezed Out of the Picture." *Washington Post*, May 17, 2009.

———. "Consider This: NPR Achieves Record Ratings," *Washington Post*, March 24, 2009, C01.

———. "Political Pundits, Overpopulating the News Networks." *Washington Post*, February 19, 2008.

———. "The Ads That Aren't." *Washington Post*, September 11, 2008.

FCC v. Pacifica Foundation. 438 U.S. 726 (1978).

Fite, Katherine. "Television and the Brain: A Review." Study by the Children's Television Workshop, 1998.

Fitzgerald, Michael. "Dixie Chicks Axed by Clear Channel." *Jacksonville Business Journal*, March 18, 2003.

"Future of Wireless Technology." *New York Times*, May 7, 1899. http://earlyradiohistory .us/1899futr.htm (accessed June 11, 2008).

Gershon, Richard A., and Ratnadeep Suri. "Viacom Inc: A Case Study in Transitional Media Management." *Journal of Media and Business Studies* 1, no. 1 (2004): 47–69.

Gibson, Rachel. "Elections Online: Assessing Internet Voting in Light of the Arizona Democratic Primary." *Political Science Quarterly* 116 (Winter 2001–2002): 561–583.

Ginocchio, Paul. "Newspaper Circulation, Deutsche Bank Securities Analyst's Report." *Project for Excellence in Journalism: The State of the News Media 2008*, November 6, 2007.

Goff, Keli, and Pat Buchanan. Interview by Dan Abrams. Live Television, New York, NY, March 12, 2008.

Goren, Paul. "Party Identification and Core Political Values." *American Journal of Political Science* 49 (October 2005): 881–896.

Gough, Paul J. "MSNBC Votes Off Feuding Anchors." *Washington Post*, September 8, 2008. http://www.washingtonpost.com/wp-dyn/content/article/2008/09/08/AR2008090802835.html.

Graber, Doris. *Mass Media & American Politics*, 6th edition. Washington, D.C.: CQ Press, 2002.

———. *Media Power in Politics*, 5th edition. Washington, D.C.: CQ Press, 2007.

Haberman, Zach. "Newsday Pleas: Execs Cop to Fraud for Fleecing Advertisers." *New York Post*, May 27, 2006.

Halper, Donna. "The Pitfalls and Promise of Progressive Talk; Surviving and Thriving on the Left End of the Radio Spectrum." *Extra*, January 2007.

Hamby, Peter. "Members of Congress Twitter Through Obama's Big Speech." *CNN Political Ticker Online*, February 25, 2009. http://politicalticker.blogs.cnn.com/2009/02/25/members-of-congress-twitter-through-obamas-big-speech/ (accessed May 26, 2009).

Hannity, Sean. *Deliver Us from Evil: Defeating Terrorism, Despotism and Liberalism*. New York: Harper, 2005.

Harnden, Toby. "John McCain 'Technology Illiterate' Doesn't E-mail or Use Internet," *Guardian UK*, July 18, 2008. http://www.telegraph.co.uk/news/newstopics/uselection2008/johnmccain/2403704/John-McCain-technology-illiterate-doesnt-email-or-use-internet.html (accessed July 25, 2008).

Helman, Scott. "Internet-Based PAC Driving Democratic Push Small Donors Fuel Big Support Drive." *Boston Globe*, August 7, 2007.

Hinckley, David. "Bush Welcomes Right-Wing Talkers to the West Wing." *New York Daily News*, August 2, 2007. http://www.nydailynews.com/entertainment/tv/2007/08/02/2007-08-02_bush_welcomes_rightwing_talkers_to_the_w-2.html (accessed May 15, 2009).

Hollihan, Thomas. *Uncivil Wars: Political Campaigns in a Media Age*, 2nd edition. New York: Bedford/St. Martin's, 2008.

Hopkins, Andrea. "Republicans Turning to Radio to Get Out the Vote: Medium Remains Predominantly Conservative." *National Post* (Canada), October 26, 2006.

Huffington, Arianna. "10 Questions." *Time*, July 14, 2008.

Hurwitz, Roger. "Who Needs Politics? Who Needs People? The Ironies of Democracy in Cyberspace." *Contemporary Sociology* 26 (November 1999): 655–661.

Isaacson, Walter. "How to Save Your Newspaper." *Time*, February 16, 2009, 30.

Ingraham, Laura. Fox News Interview. *Hannity & Colmes*, June 27, 2007.

Jackson, David, "White House Hosts Mass Talk Radio Event; Airwave Celebrities Gather Under Tent on Front Lawn as Cheney, Others in Administration Appeal to GOP Base." *USA Today*, October 25, 2006.

Jacoby, William G. "Issue Framing and Public Opinion on Government Spending." *American Journal of Political Science* 44, no. 4 (October 2000): 750–767.

Jamieson, Kathleen Hall, and Joseph Cappella. *Echo Chamber: Rush Limbaugh and the Conservative Media Establishment*. New York: Oxford University Press, 2008.

Jensen, Elizabeth. "Sinclair's Shadow: Canned News and Conservative Commentary." *Columbia Journalism Review* (May/June 2005). http://cjrarchives.org/issues/2005/3/jensen.asp (accessed May 12, 2008).

Johnson, Sasha, "Jon Stewart Lectures Reporters on Coverage." http://politicalticker.blogs.cnn.com/2008/08/25/jon-stewart-lectures-reporters-on-coverage/ (accessed August 25, 2008).

Jurkowitz, Mark. "Did Talk Hosts Help Derail the Immigration Bill?" Project for Excellence in Journalism, June 18, 2007.

Kang, Cecilia, "Merger Plans for Comcast, NBC Ignite Battle over Television Access," *Washington Post*, December 4, 2009.

Kellner, Douglas. "Network Television and American Society; Introduction to a Critical Theory of Television." *Theory and Society* 10, no. 1 (1981): 31–62.

Kirkpatrick, David. "Feeding Frenzy for a Big Story, Even if It's False." *New York Times*, January 29, 2007, A2.

Klein, Joe. "Beware the Bloggers' Bile." *Time*, June 18, 2007, 25.

Knowles, David. "Colin Powell/Rush Limbaugh War Rages On." *Politics Daily*, May 7, 2009. http://www.politicsdaily.com/2009/05/07/colin-powell-rush-limbaugh-war-rages-on/ (accessed May 15, 2009).

Kubey, Robert, and Mihaly Csikszentmihalyi. "Television Addiction is no Mere Metaphor," *Scientific American* 2003. http://www.simpletoremember.com/vitals/TVaddictionIsNoMereMetaphor.pdf (accessed January 20, 2008).

Kuhnenn, Jim. "Paul Raises More than 3.5 Million in One Day." *Fox News Online*. http://www.foxnews.com/wires/2007/Nov05/0,4670,PaulFundraising (accessed November 5, 2007).

Kuhnhenn, Jim, and Charles Babington. "Obama Says Remarks on 'Bitter' Working-Class Voters Ill Chosen." *Boston Globe*, April 13, 2008.

Kurtz, Howard. "National Review Cans Columnist Ann Coulter." *Washington Post*, October 2, 2001, C.01.

———. "Blogging without Warning." *Washington Post*, June 19, 2008. www.washingtonpost.com/wp-dyn/context/article/2008.

———. "For the Candidates, Not Just Any Brand of Soapbox Will Do." *Washington Post*, August 13, 2007, C01.

———. "Fox Puts Its Money on 'Fun' Business Channel." *Washington Post*, October 15, 2007.

———. "Hardbrawl: Candid Talker Chris Matthews Pulls No Punches." *Washington Post*, February 14, 2008.

———. *Hot Air: All Talk All the Time*. New York: Basic Books, 1996, 107.

———. "MSNBC Leaning Left and Getting Flak from Both Sides." *Washington Post*, May 28, 2008. http://www.washingtonpost.com/wp-dyn/content/article/2008.

————. "The Post-Russert Era." *Washington Post*, June 30, 2008. http://www.washington post.com/wp-dyn/content/article/2008/06/30/AR2008063000222.html.

————. "Winds of Change in Chicago News." *Washington Post*, April 1, 2009, C01.

Lamb, Brian. October 17, 2007. Personal interview with author.

Liasson, Mara. "Political Left Launches Its Own Attack." *NPR*, June 19, 2007. http://www.npr.org/template.story.story.php?storyId=11181167&sc=emat (accessed June 19, 2007).

Lichtenberg, Judith. "Foundations and Limits of Freedom of the Press." *Philosophy and Public Affairs* 16 (1987): 329–355.

Lillington, Karlin. "Reading between the Lines of Google Books Settlement." *Irish Times*, May 8, 2009. http://www.irishtimes.com/newspaper/finance/2009/0508/1224246114910.html (accessed May 11, 2009).

Lister, Sara. July 2008. Personal interview with author.

Luntz, Frank. *Words That Work: It's Not What You Say, It's What People Hear.* New York: Hyperion, 2007.

Luo, Michael. "Democrats Take the Lead in Raising Money Online." *New York Times*, July 13, 2007. http://www.nytimes.com/2007/07/13/us/politics/13internet.html?_r=1&oref=slogin.

Mackey, Robert. "Former CNN Anchor Moves to the Onion." *New York Times*, March 25, 2009.

Malbin, Michael. "Small Donors, Large Donors and the Internet: The Case for Public Financing after Obama." *The Campaign Finance Institute April* 2009. http://www.cfinst.org/president/pdf/PresidentialWorkingPaper_April09.pdf (accessed May 24, 2009).

Mann, Thomas, and Norman Ornstein. *The Broken Branch.* New York: Oxford University Press, 2006.

Martin, Jonathan. "Limbaugh Blasts Steele, the RNC." *Politico*, March 2, 2009. http://www.politico.com/news/stories/0309/19498.html (accessed May 15, 2009).

Mayer, William. "The Myth of a Conservative Media." Paper presented at the American Political Science Association Annual Conference, Chicago, August 28–September 1, 2004.

McKay, Adam. "We're Gonna Frickin' Lose This Thing," *The Huffington Post Online.* http://www.huffingtonpost.com/adam-mckay/were-gonna-frickin-lose-t_b_124772.html (accessed September 15, 2008).

Medved, Michael. "Why Conservatives Dominate Talk Radio," November 2002. http://www.michaelmedved.com/site/product?printerFriendly=true&pid=19056 (accessed July 9, 2007).

"Mellencamp Asks McCain to Stop Using Tunes." *Rolling Stone*, February 4, 2008. http://www.rollingstone.com/rockdaily/index.php/2008/02/04/mellencamp-asks-mccain-to-stop-using-tunes/ (accessed May 19, 2009).

Meredith Corp. v. FCC. 809 F.2d 863, 873 (D.C. Cir. 1987).

Miller, Martin. "No Hard Questions We Promise." *Los Angeles Times*, November 12, 2004, E27.

Miroff, Nick. "Muscling a Website into a Social Movement." *Washington Post*, July 22, 2007.

Mitchell, Alison. "Clinton Takes Aim at Critics on 'Right-Wing' Talk Radio." *New York Times*, December 16, 1996.

Mortman, Howard. "C-SPAN Shares Lamb Skewers on Air." *Politico*, June 21, 2007.

Mosk, Matthew. "An Attack That Came Out of the Ether." *Washington Post*, June 28, 2008, C01.

Mutz, Diana C., and Byron Reeves. "The New Videomalaise: The Effects of Televised Incivility on Political Trust." *American Political Science Review* 99, no. 1 (2008): 1–15.

Naughton, John. "How the Nets Political Dirt Corrupts Mainstream Media." *Observer*, June 8, 2008.

Near v. Minnesota 283 U.S. 697 (1931).

New York Times v. United States 403 U.S. 713 (1971).

New York Times v. Sullivan 376 U.S. 254 (1964).

"News Audiences Increasingly Politicized." *The Pew Center Research for the People and The Press* 2004: 834. http://people-press.org/reports/display.php3?PageID=834 (accessed January 15, 2007).

"Newspaper Online Advertising Spending Jumps 19%, Print Ads Down 9%." http://www.marketingcharts.com/print/newspaper-online-advertising-spending-jumps-19-print-ads-down-9-4024/ (accessed September 8, 2008).

Novak, Robert. "Mission to Niger." *Washington Post*, July 14, 2003, A21.

NSC Staff. "Newsday Execs Plead in Circulation Scandal." *The Street.com*, May 2006. http://www.thestreet.com/stocks/media/10288651.html (accessed September 24, 2008).

Obama, Barack. White House Correspondents Association Dinner Speech. Transcript. May 10, 2009. http://blogs.suntimes.com/sweet/2009/05/obama_at_the_white_house_corre.html (accessed May 11, 2009).

O'Brien, Jennifer. "Putting a Face to a (Screen) Name: The First Amendment Implications of Compelling ISPs to Reveal the Identities of Anonymous Internet Speakers in Online Defamation Cases." *Fordham Law Review* (2001).

O'Brien, Michael. "Cheney Picks Limbaugh's Version of the GOP." *The Hill*, May 10, 2009. http://thehill.com/leading-the-news/cheney-picks-limbaughs-version-of-the-gop-2009-05-10.html (accessed May 15, 2009).

Owyang, Jeremiah. "Web Strategies of the 2008 Presidential Candidates." *Web-Strategist.com*. http://www.web-strategist.com/blog/2007/04/05/web-strategies-of-the-2008-presidential-candidates/ (accessed June 11, 2008).

Paletz, David. *The Media in American Politics*. New York: Longman Publications, 2002.

Perez-Pena, Richard. "More Readers Trading Newspapers for Web Sites." *New York Times*, November 6, 2007, C9.

Pfeiffer, Eric. "Online Donations to GOP Trail Rivals; Democrats Link Web to Strategy." *Washington Times*, April 20, 2007.

Poniewozik, James. "CNBC's Bull Market." *Time*, March 23, 2009, 28.

———. "Fox on the Run." *Time*, April 7, 2008, 22.

———. "Sean Hannity." *Time*, November 11, 2002.

———. "The Rise of the Anger Industry." *Time*, December 1, 2003.

———. June 9, 2008. Personal interview with author.

Popplewell, Brett. "Organizing News of the World." *Toronto Star*, May 9, 2008, B04.

Porter, Tim. "What's the Point?" *American Journalism Review* (October/November 2004).

Postman, Neil. *Amusing Ourselves to Death*. New York: Penguin Books, 1985.

"Primary Choices: John McCain." *New York Times Editorial*, January 25, 2008. http://www.nytimes.com/2008/01/25/opinion/25fri2.html?pagewanted=print.

Prior, Markus. "Liberated Viewers, Polarized Voters—the Implication of Increased Media Choice for Democratic Politics." *The Good Society* 11 (2002): 10–16.

———. "News v. Entertainment: How Increasing Media Choice Widens Gaps in Political Knowledge and Turnout." *American Journal of Political Science* 49, no. 3 (July 2005): 577–592.

———. "The Real Media Divide." *Washington Post*, July 16, 2007, A15.

Reno v. ACLU. 521 U.S., 844, 870 (1997).

Rich, Motoko, "Potter Was Still Magical, but Not All Books Rose." *New York Times*, May 30, 2008.

———. "Waiting for Blockbusters, U.S. Book Sales Struggle." *New York Times*, June 1, 2007.

Riddell, Kelly. "Fox-Time Warner Cable Deal Could Mean Billions for Broadcasters." *Washington Post*, January 2, 2010.

Ruffini, Patrick. "Epic Text Message Fail? Media Gets Biden News Hours before Supporters." *Tech President*, August 23, 2008. http://www.techpresident.com/blog/entry/28891/epic_text_message_fail_media_gets_biden_newshours_before_supporters (accessed August 25, 2008).

"Sarah Palin Sent Legal Letter by 'Barracuda' Singers." *US Weekly Online*, September 5, 2008. http://www.usmagazine.com/news/sarah-palin-Slammed-by-Barracuda-Singers-for-Using-Song (accessed November 8, 2008).

Scarborough, Rowan. "Top Army Woman Quits after Uproar; She Said Marines Are 'Extremists.' " *Washington Times*, November 15, 1997.

Schudson, Michael, and Danielle Haas. "Getting Bit: When Sound Bites Get Snack-sized." *Columbia Journalism Review* (May/June 2008).

Seelye, Katharine Q. "The Online Candidate Confronts Critical Netroots." *New York Times*, July 16, 2008. http//www.nytimes.com/2008/07/16/us/politics/16web-seelye.html (accessed July 28, 2008).

Sella, Marchal. "The Red-State Network." *New York Times*, June 24, 2005.

Shear, Michael D., and Jose Antonio Vargas. "Candidates' E-mails Have a Bottom Line." *Washington Post*, November 25, 2007.

Shenkman, Rick. "The Dumbing Down of Voters." *Boston Globe*, June 15, 2008.

———. *Just How Stupid Are We? Facing the Truth about the American Voter*. New York: Basic Books, 2008.

Shields, Mark. "Yahoo!'s Newspaper Consortium a Hit with Users." *Media Week*, July 30, 2008.

Shirky, Clay. "Newspapers and Thinking the Unthinkable," http://www.shirky.com/weblog/2009/03/newspapers-and-thinking-the-unthinkable/ (accessed May 11, 2009).

Sidhu, Dave. "Media and Muslims." *Sanford Cyberlaw*, December 21, 2006. http://cyberlaw.stanford.edu/node/5074 (accessed July 28, 2008).

Simon, Roger. *Showtime: The American Political Circus and the Race for the White House.* New York: Crown, 1998.

———. "Showtime: The American Political Circus and the Race for the White House." CSPAN, February 1, 1998.

Smith, Tom W. "Liberal and Conservative Trends in the United States since World War II." *Public Opinion Quarterly* 54 (1990): 479–507.

Sniderman, Paul M., and Sean M. Theriault. "The Structure of Political Argument and the Logic of Issue Framing." *Studies in Public Opinion Attitudes, Nonattitudes, Measurement Error, and Change.* Princeton, NJ: Princeton University Press (2004): 133–165.

Spiegel, Brendan. *Ron Paul: How a Fringe Politician Took over the Web. Wired.* http://www.wired.com/politics/onlinerights/news/2007/06/ron_paul (accessed May 12, 2008).

Stanley, Alessandra. "Waving the Flag at the Bunny Ranch." *New York Times*, January 30, 2007.

State of the News Media 2007, The Project for Excellence in Journalism. http://www.journalism.org/.

Stelter, Brian. "ABC Reshapes the Evening News for the Web." *New York Times*, October 12, 2007.

Stross, Randall. "Freed from the Page, but a Book Nonetheless." *New York Times*, January 27, 2008, BU8.

Sullivan, Andrew. "Why I Blog." *The Atlantic Monthly*, November 2008, 106–113.

Sunstein, Cass. *Republic.com.* Princeton, NJ: Princeton University Press, 2002.

Svensson, Peter. "Sony Opens Up e-Book Reader to Other Booksellers." *The Associated Press*, July 24, 2008.

Sweney, Mark. "Fox News Anchor Taken Off Air after Obama 'Terrorist Fist Jab' Gaffe." *The Guardian*, United Kingdom, June 13, 2008.

"Talk Radio Research Project 2008." *Talkers Magazine*, 2008. http://talkers.com/online/?p=98 (accessed February 21, 2009).

"The Associated Press and Intellectual Property Protection." *Webwire*, April 13, 2009. http://www.webwire.com/ViewPressRel_print.asp?aId=92326 (accessed May 13, 2009).

"The Top Talk Radio Audiences." *Talkers Magazine*, 2007. http://www.talkers.com/main/index.php?option=com_content&task=view&id=Itemid (accessed July 16, 2007).

Trippi, Joe. *The Revolution Will Not Be Televised: Democracy, the Internet and the Overthrow of Everything.* New York: Regan Books, 2004.

"Today's Journalists Less Prominent." *PEW Center for People & The Press.* March 8, 2007. http://people-press.org/report/309/todays-journalists-less-prominent (accessed October 1, 2008).

Tolbert, Caroline J., and Romona S. McNeal. "Unraveling the Effects of the Internet on Political Participation?" *Political Science Quarterly*, 56 (June 2003): 175–185.

Tumulty, Karen. "Can Obama Shred the Rumors?" *Time*, June 23, 2008, 40.

Vallely, Paul. "The Big Question: Why Are So Many Political Memoirs Published, and Does Anyone Read Them?" *The Independent UK*, May 13, 2008. http://www.independent.co.uk/news/uk/politics/the-big-question-why-are-so-many-political-memoirs-published-and-does-anyone-read-them-827085.html (accessed June 13, 2008).

Vanacore, Andrew. " 'Broadcasters' Woes Could Spell Trouble for Free TV." *Washington Post*, December 29, 2009.

Vargas, Jose Antonio. "Campaigns Experimenting Online to See What Works." *Washington Post*, February 3, 2008.

———. "For Candidates, Web Is Power and Poison." *Washington Post*, November 8, 2007.

———. "In Texas, the Right Boots Up to Gain Strength Online." *Washington Post*, July 18, 2008.

———. "Liberal Bloggers Brace for Victory." *Washington Post*, July 21, 2008.

———. "Obama's Wide Web." *Washington Post*, August 20, 2008.

———. "The Medium Is the Message." *Washington Post*, September 14, 2007. http://voices.washingtonpost.com/the-trail/2007/09/14/the_medium_is_the_message.html (accessed July 28, 2008).

Vistica, Gregory, and Evan Thomas. "At War in the Pentagon." *Newsweek*, December 8, 1997, 44.

Wagner, Vit. "Pinning Hopes on the Next Megaseller." *Toronto Star*, February 23, 2008, E01.

Walker, Dave. "Rush's Quiet Diet Tribe: Have Diners Had Their Fill of Limbaugh?" *Phoenix New Times*, May 26, 1993.

Weaver, David. "What Voters Learn from Media." *Annals of the American Academy of Political and Social Science* (546 Annals 34, July 1996).

Weisman, Jonathan, and Shailagh Murray. "Some Republicans under Attack from . . . Talk Radio?!" *Washington Post*, June 24, 2007.

White, Joe Slade. "Wavelength Winners: 12 Rules for Better Political Radio Ads." *Campaigns & Elections*, June–July 1993. http://findarticles.com/p/articles/mi_m2519/is_/ai_14321245 (accessed October 1, 2008).

Williams, Juliet. "On the Popular Vote." *Political Research Quarterly* 58, no. 4 (December 2005): 637–646.

Wilson, James Q. "How Divided Are We?" *Commentary Magazine*, February 2006.

Woodward, Gary. *Perspectives on American Political Media*. New York: Allyn and Bacon, 1997.

Zelezny, J. D. *Communications Law: Liberties, Restraints, and the Modern Media*, 5th edition. Belmont, CA: Thomson Wadsworth, 2007.

Zogby, John. "Politics at the Speed of Light." *Politics Magazine*, June 2008, 54.

Index

ABOUT THE AUTHOR

Alison Dagnes began her career as a producer at C-SPAN in Washington, D.C. She moved on to academia, earning her doctorate in Political Science from the University of Massachusetts at Amherst. She is currently an associate professor in the Shippensburg University Political Science Department, where she teaches courses on American government and politics. Dr. Dagnes's research interests concentrate on American political behavior, and she has recently focused specifically on the American media and on ideology in modern American politics.